UNORTHODOX: My Life in and Outside Psychoanalysis

UNORTHODOX:
My Life in and Outside Psychoanalysis

A Memoir

Arnold D. Richards, MD

International Psychoanalytic Books (IPBooks)
New York • http://www.IPBooks.net

Published by IPBooks, Queens, NY
Online at: www.IPBooks.net

Cover art by Sophie Taeuber-Arp, *Quatre espaces à croix brisée*, 1932. Painting in the Musée national d'art moder

ISBN: 978-1-956864-50-2

*To Tamar Schwartz and Lawrence Schwartz
who made this achievement possible*

*And to my beloved family,
Stephen, Carol, Joshua, Justin, Rebecca, and Arlene*

Acknowledgements

A memoir is a labor of love. It is also a second analysis, a self-analysis. It requires honesty, and good memory, but neither of those can be perfect. A lot is included in this volume but I'm sure a lot is left out.

I want to acknowledge all my family and friends who contributed to this project and who have also made my life special. Thanks to Michael Takiff, my editor, whose contributions to this memoir were invaluable. Last, but not least, is my gratitude to my first and only analyst, Heinrich Henry Lowenfeld.

Free Association Appreciation for Arnold Richards: "What Comes to Mind?"

Nancy R. Goodman, Ph.D.

I was invited to write an appreciation for Arnie Richards and feel honored to do so. And, it is true, I appreciate Arnold Richards, and in fact I love Arnold Richards for his capacity to love, nurture, and get involved with people, psycho-analysis, and ideas. Arnie is tenacious in pursuing what he loves, in putting in effort, time, and a special alertness to what matters. I have recently been immersed with others in thinking about what remote treatment and training bring to the psychoanalytic experiences we have all had now through the need for COVID carefulness. Many of us tend to get concrete as we list what is the same and what is different from our in office sessions, as if we try to evaluate by making categories. I heard Arnie chime into these conversations, eloquently, with a steady pure psychoanalytic perspective. He reminded us that all people have experiences of feeling that they cannot get into the room, or that being in the room is too overwhelming and that distance is protective, and they have fantasies activated no matter what. Each individual has a story about closeness and distance, whether in the physical or virtual room. He was telling us that subjectivity, affect, and unconscious resonances will appear on Zoom. Whatever the modality, there is the psyche, curiosity, and contact of minds. This is why I love Arnie, he has room in his mind for the individual and for the universality of psychoanalytic knowing.

In the psychoanalytic way of finding meaning, I go forward here by asso-ciating to 'Arnold Richards' bringing me to song, memories, and all that Arnie does. Of course, one of the prominent associations to Arnie is Arlene Kramer Richards who is always in dialogue with Arnie about psychoanalytic matters with their companion poodle, Winnie the Pooh (now R.I.P.).

When it comes to thinking about Arnold Richards and how to write an appreciation, there is for me a flood of memorable stories I have been told by Arnie, by Arlene, and ones I have collected in my own right through our friendship and intellectual collaborations. When I first thought about what to include in my appreciation, a tune played in my mind—apparently only music can accompany thinking about Arnold Richards. I could hear the song, *I Will Follow You*. A quick search for the lyrics led me to the discovery that it was Ricky Nelson who sang this tune in 1963, when I would have been in college. There is something about Arnie that brings one to hear song and to feel young and energetic. The lyrics about "following" are central to my appreciation. For those who were also rocking and rolling in the 1960s, you can hear the tune, and the lyrics which work especially well when putting in the word psycho-analysis here and there.

We can transpose the lyrics into love for psychoanalysis and for the ever-energetic love for Arnie and his love for psychoanalysis. Arnie has led many across the ocean and over the mountains of conflicts in the intellectual development of psychoanalysis and the tensions between institutions. He wants to expand the world of psychoanalysis, enliven deep understanding, and keep the music playing. When knocked down by the politics of psychoanalysis, Arnie always perseveres and dreams up new ideas and new formats for learning and trans-mitting ideas that have gathered large followings. I think he believes that the destiny of psychoanalysis depends on change and transformation, or else it could atrophy and die. Arnold Richards is a compelling force who creates and then invites others to join him in new psychoanalytic adventures, hard work, and inspiration. It is impossible to resist. We want to follow him.

Commitment, hard work, and bringing others too

I review here, many of the projects Arnold Richards dedicated himself to as he made psychoanalysis better for all by opening doors for including others. I review many of his projects here using my own impressions and information gathered in an interview I conducted with Arnie in September, 2021 about his reflections on all that he has developed and keeps developing.

Editor of *JAPA:* The fax machine and agent of change

The first time I visited Arnie and Arlene in Manhattan, I learned about the sound of a fax machine when it is continually producing paper after paper after paper and taking up the space of the counter in the kitchen. Arnie was receiving manuscript submissions for *JAPA.* and he was enormously busy. Arnie became editor of *JAPA.* in 1994, remaining in that position until 2004. He had a new vision for the journal which he presented in his interview for the position. He was innovative in wanting to open the journal to the intellectual life of a wider community of psychoanalysts than the American Psychoanalytic Association whose members were the mainstay of the writers of the journal articles, as well as its subscribers, up until this time. This is how Arnie describes the experience:

Arnie: So I came and presented for my interview and, of course, my presentation was brilliant. I told them stuff about *JAPA* that they didn't know. So according to everyone on the committee I was selected unanimously. But it is hard to know.

Nancy: So what was it you told them? You told them brilliantly, *something…*

.

Arnie: I told them about the history of the journal, when it got started and so forth, and what it needed. Because before me was Ted Shapiro and before him was Harold Blum. It was a house organ. And the first thing I did was open it up to everyone. There was such a backlog of papers that most of the papers, the first year, were from people from IPTAR.

Nancy: Oh, that is interesting.

Arnie: Yes.

Nancy: Well, the papers had always been there, but you looked at them.

Arnie: Right, and accepted them.

Nancy: That is really breathtaking.

Arnie: So, people would not submit anymore because they thought they wouldn't be accepted.

Nancy: You said that it was a house organ, then it was the organ of the American Psychoanalytic Association?

Arnie: Right.

Nancy: And there really wasn't another journal of IPTAR or the Freudian Society.

Arnie: So I increased circulation from about 2,500 to at the top 5,200, which is a big accomplishment.

Nancy: That is because you opened things up.

Nancy: So, I am going to follow up just a tiny bit on *JAPA*. So you knew, even before you were the editor, that you would change the journal? Open the pages of the journal to new writing?

Arnie: Right.

Nancy: And no one else was doing that. No one else would have done that.

This is one example where Arnie is an agent for change and a force to bring about his vision of change. I remember the feelings of my study group when we got an invitation, *via* Harriet Basseches, from Arnie, to submit a paper for the issue on femininity. We responded, conducted research on femininity, and published in *JAPA*. Many psychologists and social workers, and women in psychoanalytic Institutes followed Arnie to the pages of the journal he now edited. It makes a difference if someone is wanting your participation and respects your work—or if they ignore and reject your thinking because of the politics of exclusion.

I "will follow you" (day and night) to the blog: Internationalpsychoanalysis.net

Arnie started the blog in 2007. The beginning of this venture is worth talking about because the new idea for a psychoanalytic blog grew out of a rejection. Arnie was being considered for the editorship of International Journal of Psychoanalysis (*IJP*), and when he did not get the job, he developed his own idea of how to gather and spread psychoanalytic knowledge to all corners of the globe. The blog was born. Arnie recognized that the blog format could provide something that a journal could not. As of this writing in 2023, the blog is going strong. It is a place for ideas, for commentary on psychoanalytic topics and sociological and political topics. Discussion and reports have been archived and can be found. This is a democratic stronghold—if you have something to say, let Arnie and his team know, and space will be made. From its inception, the virtualpsychoanalyticmuseum.org (Director, Nancy Goodman; Curators, Batya Monder, Paula Ellman, and Marilyn Meyers) was supported by the blog and by Arnie. The blog is not only a part of our psychoanalytic landscape from morning to night, but has created a landscape where we can wander and discover.

I "will follow you" to IPBooks

Arnie started IPBooks in 2009 with the publication of *Beginning to Grow: Five Studies* by Sylvia Brody, with what he calls the best team in the world, Tamar Richards Schwartz and Lawrence L. Schwartz. I recall seeing the first table with their books for sale at American Psychoanalytic Meetings when IPBooks was just beginning—a small table with Arnie seated next to hot-off-the-presses new titles. The variety of books, and the sheer number of books has greatly increased so that in London, at the IPA Congress in 2019, the press was prominent and attracting crowds. IPBooks titles also traveled to Cartegena with Arnie to the IPA Congress when few other publishers managed to bring theirs. IPBooks has now published more than 225 books and authors have "followed" Arnie to the Press for books on psychoanalysis, poetry, novels, memoirs, and sports, for example. The breadth of topics speaks to the openness and reach of Arnie's vision of what is possible.

IPBooks continues to grow, including the recent addition of a new type of journal. Arnie describes this as follows:

Arnie: I think my most recent thing is the *International Journal of Controversial Discussion*. Issue #4 of Volume #1 is about to come out as a book and Volumes #1 and #2 and #3 are in the works. (The titles of the IJCD Issues are: Vol 1, #1 *Psychoanalysis Art or Science* Edited by Daniel Benveniste in March 2020; Vol 1 #2 *Organizational, Educational, and Institutional Psychoanalysis* edited by Douglas Kirsner in August 2020; Vol1 #2 Supplement, Also edited by Douglas Kirsner; Vol 1 #3 *Psychoanalysis and Feminism: Rage and Creativity* Edited by Lucille Spira, and in September 2020; Vol 1 #4 *Psychoanalysis: Art Science or Ideology* edited by James Tyler Carpenter in June 2021)

Arnie: I realized that there was a need for a different kind of journal. A journal where you do not send in a paper and you wait forever and you get it approved, and blah, blah, blah…

Nancy: Yes, Yes,

Arnie: —and the peer review. So I really redefined the journal. I hope that this will be the most important journal of psychoanalysis. It is a little grandiose but so far, this current issue which we will be getting soon is really terrific. It is based on my paper, "Psychoanalysis: Art, Science, or Ideology?" It has some wonderful contributions.

Nancy: I like that way of doing it. You pick a theme and then people can comment. You bring together thoughts. I think it is very enlivening.

Arnie: Right. Otherwise, journals can be dull.

Nancy: So the one that Arlene did, on *Rage and Creativity*—

Arnie: Yes, that was issue #3. It was wonderful. And it is a great book.

Nancy: It was wonderful.

Arnie: Yeah. With some incredible contributors.

Arnie, again has an inspiration to create a new type of journal, invites creative thinkers to write articles around a paper and brings about what he was dreaming about.

I "will follow you" to Yiddish, YIVO, and remembrance

Nancy: Tell me about *YIVO*. (The *YIVO* Institute for Jewish Research is dedicated to the preservation and study of the history and culture of East European Jewry—of Yiddish culture.)

Arnie: Oh that is another story.

Nancy: Tell me what it means to you.

Arnie: Well, there was a story before that. The story before that is that we owe it all that to Arlene. And there is a story before that also. We came to New York, joined *B'nai Jeshurun,* and Steven was *Bar Mitz-vahed* there. *B'nai Jeshurun* is a conservative synagogue on the Upper West Side. We went there because the Rabbi's sister was the wife of the chaplain from Fort Lee when I was in prison service. So then Rabbi Berkowitz said that Vietnam is good for the Jews—we resigned from B'nai Jeshurun.

Nancy: So the war in Vietnam was good for the Jews?

Arnie: Yeah.

Nancy: Because of the industrial complex?

Arnie: I don't know why. It was part of a conservative sensibility.

Nancy: Okay.

Arnie: So we left and joined the S.A.J. We joined the S.A.J. (Society of Advancement of Judaism) because Lester Schwartz was a member, who was a very close friend, and it was a Reconstructionist synagogue, which is a whole other story, with Rabbi Kaplan and then Alan Miller. So that was in the late 60s. The Rabbi asked Arlene to do the Martyrology for Yom Kippur. So she did a martyrology based on Yiddish poetry: Sutzkever and Glattstein, and it went over very well and started an interest in Yiddish at the S.A.J. And so we started a Yiddish program at the S.A.J. and invited people like Isaac Bachevis Singer and Chaim Grade and so forth to come and give speeches.

Nancy: Oh, how exciting.

Arnie: And then Jim Hoberman had an article in the Village Voice about Yiddish films and Arlene said, "I would like to see some of them." So we started showing Yiddish films at the S.A.J. And then I thought, "Well, why don't we broaden this?" And I organized the first New York Yiddish Film Festival in 1972. And we brought together the 92nd Street Y, The Jewish Museum, YIVO, The Workman's Circle, the Brandeis film group, and The American Jewish Committee. These seven organizations sponsored a film series in 1972, which was extremely successful. We filled up the Kaufman auditorium which holds about 900 people. We showed all these films: *The Dybbuk* and so forth. So one of the organizations that was included there was YIVO, so that is how I connected to YIVO because I got them involved in the Yiddish Film Festival. So I met Maury Laub who was the director and I got involved with YIVO, and then they put me on the Board, and then they made me the Chairman of the Board, and then I got Bruce Slovin to take my place, and so forth. But through YIVO, that really started the Yiddish revival in New York because The Klezmatics worked for us. So a lot of what was going on after that, in terms of Yiddish came from YIVO and from me, and it was very, very, gratifying. Got it?

Nancy: I got it, and it is wonderful to hear all these projects.

Arnie: So that is a whole other thing in terms of Yiddish. And I would like to tell you, between you and me, now that I am retired, I would like to get more involved in the Yiddish Book Center in Amherst, and get more involved in YIVO again, and the Folksbiene, because those people—Actually there were two people who were with Yiddish—Moise Rosenfeld, who was the educational director of the Workman's Circle, and me. And the Workman's Circle was very important in this whole enterprise. Yossel Mlotek, whose son Zalman Mlotek, did *Fiddler on the Roof* in Yiddish, were involved in this whole enterprise.

Arnie's father following the Bolshevik army with books!

Nancy: So once in a while, when I hear you talk about all of your projects, I of course, think about all of your stories about your father bringing the books to the troops.

Arnie: Right.

Nancy: To the revolutionaries. I don't know whose side they were on.

Arnie: Well, it was the Bolsheviks. He was a Bolshevik.

Nancy: And how did he get involved with books?

Arnie: Well, he graduated from *Gymnasium* by correspondence. He was one of the only Jews. And, in fact, he and his sister started a school in *Sukoletz,* I think in 1916. My father was essentially a scholar, an academic. He could read and he loved Pushkin, and Turgenev, and Chekov, and so forth. In fact, I sponsored an exhibit at YIVO, something about Publishing for the Tzars and the Soviet Union, and if you look it up on Google, you can find it. It was a wonderful exhibit—a YIVO exhibit on publishing in the Soviet Union—that I sponsored. It was a wonderful exhibit in memory of my father. And he was essentially a scholar... he read a lot. He could read Russian, and so when he joined the revolution, that is the job they gave him. Of course, there weren't that many people in Trotsky's Army who could read.

Nancy: I love that story.

Arnie: It is a wonderful story.

Arnie holds Yiddish as a first language and also as a language/culture to preserve. When gathering contributions for my edited book *The Power of Witnessing: Reflections, Reverberations, and Traces of the Holocaust* (Goodman and Meyers, 2012, Routledge), I recognized that the enormity of loss of individual Jewish people was accompanied by the loss of culture and language: Yiddish. Was there a way to honor this loss in the book? I turned to Arnie, inviting him to please write about the loss of Yiddish culture. Who else could take on the task of witnessing such a death. Arnie, responded positively and wrote a chapter commemorating the Jewish Yiddish writers who were murdered, both known famous writers and the young upcoming poets and story tellers who never got a chance to develop their art. The ability to contain the horror of such atrocity for individuals, and for an entire culture, art, and language requires a very special person. Arnie did this and wrote from personal recall of his family and their history, and the history of Yiddish culture, mainly in Poland. The chapter, "Witnessing the Death of Yiddish Language and Culture" (Richards, 2012), is inviting because of his approach of interweaving the subjective and objective. How does Arnie get us to sing the song, *I Will Follow You,* even when it is about such an unthinkable devastating topic. He pulls together themes from a rich variety of sources in his own mind, and he takes us on a journey.

Psychoanalysis in China: Arlene is invited and brings Arnie

Nancy: So what about China? Because there is another place that you took on, that you believed in…

Arnie: But let's give credit where credit is due. That wasn't me, that was Arlene.

Nancy: Yes,

Arnie: Arlene was invited to go to China and she said, "By the way, can my husband come also?" And so they said, "Can you send us a CV?" So she sent them my CV and so they allowed me to come. So that is China, but China is really Arlene's thing. She is probably the most important psychoanalyst for 3 billion or 2 billion Chinese. She has made more of a contribution. And she is incredible in terms of the number of students she has. She has done teaching and supervision, and so forth. I am less involved, but I did do this seminar on four cultures, and we had 38,000 Chinese-speakers listening where I discussed the case. And Arlene did it also....

Nancy: What is this that you were presenting?

Arnie: It was this meeting called "Four Cultures." They invited me, and Arlene, and someone from China, someone from Israel, and someone from France to discuss a case (Arlene had another thing) and we all did that, and I was told that 37,000 people were listening, it was Chinese-speakers from all over the world.

Nancy: That is so unbelievable.

Arnie: It is unbelievable. I couldn't believe it.

Nancy: But the new technology can bring that about.

Arnie: Right, right. Arlene and I are central to this enterprise (the psychoanalytic therapy program by Dr. Tong in Wuhan) mostly because we have gotten good people like you and Lou to participate, and Dan [Benveniste] and Adriana [Prengler], Paula [Ellman], and Doug [Chavis], and Dr. Tong, and us. We really made something.

Nancy: You really did something.

Arnie: My group is still meeting, eleven years later, privately once a week. People come and go. Arlene has groups. So we really have a presence in China. China is rather problematic but somehow, they let us be. I think it happened with Arlene and the powers that be in China because of concern with the suicides of their kids, and that is why they started this program. But it isn't what it used to be for psychoanalytic psychotherapy. They are really falling back on medicine. Although I remember very vividly that we went to China in 1978, and the difference is incomprehensible. We went to *the number-one* mental hospital in Shanghai, and we presented a case, and so forth, and we discussed it, and they said, "We treat with heart-to-heart talks and Haldol." But the one in charge was very knowledgeable, he read *JAPA,* and he wanted to know about Margaret Mahler and separation and individuation. So they were knowledgeable about psychoanalysis. If you read, and you read English, you can be informed.

Nancy: I remember you telling me that your group in China asked the best questions of any group you have been a part of.

Arnie: Absolutely. They are so sophisticated, they are so smart. But I presented a case (we do one case then two papers), but they have a problem though, I mean I am talking about questions about the theory papers, but in terms of their clinical papers they do have a problem. Because they present a lot of historical stuff but not enough about feelings. And we talked about that yesterday. During a case presentation a member of the group said: "Look, you really need to find out how she feels about that relationship." So that was good.

Let's follow Arnold Richards into the future: Onward

Returning to the lyrics of *I Will Follow You* (wherever you may go), I am ready, and we can all be ready to follow Arnie, with his booming voice, to his next endeavors, we know it will take energy and fervor, and that we will be joining in on momentum that has purpose.

Nancy: I mean, you keep getting ideas. You trust that they are good ideas, and you do something with the ideas. So what new ideas are you cooking up?

Arnie: You know I was just thinking about that, as we spoke. I have to come up with something new. Well, right now I am thinking about how to promote our books and sell more books. Nothing occurs to me at this moment. Good questions. I will have to come up with something.

Nancy: Good, you will let me know. I want to thank you because I am writing my appreciation and I want to honor so much that you have done and the spirit in which you have done it. Because you keep bringing about new things. The blog is still amazing, I get messages all day and I enjoy that. It connects to things all over the world. I think it is brilliant. So I want to thank you, Arnie.

Arnie: So just let me say one thing. What I get to do is that I have a capacity for getting people to do things, to get people to work, and this latest journal is an example of that. I am the Tom Sawyer of psycho-analysis.

Nancy: And I will travel with you on the river.

Arnie: Right. And this is a good example of your doing things and I am very, very, grateful.

Nancy: I know when you have asked, people say, "Yeah, okay."

Arnie: And I am surprised about how much people do.

Nancy: And is there anything else you want to say?

Arnie: Thank you, thank you.

Thank you, Arnold Richards for your ability to love, enjoy, and create.

Foreword

Arnie Richards and his History of Making
"Good Trouble" for Psychoanalysis
by Daniel S. Benveniste, Ph.D.

Psychoanalysis is inherently subversive, and Arnie Richards is a psychoanalytic guerrilla warrior. As a therapeutic treatment, psychoanalysis exposes the primitive motives under our noble intentions. We see how our sweet dreams conceal self-interests. We discover how hostility covers vulnerability, tears hide our rage, aloofness conceals our longings, desperate attachments to others cover our loneliness. Our innocent declarations hide our complicity. Our heroic declarations disguise our fear and lack of control. In psychoanalysis we realize how our autobiographies are actually cover stories and our self-reputations, personal myths. Psychoanalysis helps us to keep as few secrets from ourselves as possible.

We speak of humanity's three great narcissistic insults: the Copernican insult that revealed how the earth is not at the center of the universe but in orbit around the sun; the Darwinian insult that demonstrated how we are not a privileged species, or even at the top of the animal kingdom, but rather just another animal among many with our own evolutionary history into our primate and mammalian past; and the Freudian narcissistic insult that says we are not captains of our ships and masters of our destiny, as we are significantly influenced by unconscious motivations.

So how does one teach this subversive psychoanalysis in an institute without falling into all the traps of institutionalization: the power dynamics, group dynamics, sexual dynamics, and all the other manifestations of the unconscious in groups?

On the boat from Europe to the United States, Freud commented to Jung, "They don't realize we are bringing them the plague." Psychoanalysis is the plague. It upsets the apple cart. It calls into question all the ideas we have of ourselves, introduces doubt, and arouses curiosity. But psychoanalysis does not upset us with something that is foreign to us. It does not bring us a germ or an assault from outside. No, it's upsetting because it helps us to discover something troubling that already exists within us, something that is already a part of us. It helps us to discover a bit of ourselves repressed into unconsciousness, a secret we have been keeping from ourselves. And while it may be unpleasant to discover and perhaps more so to contemplate, when we make the unconscious conscious, we find a way to live more comfortably, and more honestly, in our own skin.

Arnold D. Richards has dedicated his life to conducting psychoanalytic treatments of individual patients, training psychoanalytic candidates, thinking critically, writing creatively about theory and technique, facilitating the writing of other analysts as a journal editor and publisher, and challenging the status quo in psychoanalytic societies and associations in order to save psychoanalysts from themselves.

As a world-class psychoanalyst, situated at the heart of psychoanalytic institutions, he has, through honesty and critical thinking, worked his way out to the border zones of the compact majority to become one of the most outspoken critics of psychoanalytic institutions. But he's not a Freud basher, and his intentions are not to destroy the institutions of psychoanalysis. No, he actually takes his psychoanalysis seriously enough to look for the unconscious operating in the group setting, and his efforts are aimed at saving psychoanalysts from the destructive personal and group dynamics in psychoanalytic institutions. He certainly has colleagues who support him in these efforts, but he is very much a one-man army. It is in this sense that I call Arnie Richards "a psychoanalytic guerrilla warrior." He works largely on his own but, of course, recruits partisans along the way. The first time I called Arnie a psychoanalytic guerrilla warrior he was naturally pleased and fired back, "Well, of course. I'm the son of a Bolshevik!"

A Freudian and a Fleckian

When not talking about the unconscious psychodynamics of a patient, Arnie Richards is talking about unconscious power dynamics of psychoanalytic institutions. He has carefully read Freud's collected works from cover to cover from volume 1 through volume 23 three times. But he has also studied the works of Ludwik Fleck (1896–1961). Fleck developed a system of historical philosophy and a sociology of science. He said the way we think of things and come to know what we know is a collective activity that gives rise to a "thought collective" in which a mood and thought style develops. It is characterized by active elements, including methods of knowing, which shape the way members of the thought collective see and think about the world, and passive elements, which are perceived as objective reality. Facts are social constructs, and the facts of one thought collective are often seen as false, meaningless, or insignificant to another thought collective. Think of how the thought collectives of psychoanalysis, medical psychiatry, family systems theory, and cognitive behavioral theory regard themselves and each other.

Arnie Richards sees psychoanalysis as a thought collective embedded in the personalities, publications, institutions, and rituals of psychoanalysis. It's a thought collective that changes with its history and with developments within the discipline. The thought collective is also defined by what it can and cannot address scientifically and who is and is not allowed to participate in the enterprise. Thomas S. Kuhn said that Fleck's work anticipated many of the ideas Kuhn put forth in *The Structure of Scientific Revolutions* (1962).

If Richards didn't have Fleck's formulation of the "thought collective," he would have organized much of his independent thinking about the group around the importance of psychoanalytic history, of which he is a scholar and to which he is a contributor. It is in the history of psychoanalysis and psychoanalytic institutions—its innovators, integrators, and critical thinkers—that psychoanalysis lives, grows, and develops. But Fleck's concept of the thought collective allows us to consider history from outside the history. Psychoanalytic modes of knowing are not Wundtian or psychiatric modes of knowing. They are specifically psychoanalytic, and the psychoanalytic vocabulary born of its technique allows us to speak of things we could not speak of without it. And then comes the deceptively simple question of who gets to join in this conversation. Medical doctors? Men? Austrians? Foreigners? Women? Psychologists? Teachers? Art historians? Lawyers?

In mid-July 1914, Freud's "On the History of the Psychoanalytic Movement" was published. The psychoanalytic movement was still small but receiving international attention. When revisionists came up with new ideas, there was no way for the public to separate the wheat from the chaff. With this essay Freud defined the borders of psychoanalysis so clearly that the positions of the revisionists also became clearer. Those borders around the psychoanalytic thought collective continue to be renegotiated, and while the psychoanalytic thought collective has expanded widely in terms of the psychopathologies treated, theories applied, techniques employed, and candidates welcomed into training, not all developments are welcomed by all, and so the struggle continues.

Within the psychoanalytic thought collective there are multiple roles to fill, including upholders of the tradition, foot soldiers, innovators, integrators, and critical thinkers. I can see Richards in all categories, but primarily I see him as a critical thinker who helps us think about the innovations and integrations of others in the context of modern conflict theory and in relation to the other innovations and integrations. Instead of looking at the world through one pair of lenses—that is, one theory—he helps us to approach the material through multiple lenses and see how some theories bring into high relief some aspects and put other aspects into low relief, into the background.

Arnie Richards's Personal Thought Collective

Arnie Richards's credentials begin with the begats—that is, his lineage. He associates his orthodox Jewish upbringing in Brooklyn with his orthodox psychoanalytic training at the New York Psychoanalytic Society and Institute (NYPSI). While his orthodox Jewish upbringing was explicitly religious, his orthodox psychoanalytic training was secular but deeply influenced by Jewish—specifically, Eastern European Ashkenazi—culture. Interwoven in both were explicit and implicit socialist trends. His father was a Bolshevik, and many of his teachers and his analyst were either members of the Communist Party or held strong socialist values.

His instructors at the NYPSI included Robert Bak, Ruth Eissler-Selke, Otto Isakower, Edith Jacobson, Rudolph Loewenstein, Margaret Mahler, Jacob Arlow, Charles Brenner, Martin Stein, and Nicholas "Nick" Young, Phyllis Greenacre, and his analyst was Henry Lowenfeld. His supervisors were David Beres, an ego psychologist; Ted Lipin, who followed Paul Gray's "close process monitoring" approach; and George Gero, embedded in the earlier topographical model, who looked for unconscious fantasy.

As I briefly describe each of these analysts who were so influential to Arnie's formation as an analyst, notice the recurring themes of left-wing politics, writing, publishing, historical context, and theoretical innovations and integration. The first six on the list below were European émigrés who belonged to the second generation of psychoanalysts in Vienna and Berlin, most of whom probably had some direct contact with Sigmund Freud and his immediate circle, as did his analyst Henry Lowenfeld and his supervisor George Gero.

Robert Bak (1908–1974) was a psychoanalyst from Hungary. He came to the United States in 1941 and later became president of the New York Psychoanalytic Society. He was president of the NYPSI from 1957 to 1959.

Ruth Eissler-Selke (1906–1989) was born in Odessa, Ukraine. She was educated in Germany, where she became a psychiatrist and did her analytic training in Vienna in the 1930s, taking her analysis with Theodore Reik and Richard Sterba. She and her husband, Kurt Eissler, emigrated to the United States in 1938 and moved to New York in 1948.

Otto Isakower (1899–1972) was the innovator of the Isakower phenomenon. This was his observation of the hypnagogic states and body-ego regressions that take place while falling asleep. Isakower was selected to co-edit Sigmund Freud's collected works (*Gesammelte Werke*) that Anna Freud carried on from London. Otto Isakower was on the New York Psychoanalytic Society and Institute's Curriculum and Library Committees. He gave the course on dreams.

Edith Jacobson (1897–1978) creatively integrated the structural model, drive theory, and object relations. She was a member of the political left, actively opposed the Nazi regime, and was imprisoned for a time. She was president of the NYPSI from 1954 to 1956.

Rudolph Loewenstein (1898–1976) participated, in 1927, in the creation of the French psychoanalytic society's journal, *La Revue Française de Psychanalyse*, and in 1928 he and Marie Bonaparte translated Freud's case study of Dora into French. Loewenstein is known, along with Ernst Kris and Heinz Hartmann, as one of the foremost innovators and developers of ego psychology. He was president of the NYPSI from 1959 to 1961.

Margaret Mahler (1897–1985) was the innovator of separation-individuation theory in early child development. Her research and writings had great theoretical and technical influence. She trained in Vienna and was closely associated with August Aichhorn, among others. She was president of the NYPSI from 1971 to 1973.

Jacob Arlow (1912–2004) was an American-born psychoanalyst. He was editor of the *Psychoanalytic Quarterly* and wrote on psychoanalytic history. In perhaps his most significant theoretical contribution to psychoanalysis, Arlow explored the role of unconscious fantasy from the point of view of ego psychology, both subsuming its use in Kleinian theory and providing the building blocks for Charles Brenner's later development of conflict theory.

Charles Brenner (1913–2008) was an American-born psychoanalyst. He made important contributions to drive theory, the structure of the mind, and conflict theory. Brenner was notable for his eagerness to challenge psychoanalytic dogmas, which was most apparent in his late revision of Freud's structural theory, culminating in his article "Conflict, Compromise Formation, and Structural Theory" (2002), which he considered "the most useful and valuable contribution I have been able to make to the field of psychoanalysis." He was president of the NYPSI from 1961 to 1963.

Martin H. Stein (1913–2000) was an American-born psychoanalyst. He wrote about analysts who write for publication. He also wrote on acting out, masochism, states of consciousness, character theory, moral issues in psychoanalysis, mental health, the psychology of dreams, and more. He considered the transference implications of patients discovering the articles and books written by their analysts and encouraged analysts to write nonetheless. He was president of the NYPSI from 1963 to 1965.

Nicholas "Nick" Young (1914–2005) was instrumental in the education program of the New York Psychoanalytic Society and Institute. He was a highly esteemed teacher and a mentor to many. Arnie remembered him as being particularly interested in dreams.

Phyllis Greenacre (1894–1989) was a distinguished American-born psychoanalyst. Her interest in psychoanalytic training led her to issue strong warnings against boundary transgressions in relation to transference. This was a concern that would lead her to oppose analysts taking political stands publicly that might be seen by the analysts' analysands. She was president of the NYPSI from 1956 to 1957.

Henry Lowenfeld (1900-1985) was Arnie's psychoanalyst. Lowenfeld was a member of the Freudian left in Germany along with Otto Fenichel, Edith Jacobson, George Gero, and Elizabeth Santos. He was highly respected by all but was not part of the oligarchy that ran the institute.

David Beres (1902–2003) wrote on the structure and function of psychoanalytic theory, on empathy, and on fine literature. He was president of the American Psychoanalytic Association in 1963 and president of the NYPSI from 1969 to 1971. He was one of Arnie's supervisors, and his focus was on the unconscious conflict.

Theodore Lipin (1914–2005) was a German-born psychoanalyst but came to the States when he was 10. He was a very important analyst at the New York Psychoanalytic Institute. His focus was on close process monitoring. He was Arnie's supervisor. Arnie recalled that Lipin never said anything about the patient but just focused on monitoring the process, in the Paul Gray tradition.

gl fh!

George Gero (1901–1993) was strongly identified with Freud's drive theory. Originally from Hungary, he was trained at the Berlin Institute, where he was analyzed by Sandor Rado and Wilhelm Reich. Escaping Nazi Germany, he went to Copenhagen in 1934; traveled on to Tucson, Arizona; and eventually settled in New York. He was one of Arnie's supervisors and was classical in his approach, focusing on Oedipal conflict.

Arnie's personal thought collective, comprised of the books and people with whom he associated throughout his training and subsequent career, is a subgroup of the wider American and international psychoanalytic thought collective. His interest in the psychoanalytic thought collective implies that he didn't take in psychoanalytic dogma uncritically. He could be both a participant and an observer—a critical observer, a critical thinker. Psychoanalysis is a lens, a way of looking at things that by its nature insists that a perception of reality is always an interpretation, and from a Fleckian perspective that perception is based on the views of a thought collective embedded in its history. Arnie Richards's commitment to psychoanalytic history is pervasive in his writing. With his eye on psychoanalytic history, he helps us to contextualize theory and technique within its personal and historical contexts.

Psychoanalysis on the Front Lines

As a clinician Arnie Richards is a classical New York psychoanalyst, but he has also worked in the trenches offering psychotherapy behind prison walls; offering crisis counseling for survivors of the September 11, 2001 terrorist attacks on the Twin Towers in New York City; working analytically with patients in the People's Republic of China; and being a pioneer in providing psychoanalysis and psychotherapy via video conferencing. He frequently quotes Brenner to tell his students, "Psychoanalysis is not about furniture or frequency."

Writing the Ship

While many psychoanalysts practice the art and discipline of psychoanalysis, the theoretical and technical growth and development of psychoanalysis is left to those whom I would describe as the innovators, the integrators, and the critical thinkers who oversee it all. From my perspective, Arnie Richards is first and foremost a critical thinker. His volumes of selected papers cover a wide range of topics, but a recurring theme is the critical evaluation of different theories in relation to one another and in relation to modern conflict theory.

We could say that Sigmund Freud's drive theory gave rise to his ego psychology, which was then developed by Anna Freud, Heinz Hartmann, Ernst Kris, and Rudolph Loewenstein. Ego psychology then gave rise to Jacob Arlow and Charles Brenner's modern conflict theory, and Arnie Richards is one of the distinguished heirs of this tradition. He stands firmly on the shoulders of Arlow and Brenner—and Leo Rangell as well.

Richards has taken it upon himself to compare and contrast the theories of modern conflict theory, self-psychology, relational psychology, and object relations theory. The intention has been to avoid the typical splitting of psycho-analytic organizations into camps and personality cults and instead create an open conversation within the psychoanalytic thought collective to profession-ally (or even scientifically) evaluate innovations to see if they are worthwhile extensions and elaborations of theory. If not, they may just be old resistances coming back to us in new forms.

The worthwhile innovations often extend psychoanalysis, but when the old resistances come back to haunt us, they are typically new forms of the familiar and age-old denials of infantile sexuality, unconscious motivation, transference, countertransference, and so on. Many who call themselves psychoanalysts these days even take pride in repudiating these pillars of psychoanalytic theory.

It is indeed startling to see how psychoanalysts routinely fall into narrow-minded group think. Books and authors organize themselves into theoretical neighborhoods, and the rival psychoanalytic theories become associated with the rival gang across town. It is the narcissism of minor differences within psychoanalysis. Then the various groups start journals of their own where their thought collective can develop and define itself as different from the rest. And then new institutes emerge.

Richards has resisted this tendency and made a point of calling for dialogue between competing theories. For this he has earned the respect of many and the mistrust of others.

Facilitating the Writing of Others

In a letter to Max Eitingon dated April 27, 1932, Freud wrote of his pleasure in hearing that Edoardo Weiss had founded a psychoanalytic journal in Rome: "The personality of the leader [Weiss] is a sure guarantee for the development of the group, he alone is worth a group, and one cannot make any further demands upon a society which publishes a Rivista [a journal]."

In 1918 Anton von Freund, a former patient of Freud, set up a foundation to subsidize the Internationaler Psychoanalytischer Verlag (International Psychoanalytic Publishing House). His support of psychoanalytic publishing helped assure the ongoing development of psychoanalysis. In time Freud and von Freund became friends, and at one point Freud gave von Freund a ring engraved with an ancient intaglio, as he had with several other close associates within his inner circle.

During the course of his career, Arnie Richards has been editor of the *American Psychoanalyst* as well as the *Journal of the American Psychoanalytic Association*. During both editorships, he actively worked to broaden the range of voices publishing in these two principal journals of American psychoanalysis. He later founded the website InternationalPsychoanalysis.net, where he publishes countless articles online. And in 2020 he also launched the online

International Journal of Controversial Discussions. It is what I call a "psycho-analytic village square," where analysts of different persuasions come together to compare and contrast their divergent views of various themes. While von Freund founded the Internationaler Psychoanalytischer Verlag, Arnie is founding editor of International Psychoanalytic Books, which has by now (in early 2023) published well over 250 books.

A Psychoanalytic Guerrilla Warrior Making Good Trouble

Representative John Lewis (1940–2020) was an American statesman who served in the U.S. House of Representatives and was a leading light in the American civil rights movement. He described his involvement in nonviolent protests against racial injustice as "good trouble, necessary trouble." Good trouble is the disruptive activism that shakes up the status quo and leads to social and institutional change. I see Arnie Richards as making good trouble, necessary trouble, on behalf of psychoanalysis and psychoanalytic institutions. As an analyst, teacher, writer, editor, publisher and institutional activist within psychoanalysis, Arnie is a one-man army.

One of the ways he has created good trouble within psychoanalysis is his extensive participation in Douglas Kirsner's project to interview psychoanalysts at four major American psychoanalytic societies (New York, Boston, Chicago, and Los Angeles) to get behind-the-scenes accounts of the power dynamics, plots, vendettas, rivalries, and damaging narcissistic personalities that drove these institutions. The conclusion of Kirsner's work is his classic *Unfree Associations: Inside Psychoanalytic Institutes* (2000/2009). It is astounding to see how many people wanted to talk to Doug and just how open they were with him. It seems the analytic reserve of professional psychoanalysts was cast aside when they were invited to speak, on the record, about all the power moves, personality dynamics, and shenanigans that took place in their societies and institutes. Much of the bad behavior described could be seen as surprising and disappointing for some, but for others there has been no surprise, as it is just the unconscious making itself known in the group setting. Psychoanalytic societies and associations are groups no different from small towns, religious orders, companies, or other professional communities. The unconscious always seeks expression in dreams, fantasies, and, of course, in group dynamics. Arnie was a significant contributor to Kirsner's research into the power dynamics of the New York Psychoanalytic Society and Institute. He spoke up not in revenge or in an effort to destroy but rather to revolutionize, change, and overthrow the status quo. He spoke up to open the society and institute to diverse candidates, theories, and disenfranchised voices.

In 1996 I had the opportunity to moderate a presentation by Doug Kirsner, with Nathan G. Hale Jr. as his discussant. Doug's book had not yet been published, but he was presenting that evening some of his startling findings. Hale was the leading authority on the history of psychoanalysis in the United States and was also a conservative defender of classical psychoanalysis. I recall that Hale, at that point, was critical of Kirsner and suspicious that he might be yet another Freud basher. But after reading Kirsner's completed manuscript, Hale wrote a blurb for it: "Using extensive interviews and documents Kirsner has written an arresting, definitive account of the internal politics of psychoanalytic institutes and their sometimes paralyzing effects on policy and research."

The idea that the group dynamics of the thought collective could have paralyzing effects on policy and research goes to the heart of the kind of "good trouble" Arnie Richards has always sought to create. Kirsner's critique and Arnie's efforts demonstrate how organized psychoanalysis has sabotaged its own survival, facilitated its own decline, betrayed its own candidates and members, and fallen victim to rivalries, splits, exclusionary politics, and unadulterated nastiness.

Thus, the critique is aimed at saving psychoanalysis from the psychoanalysts themselves—to liberate policy, research, theory, technique, and training from the constricting and paralyzing effects of institutional life.

Sometimes outrage and disappointment follow the disillusionment from such revelations. We admire and are grateful to our teachers, our supervisors, our distinguished writers, and our analysts, and we value the insights we have each gained from psychoanalysis. So when met with the unequivocal truth about our elders and our institutions, we are left with three choices: (1) fight to defend our elders and preserve our idealizations; (2) become disgusted with our elders and denigrate everything associated with them, including psychoanalysis; or (3) appreciate and be grateful for what our elders gave us, accept their limitations, pick up the torch of psychoanalysis, and carry it forth yet another generation.

Richards says he suffered two disillusionments: the fates of psychoanalysis and communism. He observed that many of the early psychoanalysts, including his teachers, adhered closely to left-wing politics. Both psychoanalysis and communism are committed to the psychological and political liberation of people everywhere, and yet psychoanalytic associations and communist governments are both well known for their visionary beginnings and their subsequent oppression under the domination of power elites.

Political movements on the right and left often begin with democratic ideals but often succumb to totalitarian ambitions. If I ask myself, "What is necessary to keep the democratic spirit alive?" the first things that come to mind are a free press, alternatives, and critical thinking. And these are what Arnie Richards has been promoting for decades through his good trouble: freedom of thought, freedom of expression, openness to alternative views, and critical thinking to evaluate the various alternatives. It's not enough to have alternatives and be uncritically open to them all. One needs to employ critical thinking to evaluate the usefulness and limitations of each. I once heard it said, "The only problem with having an open mind is that anything can fall into it." Critical thinking helps us to see how the new idea brings some things into high relief and recesses others into low relief.

The Near-Death Experiences of Psychoanalysis in the United States

There have been numerous threats that have challenged psychoanalysis over the years. One need only think of the introduction of psychopharmacological drugs, managed health care, and cognitive behavioral approaches to therapy. But these were all external threats that would have been much easier to deal with if organized psychoanalysis were not so compromised by internal threats. The internal threats were the exclusion of lay analysts from the practice of psychoanalysis; the tendency of psychoanalytic groups to cling to rigid psycho-analytic dogma; the exclusion of rival psychoanalytic theories; the power dynamics in psychoanalytic organizations that bring about the development of in-groups and out-groups; the exclusion of women, people of color, and those with alternative theoretical viewpoints; and the training analyst system that promotes theories and techniques based on a dogmatic self-perpetuating in-group. Arnie Richards has been dedicated to challenging these internal threats to psychoanalysis for most of his career as a psychoanalytic guerrilla warrior.

Now this may sound like a non-sequitur, but I have long been fascinated by the Oedipus complex. I think it was a startling bit of insight and clearly one of the best examples of Freud's genius. My only critique is that it is often regarded too literally and not metaphorically enough.

Aside from that, I have an observation of the relationship between the Oedipus complex and American psychoanalytic organizations in the 20th century. My observation is that American psychoanalysis was significantly influenced by the same cultural trends that gave rise to the Generation Gap observed in the second half of the 20th century. It was the generation gap between the fathers, or the establishment, and their sons, the next generation, in American psychoanalytic organizations. Now I am an outsider to American psychoanalytic organizational life but as a psychoanalytically oriented clinical psychologist, a colleague of many analysts, and, more importantly, as a psycho-analytic historian I have observed the tendency of the fathers, or the leaders of American psychoanalytic institutes, to raise the standards which in turn raised the age of admissions to institutes. They found reasons to exclude candidates, reasons to keep them in training for seven, eight, nine, ten years; and to demand that candidates conform to the theoretical and technical demands of the fathers. The desires, ambitions, and creativity of the candidates were often seen as manifestations of the Oedipus complex, efforts to kill the father without recognizing that the only way for psychoanalysis to continue would be for the fathers to teach the candidates well and pass the torch of psychoanalysis to the next generation. This tendency of the fathers, the organization, to stifle creativity, snuff out ambition, exclude candidates, hold back advancement, and in other ways limit the next generation of psychoanalysts is what I call a manifestation of the Laius complex in American psychoanalysis.

You'll recall that Laius was Oedipus's father. But Laius had a history before Oedipus was even born. Laius was entrusted to teach a young boy, Chrysippus, how to drive a chariot and instead of doing so, he raped the young boy. His punishment for this, as told to him by the Oracle, was that his first-born son would kill him and marry his wife. So, when the time came and Laius's wife, Jocasta, gave birth, Laius decided to kill his own son by having his feet pinned and then taken out and left to die on a mountainside. Now get this picture, Laius molested a young boy, tried, but failed, to have his infant son, Oedipus, killed on a mountainside, and years later when he met Oedipus on the road, he tried to kill him again!

This, from my perspective, is what organized American psychoanalysis did in the second half of the twentieth century. It was possessed by its Laius complex. It did its very best to hold down, exclude, and limit the creativity of the next generation and by the 1980s they almost drove psychoanalysis into extinction. And you know something interesting? They didn't to do that in Latin America –and I don't think they do that so much anymore in the United States either. But I think in the second half of the 20th century that was fairly common, and it stunted psychoanalysis.

Some people, I have heard, think that Arnie Richards, with all his trouble making, has been trying to destroy psychoanalysis. I'd say he has a Polybus complex. Polybus and Merope were the king and queen of Corinth, who adopted the infant Oedipus and raised him to adulthood. Arnie Richards, with his Polybus complex, has been running interference between Laius and Oedipus for decades in an effort to give psychoanalysis, and the next generation of psychoanalysts, a chance at a future. And I think he's been incredibly successful in his efforts, along with others, to open the doors to lay analysts, women, people of color, and to countless Chinese mental health professionals in China. He's also published over 250 authors through IPBooks (as of February 2023). And he's engaged different theorists and invited them into the psychoanalytic village square to discuss the limits and benefits of alternative theories in relation to modern conflict theory.

In this memoir, Arnie writes about the turning points in his life when his fate could have gone in one direction or another. The "what if…" questions are of great interest to historians everywhere as they can see, better than others, that the outcomes of history are not inevitable and that sometimes small accidents or random events ended up having huge consequences. Arnie has presented these turning points in his life, which ended up making him into who he is today.

But you know something, Arnie Richards, himself, was a turning point in my life. And in contemplating the "what ifs…" in my own story I wonder, who would I have been without Arnie Richards? He only published three of my books, put a bunch of my articles on his website, proposed my honorary membership in the American Psychoanalytic Association, brought me into the International Journal of Controversial Discussions, and then shipped me off to China to teach in Wuhan.

And ya know what, I don't think I'm particularly unusual. Arnie Richards has been there for countless people opening doors for them, promoting them, encouraging them, and providing opportunities. Arnie Richards has been making "good trouble" for psychoanalysis for decades and in doing so has increased its chances of survival and further development.

Arnie Richards's Memoir

In this memoir Arnie Richards takes us on a tour of his family roots in Eastern Europe, his Jewish upbringing in Brooklyn in the 1930s, his stellar career as a student in New York Public Schools, Yiddish schools, University of Chicago, Downstate Medical School, residency at the Menninger Clinic, and analytic training at the New York Psychoanalytic Society and Institute. Up to that point, everything Arnie did was orthodox—orthodox Judaism and orthodox psychoanalysis. Then began the reflection and critique of all he had learned, which resulted in a career of literary, professorial, editorial, and political activism aimed largely at what he called "the politics of exclusion." He highlights Abraham Arden Brill's early efforts to medicalize psychoanalysis in the American Psychoanalytic Association (APsaA) as well as at the New York Psychoanalytic Society and Institute. He recalls APsaA's 1938 "resolution against the future training of laymen for the therapeutic use of psychoanalysis" and the 1945 reorganization of the APsaA establishing the hegemony of the Board of Professional Standards and the secondary status of those who were not or had not been granted training analyst status. He also finds certification to be another opportunity for exclusion of some and the control of an out-group by a self-appointed in-group.

I recall some years ago reading a psychoanalytic society newsletter announcing some newly graduating psychoanalysts. They had apt descriptions of each of their psychoanalytic emphasis areas as well as their personal interests. I couldn't help but be impressed that several of them were grandparents. Grandparents? When did they start their training? How long was their training? Will they live long enough to become training analysts? Ernest Jones, Hanns Sachs, Max Eitingon Erik Erikson, Karen Horney, Peter Blos, Ernst Kris, Sandor Rado, Anna Freud, Siegfried Bernfeld, Wilhelm Reich, Theodore Reik, and Otto Rank all began, and many completed, their psychoanalytic training before the age of 30. Anna Freud was a training analyst at 29.

One of the main questions of institutional psychoanalysis is, Who is the "real" analyst? The tyranny of the real decides who will be the real candidate, the real analyst, the real training analyst, and will that person be thinking in terms of the real theory? These illusions of the "real" are some of the internal threats to psychoanalysis that have significantly diminished it in the public's eyes and left fewer and fewer people interested in psychoanalytic training. Arnie Richards calls it "the politics of exclusion" and shows us how this got us to where we are today.

The theme of exclusion is further elaborated in Richards's critical thinking about theory and technique. He does not advocate holding tight to classical Freudian psychoanalysis or even modern conflict theory. He is open to the contributions of other theorists and innovators but not uncritically, and this is where he exercises his critical thinking to evaluate what to leave in and what to leave out. Then there is his work as a journal editor and book publisher. And just when you feel like you can't keep up with all his activities, this man in his 70s and 80s flies off to the People's Republic of China, where he becomes a Johnny Appleseed (an Arnie Appleseed), spreading the seeds of psychoanalysis in the fertile young minds of modern-day China.

In a webinar in February 2021, Arnie and Arlene Richards spoke of the history of their involvement teaching psychoanalytic psychotherapy in China dating back to their first visit in 1978. They spoke of the dramatic changes they witnessed in China, the eagerness of the students to learn, the recurring clinical themes of the one-child policy and the preference for male births, the pressure on the young for academic excellence, the common practice of children being raised by grandparents, and so much more. Their discussion of the pros and cons of a top-down society was profound and naturally carries implications for the very survival of the human species. Arnie recalled that some of the Chinese have affectionately referred to him as an Old Fossil, which is a way of showing great respect. Later one of the people in the webinar differentiated Arnie from the Old Dinosaurs at the NYPSI. I found it amusing to think that Arnie might be an Old Fossil but is certainly not an Old Dinosaur!

This book is a memoir, autobiography, and oral history. Some say oral history is "just anecdotal." I say it's history that is personally, socially, and politically contextualized.

Written history is to oral history as the cover story is to the backstory. The standard history is typically institutional and serves institutional needs or the author's needs. The oral history illuminates the subjective experience, personality dynamics, interpersonal relations, and political tensions that are often edited out of the written institutional narrative history. This does not mean that oral history is aimed at airing dirty laundry or digging up gossip, both of which are rarely of historic value. Oral history does, however, serve up anecdotes that illuminate the personal and cultural contexts of the official written histories and demonstrates that psychoanalysis is not a hard science but rather a historical discipline. It shows us that, as with any human community, we will find sloppy, unjust, mean-spirited, and petty human relations, but we also find brilliance, creativity, social commitment, an ecumenical spirit, academic excellence, and inspiring acts of courage, kindness, and compassion.

Arnie doesn't promote the illusion of psychoanalysis progressing in some sort of rational and orderly development. No, for Arnie Richards, psycho-analysis is a human tradition. It's in the hands of a thought collective that pushes and shapes psychoanalysis as a function of history, institutional politics, personality cults, rivalries, schisms, innovations, animosities, collaborations, and group dynamics. His story is unique insofar as he is an insider who became a participant-observer and then an advocate for outsiders, whether they are analysts, psychologists, social workers, mental health counselors, or even representatives of excluded theoretical perspectives.

Beyond all this, Arnie has illuminated his memoir with photos, poems, and documents that amplify his story and bring it to life. One could easily critique his memoir as just being his perspective—and indeed it is. But, oh, what a vantage point he has for conveying his perspective. So, sit back and enjoy this trip into the life and work of a real troublemaker—a world-class psychoanalyst who has made a career out of making good trouble for psychoanalysis.

February 21, 2023

Contents

CHAPTER 1

FROM GALICIA TO BROOKLYN
My Roots, My Family, and Me

I almost didn't get born. My sister Libby—she was named after my grandfather, whose name was Lieber in Yiddish—was born on March 11, 1933; I was conceived less than a year later. It was the middle of the Great Depression, and my father's paint store was not thriving. My mother had decided to have an abortion.

After she told her siblings of her intentions, she got back a letter from her older brother, Joe. She "should keep the baby," Joe argued. The baby might grow up to be someone special. She should trust that, somehow, the family finances would be okay. "Don't worry," Joe writes, "and don't lose your faith that God will want you to have another darling son. And then the blessing will come and everyone will be happy."

She took Joe's advice and decided to keep the baby—me.

But she and my father couldn't stop the bills from coming. In fact, at that time, with me on the way, my mother still had not paid the obstetrician for my sister's birth. But then fate shined on her (and me): Two spinster sisters, whose father had just died, offered my mother fifty dollars if she would name her son after their father, Aaron.

My father, who wanted to name me after his brother, David, couldn't have been pleased, but in 1934, fifty dollars was real money.

My father, Samuel (Shmuel in Hebrew) Gorodovitch, born in what is now Ukraine, had fought with Trotsky's army in the Russian Revolution. His younger

1

brother David also wanted to join the revolution, but my father convinced him that he was too young to face such danger. Tragically, the warning backfired. David did stay home, but he wound up being murdered by a gang of *Pitlura*—anti-revolutionary Ukrainian bandit strongmen—who came to the door looking for my father, the Bolshevik. They mistook David for my father, because David happened to be wearing my father's Red Army cap.

I was named Aaron—Aharon—in Hebrew, just like the spinsters' father. In English, I was named Arnold. David is my middle name in both languages. My mother used the fifty dollars to pay the obstetrician for the delivery of my sister. I don't know how she paid for my birth at Doctor's Hospital, 45th Street and 15th Avenue, Brooklyn, New York, on August 2, 1934.

That was the day Paul von Hindenburg, President of Germany, died. With Hindenburg out of the way, Adolf Hitler abolished the office of president and made himself head of both state and government, thus completing his transformation from chancellor to *Führer*.

The United States had a great president, Franklin Roosevelt, but conditions in this country were dire. The Great Depression was in its fifth year; unemployment was over 20 percent. Across the center of the country, the Dust Bowl was forcing millions to relocate or starve. In a desperate country, desperate criminals met their end: Charles "Pretty Boy" Floyd, Lester Joseph Gillis (a.k.a. Baby Face Nelson), John Dillinger, and Bonnie and Clyde all died violent deaths in 1934. Bruno Hauptmann was arrested for kidnapping Charles Lindbergh's baby. Los Angeles police chief James "Two Gun" Davis claimed movie stars contributed to the Communist Party. Overseas, the USSR, ruled by the paranoid, murderous Josef Stalin, joined the League of Nations.

A postage stamp was three cents—same as a loaf of bread.

* * *

My sense is that my almost not being born made me special for my mother, for the rest of my family, and beyond. A lot was expected of me and I was celebrated at every turn—with my report cards on the walls of the long hallway of our railroad apartment at 1320 44th Street in Borough Park, with my picture in *The Forward*, and with the enthusiastic responses of all my teachers, in both elementary school and Yiddish school.

I think my excelling helped my mother keep up her spirits during the Depression and in the years that followed. Business was not my father's thing—he was a scholar, an academic. Born and raised in the town of *Nova Ushitza* (which means "new city"), in the Podolia region of Ukraine, he was the only local boy to enroll in and graduate from the *Gymnasium,* a state-run secondary school located some miles away in another town. He took his lessons not in person but by correspondence. His report card read "religion excused."

As far as I know, although *Chasidism* took root in that part of Russia, my father's family remained secular. My father did not have a Chasidic education—Gogol and Pushkin took precedence for him over the *Mishnah* and the *Talmud.* The Jewish enlightenment had a presence in Podolia but I do not know to what extent my father's family was part of that movement.

The original family name was *Rikito,* and the original Rikito was my father's great grandfather. He was the only Jewish non-commissioned officer in the Russian Army during the Crimean War, he was killed in the siege of Sevastopol. I learned the story of my great-great-grandfather from my cousin, who learned it from *his* father, my uncle, my father's brother. (I always thought Rikito was a Sephardic name, but it isn't. It's a Ukrainian word that means low-lying bush.)

Several years ago, I found someone named Rikito who was married to a psychiatrist and lived in Boston. I spoke to him on the phone and told him the story my cousin had told me. This Mr. Rikito said that his father had told him the same story!

The name Rikito didn't last. My great-grandfather, the soldier's son, changed the family name to *Gorodovitch* at the request of someone in Nova

Ushitza. This neighbor, a Mr. Gorodovitch (which means "city dweller"), had no children, and wanted the family name to continue. (I don't know if fifty dollars—or rubles—changed hands.)

The province of Podolia dates back to ancient times. The Romans were the early rulers before the Common Era, and the barbaric tribes ran the show for five hundred years after that. Podolia was later governed at various times by Poland and Lithuania, but by the nineteenth century it was ruled by the tsars of Russia. Even so, the land was still owned by wealthy Poles, who arranged for Jews to manage their estates. My great-grandfather was one such estate manager. He patrolled the estates on horseback as he collected taxes from the common people. He was caught between the peasants and the landowners, satisfying neither, hated by both.

My father's brother speculated that some of the Jews in Podolia came from the Crimean peninsula or Iran—I wonder if that accounts for my relatively dark complexion.

My father's father was a tobacco farmer. Since Jews could not own land, he leased the property from a gentile. Interestingly, my father never smoked.

The family name of my father's mother was *Bookspan*—the Bookspans were from *Bukovina,* a region formerly part of the Austro-Hungarian Empire, now split between Romania and Ukraine. My father's mother, Branyo, died of a ruptured volvulus—a twisted intestine—when my father was fourteen. His father remarried, but his children did not get along with their stepmother.

Despite the estate managers' problems with owners and peasants, the Jews of Podolia had privileges not enjoyed by Jews in other provinces or districts. Some famous rabbis came out of the region, including my father's maternal grandfather, Shimon. The Bookspans were Orthodox; Shimon was a *Vishnever Chassid* and thus known as Shimon Vishnever. One of my father's brothers was named for him. Shimon was said to have been quite tall. One member of the family whom I knew, Simon Greenberg, was also tall. I think his mother was my father's aunt—my father's mother's sister, a Bookspan.

4

I remember another Bookspan, Bela Bookspan, probably a second cousin, from my childhood. Also, Yetta Bookspan who lived in *Czernowitz* in the Soviet Union. During the late 1920s, she wanted to emigrate to the United States. At that time, my father was trying to help his two sisters come over. He and my mother saved money and got his sister Itta a visa to come, but immigration in the US from the Soviet Union was closed that year. So his cousin Yetta Bookspan came instead, pretending to be his sister Itta Gorodovitch.

This Itta moved to Montreal where she married Jack Feldman, who was in the fur business—he sold mink coats—and had two children. In Montreal Itta became a Yiddish reader—her children established an annual Yiddish lecture at the Montreal Jewish Library in her name. I got to know her when she visited us in New York. Her son, Ruben, graduated from McGill University, then became a physiatrist and moved to Western Canada to practice. He had three children—two sons and a daughter. One son died; the other is a retired policeman, and his daughter moved to Israel—Orthodox and right-wing, she lives in the Golan Heights. Ruben's sister died of cancer at a relatively young age. My only memory of Ruben comes from when I was in high school, and he came to New York to apply to medical school. I remember he was all dressed up for the interview—he wore a shirt with a spiffy pin for the collar. I have no idea why I remember the spiffy pin. What could it be a screen memory for? I don't know. I loved his mother, she loved me, and we both loved Yiddish.

* * *

Born in 1898, in 1917 my father joined the Red Army and became a unit librarian, in charge of the cart with books, although he told me that very few of the soldiers knew how to read. My father loved to read the Russian classics: Pushkin, Turgenev, Gogol, Dostoevsky, and Tolstoy. With his unrimmed glasses, he looked a little like Isaac Babel.

In the army, my father came down with typhus—*Fleckfieber*—and was hospitalized in Odessa. When the British, from ships in the Black Sea, starting shelling the city, he and another patient commandeered a civilian parked outside the hospital and left. After the British shelling stopped, the two men returned to the hospital.

While in the hospital my father was befriended by a Jewish couple who urged him to go to medical school to become both a physician and a new Soviet Man. After the hospital discharged him, he returned home, where he related the plan to his father. My grandfather disapproved, concerned about the anti-Semitism of the Bolsheviks—not their words, as they avoided official anti-Semitism, but their actions. My grandfather urged his son to leave the Soviet Union.

And so, my father did not return to his unit. He deserted to Romania, crossing the border, formed by a narrow river, in river in a small boat, holding his rifle in his lap. When he got to the other side of the river, he told the border guards that his name was Gorodowsky, not Gorodovich, because he thought it was safer to be thought Polish, rather than Russian. (I'm not sure about this detail because I don't think my father spoke Polish.) In Romania he connected with a group recruiting young Jews to go to Palestine. Although he did not consider himself a Zionist—I think he considered himself a Russophile—in 1920 he was recruited by a Zionist youth group to settle in Palestine. And so, he found himself among a group of thirteen Jews—a dozen men and one woman—set up to be a "kvutsa," a group of people who hire themselves out as day laborers and share the earnings—who took a boat from Brindisi, Italy, to Alexandria, Egypt. In Alexandria, they caught a train to Haifa. (I recently learned that my psychoanalytic colleague Martin Bergmann and his father, the philosopher Hugo Bergmann, were on the same boat from Brindisi to Alexandria—they had started out from Prague.)

I don't know whether my father's decision to go to Palestine had anything to do with any previous exposure to Zionism. There had been an active Zionist movement in Ukraine and Russia during his youth, but I don't think he or his family was part of it.

The woman, my father told me, did the cooking. In Palestine, he changed his name to Earoni—like Gorodowsky, it means "son of the city." The members of the group worked for a year as day laborers.

After a year in Haifa, my father went to *Moshav Nahalal,* a cooperative community of farmers—a kibbutz—which had been started by Moshe Dayan's parents who had come from *Degania Alef,* the original Israeli kibbutz. My father worked draining the swamp, and in a rock quarry, where he contracted malaria. However, malaria wasn't the main problem my father had in Nahalal—the workers at this kibbutz included couples and single men but few single women. So when he received a letter from a second cousin in New York looking for a husband for his daughter, my father said yes. The relative sent him a visa and money to come to the US, which he did—in 1925, at age 27, journeying first to Canada, and from there to New York. In New York, he changed his name back to Gorodowsky.

Unfortunately for the single daughter of the matchmaking cousin, when my father met her, he decided she was not good-looking enough. Everyone agreed that my father was very handsome.

After he met and married my mother, my mother insisted that he pay back the money he'd been sent by the spurned woman's father.

* * *

It's a good thing my father didn't make the arranged match because, when he met my mother, he was thunderstruck. She, it seems, was not so instantly smitten.

"Dear Lily," he writes to her in what seems to be the earliest of the many letters I have from him to her, "I wonder why you refused to meet me this Saturday. What happened? Is it that my conduct didn't make a good impression on you and that's why you refused to see me?" Just a day later he writes again to say, "I wanted to tell you how disappointed I was when you refused to meet me. I waited impatiently through the holy sabbath for the opportunity to see you."

They did meet and/or talk on the telephone at times. But my mother did not reciprocate my father's feelings. Moments after one phone conversation, he picked up his pen, apparently convinced that he had been spurned forever by his one true love:

Dear sweet child,

I just finished talking to you on the phone. I feel the black clouds are again circling over my head.... I am so helpless, lost, dejected, having no courage. I sit in my room and tears stream from my eyes, tears which flow from a cluttered heart. Lily, dear sweet child, please reconsider and pity me, in the name of my devoted loyal love for you, stay mine. I close my letter because I cannot write anymore. It seems that my eyes can see only darkness and my head is heavy. Stay happy. I kiss your dear eyes that could have made me happy. Lily, dear sweet child, don't forget me.

Your devoted and eternal friend,

Sam

Even though they saw one another regularly, the romance remained one-sided:

Every Friday and Saturday, coming into your house is a joyful time. I could hardly wait for Friday to end, to be done with my work and to be able to come to you. I saw your glances and was sure that you felt as I did. And suddenly you made a date with another and cast me aside.

In another letter Sam laments that his beloved has, apparently, told him she has made up her mind and decided to refuse him:

> Now that you are so proud of your decision, think again what it is you are doing by driving away a friend who wants to make you happy, not with riches, or jewels or diamonds, but with true devoted love. Perhaps what you are doing you will regret one day. I close my letter. We can always talk but it is difficult to understand that you cannot understand me. Think about it. I will call you at twelve. You'll probably be busy.

Repeatedly rejected, Sam doesn't give up.

> Dear Lily,
>
> Tomorrow you will receive another letter from me. You will open it, and perhaps you will even read it, hide it in a little box where all my letters are kept. And you will probably think to yourself, "Why is he bothering me with these love stories? I don't love him. He keeps writing letters to me, he comes to visit me in my house. How I would like to be rid of him!" There I won't write you so as not to cause you any pain. At the same time it isn't pleasant to write to someone for whom your letters mean nothing. It's been three days since you agreed that you would not see me.

Continuing, he notes one of his shortcomings:

> Dancing is always bad for you because I don't dance. As I prophesied, you decided not to see me and it isn't even allowed for you to talk to me, Lily. How can you be so horrible and take everything so lightly? I will suffer until your hard heart will soften and we will be together again.

He closes that letter: "Your suffering, Sam."

The romance is on again. Then it's off again. Dad appeals to the man he hopes would be his father-in-law.

> Mr. Lieber, I believe you are a devoted father and you want Lily to be happy. Believe me, I am loyal to your child. I am prepared to do everything possible that her life be full of satisfaction. Now Lily is confused and doesn't know what to do. She finds it difficult to refuse me and also to make up her mind that we should remain eternal friends. The reasons for her confusion are that I have two shortcomings. I don't yet know how to dance, and I am not Americanized. My request of you is to convince Lily to understand that life is more serious than just dancing.

But finally, Sam's two left feet notwithstanding, there is a happy ending. "Because you were so haughty," he writes to my mother,

> so mean to me, all my hopes were lost and I surrendered to my sad destiny. And suddenly, it was once again bright. The dark clouds dispersed over the oceans. We met, with even more warmth and love, I felt your body close to mine. And now I am thrilled.... Lily, be strong and decide that we will both remain eternal friends and devoted companions for each other. I am sure you will be happy with me, because I and convinced that I will always remain devoted to you.

They were married on June 8, 1932.

* * *

My mother's family, the Ehrenbergs, came from *Lanowitz*, a tiny shtetl near *Lviv*, Ukraine—later called *Lvov*, between the wars, when it was part of Poland, although my mother always referred to the city as *Lemberg,* as it was known before World War I when back when it was ruled by the Austro-Hungarian Empire. Her shtetl was less than one hundred miles from Nova Ushitza—that proximity must explain why my parents spoke such similar dialects of Yiddish.

My mother, Leiche (known as Lillian here), born in 1909, was sixteen when she came to this country. She was the youngest of five siblings, with two sisters and two brothers. Her uncle Yerich Seftel—Seftel was the family name of my maternal grandmother—was the first of the family to come to the United States, arriving before World War I. I don't know much about him except that he did well financially and was responsible for bringing the rest of the family here. Fanny, the eldest of the siblings, came to the US first. Then the next eldest, my mother's brother Joe, came. Then Bessie, the other sister, came with my mother, their brother Irving, and their parents in 1925. They sailed on the SS *Finland* from Hamburg, on the Hamburg line, which was run by a Jew. In fact, the hamburger we eat is so named because the ship company provided a meat patty—kosher—to the Jews on board its ships. My mother prided herself on the fact that her family did not have to go in steerage, and because second-class passengers didn't go to Ellis Island, they landed in New Jersey.

My mother was the favorite in the family. I have about a hundred pages of correspondence between my grandfather, Lieber Ehrenberg, in Poland and Uncle Joe and Aunt Fanny in the United States. His letters include many references to my mother: how lovable she was, how adorable. It occurs to me that her position in her family of origin is comparable to my position in mine.

Dear Faiga [Fanny],

I can write that Leiche is a very sweet child. She's walking and can say many words. She is as bright as the day.

Israel [Irving] brings us no pleasure. He doesn't want to learn or write. He causes us much pain.

Basya [Bessie] goes to school and afterward she works at the cinema.

Mother looks very bad because the children "eat her up." They don't listen. They fight and she worries about them.

The letters describe the comings and goings of the family—their relationships, their marriages, their business dealings, their travels. In more than one letter, my grandfather notes that his son Israel—known in America as Irving—was an ongoing problem to his parents. "He has no overcoat because everything has become small on him," my grandfather writes to Fanny in 1908. "He can't earn because I didn't educate him. I thought that he would help me. In the end I have more trouble from him than joy. If God were to bring better times to America, you could send for him, dear daughter! … When parents are close they can see with their own eyes that their child is decent, or God forbid, not."

The domestic situation seems to have overwhelmed my grandmother. "Mother is very busy and has not time," my grandfather writes Fanny. "The beds are unmade, the house unswept. Doing laundry is out of the question."

Before emigrating, Joe—known as Yehuda in the Old World—writes to his sister, who has already left home. "Received your wonderful photographs and $17. Now we must talk about my coming to America. This is my goal, too. And to leave after Pesach. You can send my tickets. Don't be afraid."

Around the same time Joe writes to Uncle Yerich. Here's the entire letter:

Dear Uncle Yerich:

    I am planning to go to America. Tell me if I should.

    Your nephew,

                             Yehuda Ehrenberg.

It is remarkable that everyone left by the mid-1920s—there were some references to thinking about going to Palestine but as far as I know, few or perhaps none did. There's one letter lamenting the fact that almost everyone has left.

My mother's father supported himself by commodity speculation, buying grain at a certain price for selling in the future at a higher price—sometimes the plan worked, sometimes it didn't. The letters he wrote to Joe and Fanny describe his business ups and downs. "This year there's nothing to invest in because there is no grain," he writes in 1907. "There never was such a time, and people can't remember such inflation ever." But in 1908 fortunes seem to be improving. "Wheat is now cheaper than it was. We hope for a better year." The family will depend on what looks to be a good crop at home: "onions, beets, carrots, parsnips in the garden."

A learned man, my grandfather. spoke and wrote German—an unusual skill for Jews who lived in the Austro-Hungarian empire—and traveled often to Berlin. It's clear that some of the family were fluent in German—there's a letter in which someone apologizes for writing in German rather than Yiddish. My mother told me a story about him from World War I: One day German soldiers came to his house and wanted his boots; he surrendered them reluctantly but without resistance.

My grandfather acknowledges that life in America may not always be easy—especially when one is depending on an undependable family members:

Thank you for your letter and pictures. How happy they made us. We are delighted that you wrote of the welcome you received from the uncles, especially from Mordechai Israel. Remember how Mother used to fantasize that Uncle Mordecai Israel is a rich man and when you arrive he will welcome you and care for you as his own child and how happy you will be. It's exactly the way it happened, in reverse, I think. It shouldn't surprise us because ... in his thoughts he is always building air-castles. God should help you."

At times, my grandfather sends money—a few guilders—to America. But more often, Joe and Fanny send money back to Europe, perhaps to help out, perhaps just for safekeeping—my grandfather promises to invest his children's funds at interest ("for a percent"). "I received the 75 guilders you sent, on the 16th," he writes to Fanny in March 1908.

> Uncle Yerich wrote that you sent 100 guilders on 2/12 which arrived on 3/12. Did it really take that long or did you send it later than he wrote? I want to know. You wrote that I shouldn't be angry at you for keeping 25 guilders. You wanted to get something for yourself for Passover. Of course we're not angry, but don't go shopping by yourself. Take Aunt Freyda along because she is older and has more understanding.

He ends the letter by comparing the troubles of his young daughter in America to his own, middle-aged, troubles in the old country:

> You closed your letter with, "I can't write any more, I'm very tired."
> Why are you so tired? Are you working too hard? You don't have to. Your children aren't asking for food.

Among all the letters I have, the saddest comes from my grandmother's sister Chaya. Writing to my uncle Joe in September 1922, she tells of being swept up in the Russian civil war and seeks help from America, where the streets, presumably, are paved with gold. Here's the letter in full:

> Dear Nephew Yehuda,
> This week your mother, my dear sister, was here to visit our parents' graves. She saw our poverty and shame. We have no clothes or shoes to wear. We weren't at home for 4 years. During the war we had to escape and before we ran, they robbed us. When we returned we found

14

nothing was left. Then everything was taken from us and burned. We wandered through the streets and a farmer took pity on me, my husband and child and took us in. Now he wants to throw us out. I don't have the means to rent an apartment.

We have 7 children and are starving to death. When my dear sister was here, she cried with me. She gave me your address and asked me to write and ask if you could send us something and also told me to let you know that the package you sent here took 2 years to arrive.

Dear Yehuda, I ask you to take pity on your aunt Chaya and you and your sisters should send us something. Times are very bad. Please take pity on me and my husband and children. We are hungry, we have no clothes and winter is coming. The children need warm clothes to be able to go in cold weather.

Don't forget me, your bitter, lonely aunt who is so very poor. When you mother comes to you, she will tell you about our poverty.

Etc., etc.

Your poor Aunt Chaya.

My grandfather was also a religion teacher for many children and young grownups in Lanowitz. These pupils were children of a group of people who became an extended family for my mother in Europe, and when they all came to the US. Their names were Mieselman, Lassner, Metsker, and Gross. They lived in Elizabeth, New Jersey—Aunt Bessie moved there, too (to be with them, I think). Julius Lassner worked for the CIA; his cover was a used-car dealership in Colombia, South America.

Another of that group was Izzie Metsker, who became a Yiddish writer. The story goes that he stowed away on a boat to come to America. He worked for *The Forward* and edited a column, *Das Bintle Brief* (A Packet of Letters), a Yiddish Dear Abby column. He also wrote books in Yiddish for children.

I remember one, *Toli and Toby*. But his most important book was called *Oif Zeiden's Felder*, published in English as *Grandfather's Acres*. On the cover of the book is a photograph of a dozen people connected with him, including my mother who I think was eight years old when the picture was taken. Some considered this book—a novel depicting life in rural Jewish Ukraine before the turn of the century—one of the best books written in Yiddish after the war.

Meyer Shticker, reviewing *Oif Zeiden's Felder* in *The Day*, called it "a book of great scope—in the ethical descriptions as well as in the quiet flow of lyricism. Now in the abundance of Yiskor books to commemorate our destroyed cities and towns, I. Metzker has managed in truly artistic form to erect not a gravestone, but a building, a piece of Jewish farm life that will never be forgotten."

Elie Wiesel, in his 1960 review in the *Forward* of *Oif Zeiden's Felder* on the occasion of the book's translation into Hebrew, wrote, "This is the strength and the sign of the real artist—he takes one into his world, his right of the individual, into his fenced-in garden. And for two hours, two days or two years—one goes along with his laws, his logic, his truths … It is not a novel of suspense where a word can decide fates and lives. It is a pastoral symphony where the trumpets and drums play the smallest role. It is a song for string instruments."

Izzie Metzker was important for another reason in my family. As a member of the *Forward* staff, he could arrange for my picture to be published in that paper after some achievement—a graduation, an award, etc. Of course, the idea would originate with my mother. My picture in the paper was something she could show to family, friends, and neighbors.

My mother took great delight in my excellent school performance—she cultivated relationships with all my teachers in elementary and junior high school. She saved every report card, every diploma, every acknowledgement I received and pasted them on the wall. Only my accomplishments, none from

16

my sister. I wonder how *she* felt about this; I should ask her now that she lives nearby. My mother's adulation made me feel special, favored. My sister was proud of me—she would boast to her friends about her smart brother.

* * *

But to return to the Ehrenbergs: My uncle Joe married my aunt Ada—both were named Ehrenberg—they must have been distant cousins. They had three children: Marvin, Sherman, and Gloria. Marvin flew twenty-nine missions as a navigator on a B-29 during World War II. After the war he attended Purdue University to study engineering. I remember fondly the Purdue Boilermakers t-shirt he sent me, with an embossed boilermaker figure on the front. Sherman changed his name to Brad Sherman and became a broadcaster, working for thirty-nine years at the New York all-news station WINS. ("You give us twenty-two minutes, we'll give you the world.") My family would listen to him all the time. Gloria was an artist—a painter—but never pursued a career as one. When I was running for seventh-grade vice president of the Montauk student government she made a poster for me which I hung in a school hallway: "Vote for Arnold Gorodosky for 7th-Grade Vice President."

During the war, my mother would send me to Aunt Ada and Uncle Joe during the summer. Marvin and Sherman were away in the service. Gloria—she later became Glory—was at home. She would take me to the movies—the Loew's Kings, on Kings Highway. Glory and her brothers were in the first classes of Midwood High School. Uncle Joe, Orthodox and observant, would take me with him to synagogue. Since I read Hebrew and knew the prayers, I become his favorite—he preferred me even to his own children, who had no interest. Their house, with its backyard, was for me an oasis of affluence within the poverty of my nuclear family. Uncle Joe's business was buttons—he owned the Western Button Company on West 26th Street in Manhattan, where I would sometimes go to do errands. He was a jobber, buying lots of buttons, and sorting them according to quality. My mother worked for him as a sorter, sometimes on 26th Street but more often at home. Uncle Joe's brother, my uncle Irving, was also in the button business—he owned Arrow Button at 1199 Broadway. I would go there frequently, too. I started riding the subway by myself when I was eight or nine. I am not sure my wife and I would have allowed our children to ride the subway at that age. But for some reason I still don't understand, my mother and father allowed me to go wherever I wanted whenever I wanted. I felt I was free to navigate the city from a tender age.

Uncle Irving did not do as well in business as his brother did. I would go to Irving's one-room office filled with boxes of buttons and help him make packages and send bills for his few sales. He and his wife Essie—I'm not sure when they married—had two daughters, Jeanne and Toby, but separated early on. Irving then came to live with us—I was quite young. Until my sister got married and left to live with her new husband, Irving and I slept together in the same bed. Before that, I had slept in a crib in my parents' bedroom until I was six or eight. It may have been eight because I remember being in the crib when I arrived home from the hospital after my appendectomy at that age. The appendectomy was performed by Adrian Kantrowitz, a famous cardiac surgeon—my mother insisted that I have the best surgeon in Israel Zion Hospital. I remember the ether, counting back from 100. I think I got to 89. My other memory of the surgery is that when I came home, the neighbor upstairs, Willie Rabinowitz, who owned Ike Zola luncheonette on 34th Street in Manhattan, had bought me a wooden model of a battleship. My appendicitis and my polio were the two major medical events of my childhood. I also suffered from hay fever from mid-August to late-September. My hay fever contributed to my becoming a psychoanalyst because I read Flanders Dunbar's *Emotions and Memory* and learned that hay fever could be psychosomatic as well as allergic.

My aunt Bessie, before she got married, had had a botched abortion that prevented her from having more children. She therefore needed a dowry to get married. My mother accumulated a dowery for herself and had given it to her own mother. According to my wife, my grandmother gave the money to Bessie for *her* dowery. My mother may have felt that with a dowery of her own she might have wound up with a more substantial husband than my father, and lived a life of means, instead of the poverty she was subjected to for most of her marriage.

With the dowery, Bessie married Joe Gross. They opened an appetizer store, Superior Delicatessen, on Elmora Avenue in the Elmora section of Elizabeth. After they sold that business, they opened a liquor store in Teaneck, NJ. Their house was another place my mother would send me to get away from the hot streets of Borough Park. Aunt Bessie and I loved each other very much; in fact, she would send me money every week when I was at the University of Chicago.

Fanny married Jack Brenner, an immigrant from Romania—they owned a candy store on 13th Avenue and 39th Street, at the Culver Line elevated station. Jack liked manzanilla olives and mamaliga, a Romanian dish similar to polenta. Aunt Fanny and Uncle Jack lived in the back of the candy store, which I loved to visit because of the treats I would get, like frozen twists and Mallomars and egg creams, even though Jack seemed concerned that I would eat too much free merchandise. I spent more time in the store reading than eating—I loved the comic books, especially Classics Illustrated (I remember *A Tale of Two Cities*). Of course, I had other comic book favorites, too: *Captain America, Batman,* and *Namor the Sub-Mariner.*

Fanny and Jack had two children, Harry and Herb. During the war, Herb served in the army, Harry in the navy. Both brothers were leftists—they may have belonged to the Communist Party USA (CPUSA). After the war, Harry, his wife, Judy, and their son, Eric, moved to Washington, D.C., where Harry worked for the federal government. But during the McCarthy era his political history got him fired. When Harry moved to Washington, he left his collection of books in the house of my Uncle Joe and Aunt Ada, at 1022 East 21st Street in Midwood, a house with a backyard. During summers, I'd visit and pore over

Harry's collection of radical/leftist books. That house was where my mother would send me in the summers before I went to camp at *Camp Well Met,* a Y camp, and *Camp Deal,* an orthodox camp in Deal, a shore town in New Jersey.

Herb had a daughter who worked in the school system. Herb's wife Evelyn was an artist who made huge tapestries—one of her works is in the Victoria and Albert Museum in London. I still have the pencil case she made for me. Harry and Judy's son, Eric, became a physician, enjoying a distinguished career in public health, including several years working for the UN. He and his wife live in Columbia, South Carolina. Judy retired to Hawaii, where she died. Evelyn remained creative until the end of her life at age ninety-eight.

The most famous Ehrenberg was Herman Ehrenberg, who was related more to the Ada side of the family more than to the Joe side. Born in Germany, he came to the US in the first quarter of the nineteenth century and found his way to New Orleans, where he enlisted in the New Orleans Greys, a unit that fought for the independence of the Republic of Texas from Mexico. "The Republic of Texas forever!" he is said to have yelled during his escape from enemy captivity. Herman was a surveyor and made the first map of the Gadsden Purchase, the 1854 purchase from Mexico of land in present-day Arizona and New Mexico; the land made possible the Transcontinental Railroad. Herman traveled far and wide—he visited Tahiti and was hired to survey the streets of Honolulu. In Arizona, he started a hardware store that sold supplies to the miners during the gold rush. Herman's partner in the store was a man named Goldwasser. Goldwasser became Goldwater, and Goldwater had a grandson named Barry who became a senator and presidential candidate. Barry Goldwater called Herman "one of the greatest surveyors and map makers ever to visit the Western United States." There is a statue of my notorious relative in the town named after him, Ehrenberg, Arizona. Herman Ehrenberg was murdered in 1866 in California.

So much for my mother's family. There is a lot to tell about my father's family.

* * *

After my father came to the US he remained sympathetic to the Soviet Union. That changed in August 1939 with the Hitler-Stalin Pact. I remember listening to the radio commentator Gabriel Heatter, on a Wednesday night at 9:00 pm, when I was five. Heatter would usually begin his commentary on the news with the words, "And yes, there's good news tonight." But this time he said, "And yes, there's bad news tonight: Hitler and Stalin are marching together." My father's views changed again, almost two years later, when Hitler invaded the Soviet Union—it was time to side with Stalin . Stalingrad was the turning point in the war on the Eastern Front. My father and I followed the reports of the war in *PM*, which had become our household newspaper. Every week during the war *PM* printed a picture of a Russian general on the back page of the weekend edition. I remember one of generals: Marshal Georgy Zhukov. My father's views of Stalin and the Soviet Union changed again in 1956 with the Khrushchev revelations. My father said that Stalin was an anti-Semite.

Although my father never became a Zionist, the Hebrew language was important to him. At the end of his life, he liked to read the poems of the Hebrew poet Chaim Nachman Bialik.

My father had other siblings besides David. One brother left the Soviet Union in 1925 and, because my father had written him to say that New York was not safe, emigrated to Brazil. Another brother, Simon, was an early, avid Bolshevik and a terrific orator who joined the Red Army, and made it all the way to General, before being killed in the battle for Berlin in1945. At least, that's the family lore—I'm unable to confirm this story. I also wonder how an old Bolshevik Jew managed to survive the purges of the 1930s and remain in good standing until 1945.

A sister, Milia, was very beautiful. She came to New York around 1939 and then sailed to Brazil—I have a picture of the family seeing her off on the boat. My sister and I are in the picture wearing suits Aunt Milia had made for us.

The woman remains a mystery to me. I don't know when and how she left the Soviet Union. I think she was with Yetta, who left Czernowitz in 1929. Milia was very cultured, Yetta told me, an opera lover. She returned to Brazil, to Sao Paolo, to marry a shoemaker named Pablo Wasserman. His business struggled, so he moved to *Manaus,* Brazil to work with Moshe, my father's brother. Milia and Pablo never had any children.

The story of my father's family is more tragic than the story of my mother's family. Everyone on my mother's side, without exception, left Poland before the Holocaust. Not so for my father's family.

My paternal grandfather died of natural causes before the Germans arrived. I have an image in my mind of my father sitting on the couch in our apartment on 44th Street in Brooklyn, crying when he heard the news of his father's death. My father's sister Lena and her two daughters had remained in Nova Ushitza. They were among the Jews taken to the forest outside of the city and shot by the Germans: "The Holocaust of the bullets."

A cousin Ita, then a teenager, and her parents, were among those taken to be murdered, but she survived. In the 1970s, my wife Arlene and I visited Leningrad (now St. Petersburg). Ita and a companion traveled by train to see us; we met at the Hermitage Museum. As Ita and I sat next to a painting by Leonardo da Vinci, she told me about the horrors inflicted upon our family during the war: The Germans rounded up her family and took them to the forest where they shot them all—except her "I hid behind a rock," she said, "and my parents did not look back." She was saved by some Russian partisans wearing German uniforms, who befriended her. They were traveling to *Tashkent,* where, I think, she remained for the rest of the war. After the war, she returned to Nova Ushitza and sold her house but, that night, some of the natives came and stole the money, after which she decided that this part of Russia was not for her, and so she left. She went to normal school, became a teacher, and had a good life. I asked her why she remained in the Soviet Union—in the 1970s, the Kremlin encouraged Jews to emigrate. Many thousands did, settling in the United Sates or Israel. But Ita didn't want to leave: The US was a capitalist country, she said, as was Israel. Stalin had sent her to school and defeated Hitler.

She died during the 1990s. She remained a grateful Stalinist to the end.

CHAPTER 2

RICH WITHOUT MONEY
My Youth

I was bilingual as a child. My maternal grandmother—*Bubbe,* we called her—lived with us. *Bubbe* spoke no English—she spoke to me in Yiddish, and she and my mother spoke only Yiddish to each other. My one memory of her is her saying to me, "*Avek fun der fenster,*" "Away from the window." She was always concerned that I would fall out the window.

The first year of the Dust Bowl was 1934—one storm that year was so large and so intense that the dust reached New York City. The times were as hard in New York as they were in Oklahoma. My parents struggled to survive economically. During the early thirties, they started a paint store somewhere in Brooklyn, I'm not sure where. I think they worked in the store together, and my mother took care of my sister and me as well. The business failed, but I don't know when, nor do I know what my parents did for income afterward. I remember hearing that opening the paint store had some connection to my father's having been a house painter. During World War II he worked as a painter in the shipyards in Kearny, New Jersey. It was difficult work, painting in the cramped spaces inside a ship. The hours were grueling, too: He left for work early, came back late, and went to sleep. The smell of paint on my father's clothes is one of my olfactory memories.

* * *

It was the best of times and the worst of times—I grew up in financial poverty but emotional plenty. Making ends meet was an ongoing challenge for my mother, and earning money an ongoing challenge for my father—I became aware of this reality at an early age. The situation would have been less painful for me were our dire financial straits not accompanied by my mother's constant complaints about my father's inability to support us as she felt we deserved. My mother turned to her sister Bessie and her brother Joe for financial assistance. She got donations of clothes from various sources, arranged for afterschool Yiddish and Hebrew instruction to be tuition-free, and did the same for my brief summer camp experiences. I was very much aware that everyone I knew had more money than we had; I envied my friends who had larger apartments or lived in houses with extra rooms and bedrooms. I always shared a bedroom—first sleeping in the crib in my parents' room, then sharing a different room, first with my sister, then with my uncle.

But our family's poverty—our *noit*, in Yiddish—was countered by my emotional specialness in the family, and by the recognition of me as a prodigy by my peers and my teachers for my first six grades of elementary school. I created a rich life for myself reading, listening to music, and connecting to the larger political world.

The world intruded on my awareness in December 1941 when the Japanese attacked Pearl Harbor. I heard about it from a radio broadcast coming through an open window of a house on 44th Street as I walked to school at P.S. 164. Since the attack took place on a Sunday, I couldn't have heard the news on *The Seventh*—the date which will live in infamy. I probably heard it the next day.

I followed all the battles. In our home we read the English-language papers like the *New York Post* and *PM*. My uncle Irving, then living with us, brought home the *Post* every evening. I always looked forward to reading the comics on the back page. I don't know who brought home *PM*—most likely my father, as it was a "Lefty" paper.

My education was a very important concern for my mother. She bought me the complete set of *The Book of Knowledge* encyclopedia, and I can remember reading it from cover to cover, from A-to-Z. The smell of the volumes is another olfactory memory.

Although the war ended the Great Depression, money remained a problem for my family, causing my mother to work sorting buttons for her brothers, and to sew tea aprons at home for sale. One of the most embarrassing events of my childhood was when my mother sent me out to 13th Avenue to sell aprons. The police told me to stop, then came to our house to tell my mother that my selling stuff on the street was against the law. The incident was embarrassing to me and upsetting to my mother—we needed the money. She made that fact clear often with her complaints that my father was not earning enough. She continued complaining until my father was murdered. He was seventy-seven years old.

It was the day July 3, 1975. He was coming home after a visit to the bank to pick up the cash he'd need to meet the payroll. Two of his workers—one, a man named Barker, brandishing a knife—accosted him in the hallway of my parent's apartment building. I suspect that my father resisted, and Barker stabbed him. My mother found him in the hallway. She pulled the knife out—probably not a good idea. He died in the ambulance on the way to the hospital. I was in my office when I received a call from one of my parents' neighbors.

I wrote a poem about my father and his murder—starting with this event, writing poems became the way I dealt with painful trauma. The Borough Park precinct of the NYPD mounted a concerted effort to find the murderer; he *was* apprehended and convicted. Before being sent to prison, he was sent to Riker's Island. He got a rowboat and escaped from Riker's, then fled to Florida, where he married and started a new life. After several years, the NYPD police tracked him down, and he was sent to prison again. Sometime after that, Barbara Kopple, the documentary filmmaker best known for *Harlan County USA* wanted to do a film about Barker—how he was leading a good life and that his return to prison was unfair. After my brother-in-law and I told her we would get a lawyer, she dropped the project. My mother received Victim's Compensation because of my father's murder.

* * *

World War II organized my life from ages seven to eleven. I did what I could to help the war effort.

Everyone in the neighborhood collected scrap metal—there was always a pile on 44th Street. One day I put my prized *Erector Set* (a construction toy for making metal model buildings) in the pile. I am impressed to this day with the degree of my self-sacrifice.

I started a Victory Brigade that collected scrap paper. I was always the organizer for my peers, in my neighborhood, and in school. I was class president every year—first grade through sixth. I was always humble, and was recognized as such by my teachers and classmates. The curriculum in elementary school was laced with cultural anthropology. One text we worked on was "If I Were Going"—if I were going to Lapland, Holland, Africa, etc. There were also performances, including presentations of two oratorios: the *Ballad for Americans* and *The Lonesome Train*—music for both written by Eugene Robinson, lyrics for *Ballad* by John Latouche, for *Train* by Millard Lampell. These creators were, I believe, members or sympathizers of the CPUSA. Believe it or not, in 1940, *Ballad for Americans* was performed at both the Republican National Convention and a convention of the CPUSA. Both Paul Robeson and Bing Crosby recorded it.

I suspect my sixth-grade teacher, Mr. Schuckman, was a member of the Communist Party. He would have me run the class while he sat with his feet on his desk and read *The Daily Worker*. I brought in extra books to read—like *The Good Earth* by Pearl S. Buck and *Point Counterpoint* by Aldous Huxley—because there was very little reading, writing, and arithmetic there for me to learn. We rehearsed the oratorios in class and performed them in the auditorium for the school. I can still recite the words of *The Lonesome Train*, a story about the funeral train of Abraham Lincoln:

A lonesome train on a lonesome track—
Seven coaches painted black—
They carried Mr. Lincoln down,
The train started—the wheels went round—
You could hear that whistle for miles around
Crying, Freedom! Freedom!

I remember some books Mr. Schuckman assigned me to read, especially the *Autobiography of Lincoln Steffens*, a fellow traveler, and a book about how corporate America was poisoning us.

* * *

I started writing my autobiography in the fifth grade—I still have one chapter, which reveals that I was interested in the girls in my class, and the girls in my class were interested in me. One I remember well was Helen Vishinsky, liked Russian ministers—I think her father was also leftist. I can also recall some of the girls from Montauk Junior High School: Anita Tepper, Joan Herman, Joan Itkin (who married Ted Shapiro). I recently reconnected with someone I knew not only at Montauk but in my medical school class: Michael Mossesson, a retired hematologist. We published his book, *The Fibrinogen Papers: Life of a Clot Doctor*.

In 1948, at age fourteen, I went to *Camp Well Met*; and when I returned to Brooklyn, I developed polio. I have a memory of sitting in a chair, suffering from a fever, while the doctor did the spinal tap. I was first sent to Kingston Avenue Hospital, the infectious disease hospital at Kings County. They treated me with a Priscolene, which is a vasodilator—the idea was that increased circulation would lessen the paralysis. But I did not have paralysis, only muscle weakness, more on the right side than the left. After Kingston Avenue, I was sent to the New York State Rehabilitation Hospital in Haverstraw, New York, where I edited the patient newsletter and wrote a column called "Crutch Tips." I still have a copy. I was in Haverstraw during the 1948 election. I went to sleep that night thinking Dewey had won, then awoke to find Truman had prevailed. Haverstraw was in a very Republican county—all the nursing staff were for Dewey. Only one janitor and I supported Truman. After it was clear that Truman won, the nurses were so angry, they made the maintenance man wash all the floors. But although I was rooting for Truman against Dewey, my heart was with Henry. Wallace: "Win with Wallace." I remember listening to the Progressive Party Convention that summer, when Wallace, formerly FDR's vice president, was nominated. Glen Taylor, the guitar-playing senator from Idaho, was his running mate. It was only many years later that I learned that the Progressive Party had been infiltrated by the CPUSA.

My polio hospitalization took place during my last year at Montauk Junior High, at 15th Avenue and 43rd Street in Brooklyn. In the seventh grade my run for class vice president was successful. I don't think I did much in the office but, in the spring of 1948, I decided to run for President of the GO (General Organization). After I was hospitalized in the summer, I decided to continue my campaign when school resumed in September—I thought I'd grab the sympathy vote and win going away.

I lost.

I didn't attend class; my mother brought my assignments to me in the hospital, and I completed them without any problem. I graduated on time, in June 1949. I don't remember what my position was in the class. I do remember some of my teachers—Mr. Smith for Latin. I excelled in his class and still have a copy of a letter he sent me, although I regret I didn't take French instead.

The question then was what high school I should go to. I was in the New Utrecht district, but somehow my mother, or I, or both of us, decided that Erasmus Hall was a better school.

Going out of district at that time was not easy, but my mother devised a plan. She told the Board of Education that my polio would make going to New Utrecht difficult. To get there I'd have had to use the West End Elevated, accessible only by climbing a long staircase. However, I could go to Erasmus by the Caton Avenue bus—no stair-climbing required.

Going to Erasmus had a profound effect on my life—for one thing, my wife, Arlene, went there. And while I didn't know her there, she knew of me.

"Erasmus was a high school of 5,000 students—it was giant," says Arlene. "Arnie was like two years ahead of me. It was a very good school at the time. I had a friend, Richard Reinitz, who was a friend of Arnie's as well. And Arnie was part of a small group that kind of ran the school. They were the presidents of everything. At that time, I knew he was smart. We eventually met because of another mutual friend."

We were part of an elite school group. In fact, I think I first connected with Arlene at Hunter College, when we were taking the admissions test for the University of Chicago. A friend from Erasmus, Richard Asofsky, remembers that he introduced us. She had been horseback riding that day in Central Park—she came to Hunter wearing her riding outfit, with jodhpurs.

"My father," Arlene recalls, "who was from a rural family in *Chekhanov,* was very proud that my brother and I were good riders. That day I went to Central Park in the morning, and after that went over to Hunter College to take the entrance exam. Didn't take it seriously. In fact, I was very relaxed and did well on it. And our mutual friend, who was there, introduced us. But that was it. It was a long exam and very exhausting. I went right home after."

Arlene and I didn't say much to each other that day.

"No," she says, "just hello."

How we connected, at the University of Chicago that Fall, is an account for later.

CHAPTER 3

FIRST STEPS IN THE WORLD
College, Medical School, Marriage

I prayed twice a day in high school, but my world was expanding—beyond Brooklyn, beyond my family of immigrants, beyond Judaism. Credit it to the public library. At least once a week, I went to the library at Grand Army Plaza and returned with a load of books. My awakening began with *Portrait of the Artist as a Young Man* by James Joyce, and with my discovery of Henry Miller, Kenneth Patchen, Upton Sinclair, Sinclair Lewis, and a long list of other modern writers. I remain at a loss as to who inspired me in that direction when I was that age. Certainly no one in my family. Perhaps some of my friends in high school. Perhaps Richard Reinitz, who was "with it" in a literary sense. He was famous in our high school group, which included Stanley Palumbo, Bennett Simon, Marty Willick, and Nancy Schatz (who became Nancy Willick). One day Richard and his friend Calvin Green left their books at the Erasmus Hall Lost-and-Found, and stowed away on a boat sailing for France—I think it was the SS *De Grasse*. Richard and Calvin got seasick in the middle of the voyage and gave themselves up. Their parents had to fly to France to retrieve the boys.

Richard became a scholar. Majoring in American History at Goddard College, in Vermont, he became a professor at Hobart and William Smith Colleges, and wrote about Roger Williams, founder of the Providence Plantations, which became the Colony of Rhode Island. Richard died at too young an age—he was just forty-five. Marty, Nancy, Bennett, and Stanley were the crew who ran the high school, and I was connected to them. Stanley graduated first in our class; I was second. In high school Bennett was a Latin and Greek scholar. He, Marty, Stanley, and I all became psychoanalysts. Arlene knew them and had heard of me, but I didn't know her.

Stanley's story is sad. He became a psychoanalyst but was expelled from the American Psychoanalytic Association because of boundary violations with a patient and a supervisee. He was my closest friend in the group, the smartest person I ever knew, and a wonderful poet. His book, *Dreaming and Memory*, is an important contribution to our understanding of dreams.

Marty and Bennett trained at the New York Psychoanalytic Institute, as did I. Stanley trained at the Washington Institute. Bennett was in my class there—we entered in 1964. Thirty-six people applied that year—thirteen were accepted, twelve men and one woman. The woman, Eleanor Bogach, graduated after thirteen years, which is a long time—there were four full years' worth of classes and analysis. I graduated in five years; most people didn't take more than seven to finish. She's no longer in practice. Her husband, Sam Bogach, researched cutting-edge stuff: the use of Dilantin as treatment. He did studies for Jack Dreyfus, the mutual-fund tycoon who financed research on the drug, which he considered a miraculous healing tool for a variety of maladies. Sam Bogach and Elvin Semrad, interviewed me when I applied for residency at Mass Mental Health. I was not accepted at Mass Mental Health—I'm not sure why, but I don't think it had anything to do with a quota for Jews. I know for a fact that I wasn't accepted at Columbia's medical school because I was Jewish—I got the inside scoop because the admissions director's son was a dormmate of mine at University of Chicago.

* * *

Perhaps I should pick up the story about when I graduated from high school and applied to college—to New York University in the Heights, Cornell, Harvard, and the University of Chicago. I didn't consider Yale or Princeton. I was accepted by all but could not go to any—my family did not have the money. I still have a copy of the letter informing me that I was admitted to Harvard and that I could apply for financial aid my sophomore year. To this day it is astounding to me that no one in my family was aware of how prestigious a school Harvard was. Had they known, maybe they could have tried to mobilize resources so that I could attend. Maybe they did realize what Harvard meant but my mother just preferred I not leave home.

Instead, I decided to go to Brooklyn College, starting in the fall of 1951. I remember my first day registering—I took the Brighton Beach subway line to the campus in Midwood. When I returned from my day at Brooklyn College, there was a letter from the University of Chicago awarding me a full scholarship: tuition, room, and board. The rest is the saga of my life. What would have been my life trajectory for the next sixty-eight years had I not left for Chicago? For one thing, I would not have connected with Arlene.

* * *

When I arrived in Chicago, I learned that I had placed out of all of the courses on the entrance exam but was required to take four courses for my bachelor's degree, which I received the following year, 1952, although I would spend another two years there in the Division of Biological Sciences taking premed courses. There were three others who placed out: Ernest Hartmann, the son of Heinz Hartmann, a Viennese psychoanalyst who had been a prize pupil of Freud; Howard Kremen, who became a close friend to me; and Nela Van Pesky. Ernie, Howard, and I all became psychoanalysts—an interesting fact. The best and the brightest leaned toward psychoanalytic training, and I was among that echelon in college, just as I was in high school with Stanley, Bennett, and Marty. Of course, Ernie had his father to follow. Ernie was among the first people I met on my first day on campus. He wore white buck shoes and kept his head to one side as he spoke, except he didn't really speak, he mumbled.

35

Many years later, at a meeting at the New York Psychoanalytic Association, Heinz Hartmann stood up to address the audience. He turned his head to one side and mumbled.

I lived in Dodd House, in Burton Judson Court, which was across the midway from the campus. I remember walking across the midway in the winter—the coldest weather I had ever endured. The house head was Fred Dwyer. My roommate was Dan Queen, from Swansea, Massachusetts, where his father was a local elected official. An interesting fellow, Dan ran the dorm radio station, WUC, and loved classical music, especially Mahler—in particular the great song cycles like *Kindertotenlieder* (*Songs on the Death of Children*) and *Das Lied von der Erde* (*The Song of the Earth*). Always far left in his politics, he later joined the Illinois Communist Party, became its chair, was arraigned by the authorities because he refused to name names, and spent two years in prison. Some years after that trouble, he took a conservative turn and consulted for the Saudi government. An electronics whiz, he made an amplifier for the radio station out of Wurlitzer vacuum tubes. Dan and I shared an interest in films. We both belonged to Doc Film, one of the oldest campus film societies in the United States. Some films I remember seeing on campus: *Dies Irae (Day of Wrath*, 1943, Denmark), directed by Carl Theodore Dreyer, and Ingmar Bergman's *Wild Strawberries*.

While in school, I found interesting ways to earn money. I ran the university laundry and dry-cleaning service in the basement of Dodd House, and did marketing interviews for a company called Social Research that had been started by Ernest Dichter. His wife, Jean Binstock, the company's director of recruitment, was a resident at Menninger's when I was there. I also had a job at the university staphylococcal research laboratory. The idea was to purify staphylococcal enterotoxin using the bioagent Penerotoxin, which was given to monkeys through a stomach tube.

My job was to measure the vomit time.

* * *

The University of Chicago was a special school and Dodd House a special community. The student at Dodd House who went on to become the most famous was Carl Sagan, another Jew from Brooklyn with a father born in Ukraine. We would make fun of him because of his interest in life in outer space. He earned degrees in physics and astronomy and became one of the world's most effective popularizers of science.

"Carl Sagan was a riot," Arlene recalls. "He was so funny. He was this nutcase kid who only wanted to talk about life on Mars. He was absolutely abhorred in the girls' dormitory. We would scream. 'Get out! Carl's coming!' He was totally obsessed with girls. Unable to keep his hands off. And at the same time, he wouldn't talk about anything but this strange idea of his that there was life on Mars, and we were supposed to find it, and [that] he was going to be the one to do it.

"We met him again years later when he and I were teaching at Cornell—I was the only woman on the faculty. It was really olden times. I would have my lunch at the faculty club, which was a wonderful place, because Cornell had a hotel school. They were teaching people how to be hoteliers, so the faculty club was high quality. But no one would talk to me—the guys acted like I was invisible.

"At some point Arnie came up to visit me and, at lunchtime the first day, he went over and said hello to Carl. Carl had not talked to anyone in that faculty club the whole time he was there; he was off in a corner reading the *New York Times* by himself. Arnie just went over to him, and within a week or so, had introduced him to all his fellow faculty members. It was so weird. He was an awkward person and very snobby, because he was already doing TV. He had a way of alienating people, I have to say."

Two dormmates have remained close friends: Frank Barham, who became ¨iatrist—we reconnected in Topeka at the Menninger School of Psychiatry—and Pete Rosen, who died in 2019. Pete went to medical school at Washington University in St. Louis and became a surgeon. But after surviving a heart attack at age thirty-eight, he decided to switch specialties, going into emergency medicine. Given his medical condition, he thought he should be near an emergency room. In fact, Pete established the separate specialty of emergency medicine, writing the discipline's standard textbook, which is now in its fourth revision and reprinting.

Other students in the House included Nicholas Papianis, a brilliant mathematician who supported himself playing cards on 63rd Street. I remember one quote from Nick: "Poincaré was right, the answer is philosophy." Frank Barham and I weren't the only students who became psychoanalysts—Bob Michaels, Fred Solomon, and Leon Balter all did so, too, as did Arlene.

The curriculum at the University of Chicago was made up of fourteen required courses: Social Science 1, 2, and 3; Humanity 1, 2 and 3; Natural Science 1, 2, and 3; History, Organization Methods and Principles of Knowledge (OMP), a language, mathematics and ... there was one more, which I can't now recall. I got my Bachelor of Arts after just a year at Chicago, by taking only four courses. When you arrived there, you sat for tests in all fourteen courses, and if you passed, you didn't have to take the courses. However, they wouldn't let you leave before you started, so you did have to take four courses, But then I stayed another two years to take pre-medical courses so I could go to medical school. In some ways I regret having done it that way—there were a lot of other courses I might have taken and gotten a lot out of, with some incredible professors. Anyway, I was there for one year in the college, and two years in the Division of Biological Sciences.

The four courses I took were social sciences 3, humanities 3, natural sciences 3, and OMP. Mike Nichols and Elaine May were enrolled in my OMP class, but rarely showed up. They were busy with the Compass Theater and Second City. Attendance in class wasn't mandatory—you just had to pass the

FIRST STEPS IN THE WORLD

exams. My OMP professor was Henry Rago, a philosopher and world-class poet. (He edited *Poetry* magazine for fourteen years.)

The curriculum was based on the Robert M. Hutchins and Mortimer J. Adler Great Books system, organized by Richard McKeon. I arrived at the University of Chicago just after Hutchins had left. The headline in *The Maroon*, the university newspaper, that summer was: "Hutchins Out—to Lunch." It was said that the University of Chicago was where atheist professors taught Thomist philosophy to Jews.

What was wonderful about the curriculum was that it was based on knowledge shared by all, so that we could engage in exciting intellectual exchanges. We could talk about "the Great CI"—the Great Categorical Imperative. My floor head was Donald Levine, who became a leading sociologist, as well as a dean at the college for several years.

It was at the end of my first quarter when I again connected with Arlene. But before I tell you that story, let her introduce herself.

* * *

"I was born at a place called Brooklyn Women's Hospital," Arlene says, "which was an abortion clinic covered by a maternity hospital. I lived for the first six years of my life with my maternal grandparents, who were from a town called *Chekhanov* in Poland. My mother grew up in Warsaw with her aunt, uncle, and cousin—she was farmed out there because her aunt could only have one child. That family was rich, whereas, my mother's family was poor.

"Here in America my grandfather was secretary of the Chekhanov Young Men's Benevolent Association. My grandparents wanted my mother to get married, so they invited to dinner a young man who was a member of that group, and eventually the pair got married and became my parents.

"I lived with my grandparents for a while, because by the time I was born, during the Great Depression, my father didn't have a job and my mother was supporting the family, working in the hat trade. She worked very hard and could not take care of me.

"We lived at 2027 Pacific Street in Brooklyn. I remember being taught the address when I was very young, because kids in those days would walk around the city. Just go anywhere. We had to know how to get back. You could ask people and give them your address.

"My grandfather worked as a laundry man. He would collect laundry from ladies and bring it back wet. A lot of times when my grandmother, who was depressed, couldn't take care of me, he would take me to work with him. And when I was quite little, I learned how to sort laundry. It was great.

"A very nice memory. And it enabled me to develop intellectually, like a Montessori school would. I had to sort the different shapes and colors and categories for washing. And then you had to re-sort the clothes to make sure they went to the family they belonged to. So by the time I got to kindergarten I was way ahead. And I loved school for that reason.

"One important memory: My Uncle Morris joined the army just before Pearl Harbor, and almost simultaneously he got engaged to my Aunt Sylvia. We had a big engagement party at my Aunt Sylvia's house—a Sunday afternoon dinner for about a dozen people. A family affair. And they turned on the radio—this big radio with doors on it. And there was Pearl Harbor. When Sylvia's father heard the news, he put his hands on the table, put his head in his hands, and died. He must have been in his fifties. He probably had heart disease to begin with, but that was too much for him. I was six years old at the time, and it was *verrry* scary.

"Another memory from the war: We had a neighbor whose husband had been killed in the war, just before D-Day. And when D-Day came she cried all day. I felt so sorry for her, and I tried to comfort her, but she was very angry at me. She didn't want to be comforted. She wanted to mourn.

"When I was six, I moved back in with my parents, because my father got a job as a jobber of textiles. We lived on Montgomery Street and Utica Avenue in Crown Heights. That was where I grew up from age six to age sixteen. Then, at sixteen, I went off to school at the University of Chicago, to my great relief, since I did not fit into my parents' lifestyle at all. I was very happy to be able to go off to college early.

"My parents lived the high life. They had a lot of friends who would come in and out of the house all the time. They had the first TV set in the neighborhood, so everybody in the neighborhood came in in the evenings. There was lots of socializing and lots of noise, but I was a studious kid. I wanted to read, I wanted to be quiet, and that didn't work out very well. I was really my grandparents' child in that way. So I spent a lot of my youth in a Christian Science reading room on Utica Avenue in Crown Heights, where I would go to escape. And also a lot of time escaping to my grandparents' house. That didn't sit well with my parents who felt rejected, and thought I was running away from home. Actually, I was running *to* what I wanted.

"I was not particularly interested in high school at that time. I had a *lot* of conflict about it, because my mother really *didn't* want me to become a studious girl. She wanted me to get married. So, for example, when I asked for a desk, she bought me a dressing table, with mirrors. You couldn't read at it or write on it. We had a whole different culture, my parents and I. We did not understand each other *at all*.

"My grandparents were Orthodox. My parents were militantly opposed to that. One of the ways I found to rebel in high school was to study Hebrew. My parents hated that, especially my mother. Hebrew was taught as a language at that point because Israel had just become a nation. My mother wanted me to learn French and be elegant. I think this is important in terms of Arnie because when I met him, one of the main things I was looking for in a boyfriend was someone who was Orthodox, like my grandpa. And at the time Arnie was. However, as soon as we met, he stopped being Orthodox.

"The Shoah was particularly personal, because all of my father's family was killed. He had thirteen brothers and sisters—all killed. My mother had a particularly terrible story. She had been used as a sort of companion for her cousin in her growing-up years, and one day when they were at an ice-skating lesson, her cousin said to her, 'You know, I'm the real child in this family, and you're just here as suits me. And you're nothing.' My mother kicked her cousin, who got a compound fracture, which never healed properly. Later, because this girl was a cripple, she and her parents were unable to come to the United States; eventually, they perished at Auschwitz, and my mother knew that. It was just terrible for her.

"So the Holocaust had a lot of meanings, and it was a terribly, terribly important part of why my grandmother was so depressed. In those days we knew about the Holocaust long before it was in the newspapers. We knew from letters, sent from Europe, that Jews were being rounded up and deported, never to be seen again.

"My parents dealt with all this pain by spending a lot of time at the Copacabana, by dressing up and going out with different people, by playing a lot of cards. In fact, when I told them that I was interested in Arnie and that I would like to bring him home to meet them, they said, "So is he a bridge player?" They made themselves into know-nothings. I think that was largely an attempt to cope with their terrible, terrible history. At the time I didn't realize that; I thought they were just *vilde khayes* (wild animals).

"I only spoke Yiddish until I went to kindergarten, where I learned English. I would come home and teach my grandma, who spoke no English, English words. On the other hand, my mother claimed to *not* to know any Yiddish. Would not have anything to do with it, and insisted, when I went to live with her and my father, that I speak only English. I didn't speak Yiddish again until I went to comfort my grandfather when my grandmother died. And I found I could still speak it—baby Yiddish, kitchen Yiddish, but still Yiddish (in contrast to Arnie, who had an educated Yiddish).

42

"Here's how I got to the University of Chicago: My mother suffered from intense hay fever, so my parents and I went away to a hotel in Bethlehem, New Hampshire, to escape during hay fever season. I was sitting on the lawn reading a book of poetry when a man came over to me, a much older man. (He must have been twenty or twenty-five, maybe even thirty). His name was Hyman Minsky, later a Nobel prize winner in economics. He asked what I was reading. We talked about it a little bit. And he said, 'You shouldn't stay in high school. You should go to the University of Chicago where I went. *Apply*.'

"That seemed like a good idea. And then my friend Larry Lerner, who was there as student at the time, also said I should go. So I went and took the entrance exam. And I thought, 'This is a way to get out of here. This is a way to go where I want to go.' Only Chicago and Columbia took students before they finished high school, and I was only a sophomore in high school at the time. It was a small school and that seemed great—only about five hundred students in the entire college, for all four years, so not much more than a hundred in each class. Everybody knew everybody.

"So at sixteen I went off to school at the University of Chicago, to my great relief, since I did not fit into my parent's lifestyle at all. I was very happy to be able to go off to college early."

* * *

It was my religious observance that initially got Arlene interested in me.

"At Chicago," she recalls, "early in my freshman year, I heard about this guy in Dodd House who wrapped leather around his arm and I thought, 'That's for me.' I knew what that was—*Tefillin*—but the other kids thought it was just something exotic."

We ran into each other at a student's piano recital on campus. After a brief conversation, I suggested that, since we were both going to be in New York City for the New Year's break, we should date on New Year's Eve.

"My roommate, Penny," says Arlene, "gave a Christmas party in Manhattan—we were back home on intersession for Christmas vacation. And Penny arranged for me to have a date with a friend of her family, a nice guy who was at law school at the University of Indiana, and whom she had dated but was not interested in. She invited Arnie to that party to be *her* date. And this nice guy, who was my date, volunteered to take Arnie and me back to Brooklyn, because he had a car. And he did. And Arnie and I got to talking. And afterward he called and asked me out for New Year's Eve. But in those days you didn't go out for New Year's Eve with someone you didn't really know well. So we had to have a date before that."

That was the custom, so we decided to start by going out the day before. We went to the movies, a double bill of *Pépé le Moko* and *Carnival in Flanders* at the Paris Theater.

On New Year's Eve, we went to a party at the home of someone I knew from Erasmus: Marcia Sylvan. Also present were Stanley Palombo and Arlene's friend from Green Hall, Edith Kramer. (Arlene's mother's name also happened to be Edith Kramer).

We returned to Arlene's apartment, talked a lot, slept on the floor, and decided, on New Year's Day 1952, that we would get married. Arlene says she was always an impulsive shopper.

"I mean not to get married right then," says Arlene, "but we decided that eventually we would get married. In those days, things were different. You didn't have sex with people you weren't going to marry. Look, I'm an impulsive person. Every house we have lived in, I have bought within fifteen minutes of seeing it."

Nevertheless, this quick decision needs explaining. I think what drove both of us was a need to escape from our families. When we returned to Chicago, we went to a Polynesian restaurant called The T Hut on 63rd Street, and I ate shrimp. That was the end of my being Orthodox.

"It was like our third or fourth date," says Arlene. "I ordered shrimp. I had grown up having non-kosher food—my mother thought it was old-fashioned to keep kosher. Arnie tasted my dinner, and then he got his own dish of shrimp and that was it. That was the end of everything. All his religion: *Kaput!* I was astonished—astonished that he would eat that food, and astonished that he would suddenly give all his observance up in one day. But it's not unusual, I have since learned. There's a recent novel called *Shmutz*, in which the girl eats a ham sandwich and that's it. The whole thing. All in one swoop. On the other hand, Arnie's father was not at all religious. So for Arnie, this religious thing was his own way of being different."

Arlene had been aware that I was Orthodox because she told me that she'd heard there was someone in Dodd House who wrapped leather around his arm. That someone was me. Several years later, another Dodd House resident told me that he remembered my putting on phylacteries (Tefillin) in the Dodd House bathroom—a fact I had repressed.

"The following vacation," recalls Arlene, "Arnie wanted to introduce me to his parents and visit his home, so we went there. It was in Borough Park, on the second floor of a walkup. Inside I was astounded immediately. The door opened to a long corridor. To the right were the bathroom and the kitchen, then a bedroom. On the left was this long solid wall covered with report cards, framed; with pictures from the Yiddish newspaper—of Arnie graduating from all the different schools he went to; with pictures of award events. All kinds of things, but only about Arnie. And there were four children in the family.

"This showed me that his parents valued him and *only* him. I felt sorry for his sisters and his brother. It must have been awful to come into the house you lived in, and see yourself not valued at all, and your brother worshiped."

The second year I was at the University of Chicago, Dan Queen and I shared an apartment. Arlene and I made good on our plan to get married on March 21—the first day of spring—1954. She was nineteen, I was twenty. I needed my parents' permission to get married because I was under 21; Arlene did not because she was over 18. The rules for men and women were different at that time.

We flew into a snowy New York for the wedding, spent our wedding night at the Plaza, and flew back to Chicago the next day. Very fancy. I don't know who paid for the hotel, although I assume it was Arlene's parents—certainly not mine. Mine paid for the wedding dinner at *Garfein's*, a Jewish restaurant at Second Avenue and Second Street. Peter Rosen, the future emergency medical pioneer, was my best man; Arlene's friend and Green Hall roommate Penny Leese was her maid of honor. The food at the wedding was good (Arlene's memory, not mine); the wine was Manischewitz.

"Yes, the food was very good," says Arlene. "It wasn't a very beautiful place or anything. There were thirty or forty guests."

The rabbi was a friend of Arlene's grandfather. I remember that I recited the Hebrew marriage vows from memory. We danced a lot.

Several in my family thought we were both too young to get married. My family saw my marriage as my ticket to medical school—Arlene and her parents, my family reasoned, could support me during my studies. And she did just that.

"I had to work when Arnie was in med school," Arlene recalls. "Somebody had to support us. My first job was for an insurance company. It was hard to find a job that was suitable in those days. I was nineteen years old and a college graduate. I had to be twenty to become a schoolteacher, which was the job I thought I should do, because that way I would have the most time with my kid (who would soon be on the way). So I worked for this insurance company for, maybe, eight or nine months.

"My mother-in-law and I did not get along well—that is, until Arnie graduated from medical school. Then we didn't get along at all. Her idea was that I would support him through medical school, and then he'd leave me and come back home where he belonged."

* * *

"Arnie always wanted to be a psychoanalyst—sort of," says Arlene. "Being a psychoanalyst in those days was a very glamorous profession. And a lot of smart kids did it—the smartest kids, in fact. He had read about it a little bit, so he was interested. And he was going to go to medical school because that was his mother's dream. But the last year at Chicago, just before leaving, he was taking some math course and decided that he wanted to be a mathematician instead.

"But it was too late. He was already committed to attending medical school."

It was around this time that my name changed from Arnold Gorodowsky to Arnold Richards. Here's how it happened: My brother, born when I was ten, was named Richard Jay Gorodowsky, which gave my parents the impetus to change the name of their business to the Richard Painting and Decorating Company. The name stuck—my father's customers would call him Mr. Richard. When it was apparent that I would seek to attend medical school, my mother, with the agreement of my father, decided to change the family name to Richards (and to call my brother Jay, not Richard). In retrospect, I think the reason my parents made the change was that they were concerned that I should get into medical school. This was the 1950s; they knew about discrimination. But I felt my name was taken from me, although for what my mother thought was a good reason. Still, the plan didn't entirely work—after all, Columbia College of Physicians and Surgeons rejected me because of my being Jewish. I was accepted by the University of Chicago Medical School. Arlene and I decided that we could not afford the tuition and living expenses there, but I was also accepted by Downstate Medical School in Brooklyn. The plan was that we would return to New York to live in Arlene's parents' apartment in Brooklyn where I would study for the New York State Medical School Scholarship Exam, which provided $700 a year to cover the tuition.

Although I could not be certain, I was optimistic that I would get the scholarship. I was accepted at the school before I took the test; I spent the summer studying for it. I scored seventh-highest among some nine hundred people taking the exam. It should be evident by now that I was a superb test taker—as long as there were no essay questions. Writing essays was not easy for me—my essays would be short, although I got high marks for what I wrote.

In the fall we rented an apartment at the corners of Henry and Amity streets in Brooklyn Heights, near the Long Island Hospital and the Long Island School of Medicine, where first-year classes were held. The next year the school moved to a brand-new building on Clarkson Avenue, where the second-year basic science classes were held.

I started medical school with the idea that I would become a psychoanalyst, which had been my ambition since I was a teenager and read the *Introductory Lectures on Psychoanalysis* by Freud in the red and yellow permaback addition. I did find some of the subjects in medical school interesting, particularly neuroanatomy and pathology.

In the first year of medical school, in Gross Anatomy, you bonded with your three partners around a cadaver; with me at the dissecting table were Milton Reisner, Jerry Rosmarin, Don Pinals, and me. Milton became a psychiatrist, but then developed a serious malignancy in the throat which affected his ability to speak, requiring a speech aid. He died several years ago. Don Pinals became a radiologist and recently treated the breast cancer of one of my patients. His family owned a company called *Imp Originals* that made upscale children's clothes—I remember a lovely outfit he brought for our son, Stephen. Jerry Rosmarin went into ENT (otolaryngology: diseases of the ear, nose, and throat). His brother was a psychiatrist who was the director of Linden Hill, a residential treatment center for adolescents.

I spent the summer of the first and second years doing research in pathology with the chair of the department, Patrick Fitzgerald. Arlene had not been aware that she was pregnant until Thanksgiving of 1954. In February 1955, our son was born. We named him Stephen, after Joyce's Stephen Daedalus. He was the first offspring born in our medical school class. I was still twenty years old, Arlene still nineteen.

"Once Stephen was born," Arlene recalls, "my grandfather offered us an apartment in a small four-family house he owned. So we lived there and we didn't have to pay rent. We had some wedding gifts as well as some money I had saved up from working at the insurance company. Those funds enabled us to get by." Arlene then started teaching. "While I was teaching, my mother took care of our son from nine to three, and she would bring the baby carriage at three o'clock and pick me up at school.

"First, I taught fourth grade at Williamsburg High School elementary division. I was there only a few weeks. The first two weeks I lost twenty pounds. I was throwing up all the time. These were kids who had already been tracked into vocational school by fourth grade. So were extruded from the system.

"I found it sad. For example: I started teaching school in February, and the first lesson I planned was on Abraham Lincoln, because his birthday was February 12, and celebrated in those days. I had books, fourth-grade readers, and I gave them to the kids. The book had a story about Abraham Lincoln but no one could read—which was astonishing to me. Still, I carried on. I read the story *to* them. I said, 'This is an amazing story, because it tells about how Lincoln and his sister and his stepmother and his father all lived in a one-room cabin.' And a little girl raised her hand and said, 'Teacher, Teacher. In my room we have twenty-seven people.' And it went on from there.

"These were immigrant kids living in unimaginably crowded and terrible conditions. I felt *so* sorry for them all the time. That was why I had this terrible reaction. And then I got a job at PS 189 and left. And at PS 189, I had students very much like myself, and enjoyed it a lot. I taught there for the next two and a half years.

"As long as Arnie was in medical school, I was teaching."

I was a father and a husband from day one. I was trying to pursue my professional education, but, at the same time, to take care of my family. Of course, that was not so easy in terms of earning money. I depended on Arlene.

Arlene did it all—while I was in medical school, and then later, when we came back to New York. You might say I followed the *shtetl* model: The husband studies and the wife runs the family. She did everything: three meals a day, seven days a week, and everything else. At the same time, she was pursuing her career in graduate school, and so forth. My ambition was that Arlene would belong to all the same organizations that I did. And of course, Arlene's now a Training Analyst, and a substantial professional person. She made it all on her own.

Even while I was in medical school, however, I earned money, too. For a time, I worked nights and weekends at a clinical laboratory in Manhattan. I also worked in market research for a company called Social Research that basically invented the field. I did studies for various advertising agencies. For example, we did a study for Chrysler, looking at their dealerships. I went around to dealers and asked them, "How do you feel about Chrysler?" One dealer said, "I think they're backwards." So I came up with the slogan, "The Forward Look," which the company used to market their new line of cars starting in the mid- to late fifties. Look at a '57 Plymouth and notice the long lines and the tail fins. Of course, I didn't get any credit or money for coming up with that slogan. I also did some work for Nelson Rockefeller when he was running for governor of New York. Essentially, I was doing in-depth interviewing, talking to people, and making sociological observations about them.

So, I had these part-time jobs. But, of course, the problem is that my parents weren't able to give us money. Arlene's parents were. And they helped us.

Still, it was a struggle.

* * *

I could read Yiddish when I was a young child. In fact, my earliest lexical memory is reading the Yiddish *Forward*: I recall seeing a photo of a man with a beard. The photo was captioned: "A very famous Jewish psychiatrist died." Several years ago, I looked for and found a copy of that issue of the *Forward*, from November 1939, when I was five, and it was as I remembered it: A picture of a very famous Jewish psychiatrist—in fact, the most famous psychiatrist (Jewish or otherwise), Sigmund Freud—and the announcement of his death. There was also a headline I hadn't recalled: "Warsaw in Flames." I had always remembered that Freud in the picture had a beard, and that our landlord, an older Orthodox man, also had a beard. Maybe this is transference I did not assume that Freud was Orthodox, but I did think he appeared to be a Jewish patriarch like my landlord.

Before the war, my family considered itself lucky to be in the United States; that feeling multiplied after the war: We were here, we were alive, we could live freely. To varying degrees, some members of my family wanted to put distance between themselves and the old country, between themselves and the shtetl. Some were more assimilated, some less; some modern, some less.

In the home I grew up in, ties to the Old Country were reinforced every day—in my mother's kitchen. To this day, I remember with clarity the smells and tastes of her cooking: the chopped herring, the *p'tcha*, the *kasha varnishkes*, the *vorenicas* (Ukrainian dumplings), and the borscht. *Fleyshike* borscht was like ambrosia, and I still love it. We get dairy borscht from *Barney Greengrass* and *schav* (cold sorrel soup) from *Murray's The Sturgeon King*. Jewish food has an emotional connection—and not just for me. I've heard Jews say, "The only part of me that's Jewish is my taste for gefilte fish." They call themselves "gastronomic Jews," meaning they like the cuisine although they have no place for the religion or anything else.

* * *

I grew up in a mixed Jewish and Italian neighborhood—the Italian kids beat up the Jewish kids. Since then, the area has become nearly 100 percent Orthodox. My mother, who lived there until she died, had the interesting experience of having her childhood community reconstitute around her—the people who moved in were like the people from the shtetl where she grew up. Thirteenth Avenue was replete with wig stores and Kosher butchers.

My mother sent me to Yiddish school at the *Arbeiter Ring*, known in English as the Workmen's Circle. Classes were held not far from our home, in a building—I think it was a union hall—on 14th Avenue and 42nd Street, only a couple of blocks from our home on 13th Avenue and 44th Street. The classroom was in the auditorium, which featured a stage; above the proscenium were pictures of leftist labor leaders, including Eugene V. Debs. My sister went to the *shula* also, but I don't remember her being there—I only learned of her attendance when she recently told me. On Saturdays we had singing—militantly secular—they wanted us there, not in synagogue. I recall one Saturday morning, in 1942 perhaps, when Sholom Secunda, a well-known Yiddish songwriter, came and taught us a song he'd just written: "Dona," a song of freedom, a song of liberation. A song of the hope of escape from annihilation for the Jews in Europe.

I was closer to the vernacular (Yiddish) than many others in my generation because my family had access to the Yiddish papers. I read, understood, and spoke Yiddish. Believe it or not, there were five at that time: *Der Forvitz* (*The Forward*), *Der Tag* (*The Day*), *Der Morgen Journal* (*The Morning Journal*), the *Fria Arberter Stimme* (*Free Worker's Voice*, written from an anarchist perspective), and the *Freiheit* (*Freedom*—a communist paper—essentially a Yiddish version of the *Daily Worker*). At home we got *The Day* and the *Forward*. I don't know that my father read the *Freiheit* in Yiddish. It is more likely that he read the *Daily Worker* in English.

At *shula* we read the Yiddish classics—Sholem Aleichem, I. L. Peretz, among others. I remember the names of my teachers: Mr. and Mrs. Sossel. I was their favorite.

I went to Yiddish school from 1941–1947, from age seven until I was thirteen; information about the Holocaust was part of my day-to-day experience. From what was taught and discussed at Yiddish school, from reading the Yiddish newspapers, I was aware of what was going on in Europe. I remember a Yiddish poem I learned: "We're not going to have any wheat or corn because the fields are dug up with graves." *(Mir celen vait Korn nish behoven Der Felder mit greebern bar grubin).* I made my thespian debut at Yiddish school. We performed *Dos Meserl* (*The Knife*), based on a play by Sholem Aleichem, for a large audience at PS 131. I played the lead, the little boy with the knife. It's an interesting oedipal image.

I was a precocious child; I read a lot, in both Yiddish and English. Yiddish has always been part of my *neshama*, my soul. My connection to the language, the school, the literature dates to my childhood. I mourn the loss of that language, that culture, every day of my life.

CHAPTER 4

FROM TEFILLIN TO SHRIMP
TO THE YIDDISH REVIVAL

My Jewish Journey

I had a secular Jewish education at Yiddish school, but eventually also received a religious Jewish education.

I come from a mixed marriage: My father was an atheist, my mother Orthodox. I've been told that before I was born, when my parents were living with my mother's father on New Jersey Avenue in Brownsville, my father would go to the movies on Yom Kippur just to drive his wife and father-in-law crazy. Now and then my father would take me to a Chinese restaurant—those meals were the only time I ate non-kosher food. I don't know if he told my mother about this transgression.

After I finished Yiddish school, I continued to attend Hebrew school, three-days-a-week, until age 13. On Sundays I went to a *Machzikei Talmud Torah,* on 43rd Street and 14th Avenue. Hebrew school was of little interest to me—I usually brought a book, on an unrelated topic, that I could read in class. But when I turned twelve, I needed to prepare for my bar mitzvah. Synagogues usually had someone to prepare boys for their bar mitzvahs (this was before girls were given bat mitzvahs). My mother found a rabbi in a *shtiebel,* a small synagogue below the big synagogue, the *Svardisha Shul,* on 45th and 15th—Askhenazi, even if the name is Yiddish for Sephardic. The shul was notable because of its prominent cantor—I think it was Yussele Rosenblatt or Moshe Kusivitsky. The rabbi, an old man with a beard, gave me my lessons. My *Haftorah* was from Isaiah. *"Nachamu, nachamu"* ("Hear ye, Hear ye, Israel"). The passage is famous because some of its text was spoken by Martin Luther King, Jr. in his "I have a dream" speech on the Washington Mall in August 1963, thanks to work on the speech by Stanley Levison, his adviser who had been a member of the Communist Party USA. As it happens, my birthday is in August, too—so King was saying those words at the appropriate time of the year, according to the calendar of synagogue readings. The bar mitzvah took place in the *shtiebel*. I can recall my reading of the Torah, the Haftorah, and my reciting the various blessings. When I'd finished reading, the women in the balcony, as is the custom, threw candy down at me.

After my bar mitzvah, I became Orthodox. I started to pray three times a day, I put on *tefillin* in the mornings. Eating kosher was not an issue, and there was not much to do on the Sabbath. But it is still hard for me to understand how I made the decision to be *frum* (pious, religious). Although my mother was Orthodox in her outlook, I don't think she encouraged this change in me; certainly, my father, the atheist Bolshevik, didn't.

I followed Orthodox rules through high school, and I took my tefillin in their zeckel (bag) to the University of Chicago. It's hard for me to connect with my religious self-representation at that time. It seems like it was part of an obsessional neurosis, as Freud understood religion, and must have had something to do with keeping my instinctual wishes in check, a part of sexual awakening.

* * *

At college, post-shrimp, things changed dramatically. I went to Quaker meetings and worked for the United Friends Service committee; I disconnected myself from being Jewish. Isn't that interesting? I think it was because Arlene and I were far away from home and our parents, and we were establishing a new, secular, non-Jewish identity, and when I went to medical school, I was too busy to be Jewish. I guess it had to do with emancipation, disconnection from our parents, rebellion. But a good rebellion.

We were active with the Quakers in Chicago. We volunteered for the American Friends Service Committee—among other activities, we painted apartments in Cabrini Green, a low-income public-housing development in Chicago. I recall the saying, "Urban renewal is Negro removal." We did try to help improve the neighborhood and to be of service to poor people.

I also lacked much of a connection with being Jewish in Topeka when I attended the Menninger Institute. But in Petersburg, Virginia, where I began my clinical experience as chief medical officer and chief psychiatrist at that town's federal reformatory, Arlene and I would occasionally attend a Conservative congregation, which was headed by a Rabbi Sapinsley.

We tried to invite Harry Golden, the editor of the *Carolina Israelite*, to give a talk at the synagogue, but were opposed by the rabbi and by members of the congregation, particularly those who owned some of the local department stores—they feared the reaction of local white gentiles. Golden was well known as an anti-segregationist. This was the early sixties in the still-segregated South.

Because of the fight over school desegregation, Petersburg's public schools were closed during year we were there. We had to send our kids to the Bolingbrook Country Day School, which had been set up as a so-called segregation academy. For some reason, the other parents elected me head of the PTA—which I can't understand, to this day.

"Throughout my father's life," says Stephen, "he's always been the sort of person other people choose for different leading positions, often without his actively campaigning for the job."

Arlene and I were actively involved in the civil rights movement during our time in Petersburg. We organized an integrated art show at the local teachers' college, with the works of black and white painters hung side by side. We belonged to the Southern Christian Leadership Conference and met Ralph

Abernathy, Martin Luther King's right-hand man. Arlene attended the March on Washington, hearing King's famous speech in person.

That's what those two years were about. The fight against segregation. The assassination of John F. Kennedy. The desegregation of the prisons by Robert F. Kennedy. A lot of change.

The Fort Lee army base was nearby. We knew the Jewish chaplain, Rabbi Sheldon Elster, because his wife was a friend of ours from New York. At the synagogue we met Irwin Kra and his wife, Eleanor. Irwin, who later became a renowned mathematician, was then a private in the army and stationed at Fort Lee. We met the Kras when I was invited to a bris for their son Douglas by the Fort Lee Rabbi, Sheldon Elster. I couldn't go because I was on duty, so Arlene went instead. At the reception she asked Irwin Kra's father about his last name, telling him that her grandmother came from a Polish village called Krasnosielc. After more questions and discussion, Irwin's father and Arlene figured out that his mother and Arlene's maternal grandmother were sisters, making Arlene's mother and Irwin's father first cousins and Arlene and Irwin, who was born in Krasnosielc, second cousins!—And they found this out in Petersburg, Virginia, a world away from that village in Poland!

* * *

When we came back to New York in 1964, we joined a synagogue, but what really revived my Jewish identity was my involvement with YIVO (The YIVO Institute for Jewish Research).

My interest in YIVO and Yiddish arises not only from my connection to my parents and family from Eastern Europe but also from my fascination with history. I've written about the history of psychoanalysis: an article for the *YIVO Encyclopedia* on psychoanalysis in Eastern Europe, another about Jews in American psychoanalysis for the *Encyclopedia of American Jews*, and a third in the *Encyclopedia Britannica* entitled "Psychoanalysis: Burgeoning and

Beleaguered." My wife says that when I go to a dinner party, the first thing I ask is, "Where are you from? Where were your parents from? Where were your grandparents from?" I think Freud's *Moses and Monotheism* had to do with the myth that Freud was not originally Jewish—there was the story that his family was from Cologne, not Galicia. That was a lie that Freud himself told to make it easier for him to survive as a Jew in Hapsburg Vienna.

At YIVO, I was among a number of people responsible for the Yiddish revival in New York. Two of the Klezmatics started out working for YIVO, namely Alicia Svigal and Lauren Sklandberg,

My reconnection to Yiddish began with my connection to the Society for the Advancement of Judaism (SAJ), a Reconstructionist synagogue on Manhattan's Upper West Side. When we returned to New York from Petersburg, Virginia, we joined *B'nai Jeshrun,* a huge congregation on West 89th Street. We joined BJ because its rabbi was William Berkowitz, the brother of Shalem Elster, the wife of the chaplain at Fort Lee in Petersburg. Our son had his Bar Mitzvah at B'nai Jeshrun, but we left the shul when the rabbi said that Vietnam was good for the Jews. We joined SAJ, because of a friend who belonged there, Lester Schwartz, a psychiatrist on staff at Montefiore, where I ran the OPD (Outpatient Department) when I came to New York.

The rabbi at SAJ was Alan Miller, charismatic and brilliant, but flawed. He had trouble getting along with people, including his congregants, and he published very little—a disappointing successor to Mordecai Kaplan, whom we very much admired. In fact, a group of members, including Lester, although not me, paid for his psychoanalysis. They sent him to Jack Arlow, who threw him out of treatment because he felt he was unanalyzable. He couldn't participate in the process. He wouldn't acknowledge that he had conflicts, couldn't benefit from analysis. He was too defensive. He was a difficult person who upset everyone in the congregation. Saturday mornings, instead of a sermon, he'd have an open mic. People would get up and say this or that. We later found out that he was surreptitiously recording these contributions—he had a button, just like Nixon. His idea was that he'd use what people said in a paper or book, but nothing ever came of the idea. He didn't write much—something I faulted him for.

Before the High Holidays one year, Rabbi Miller asked Arlene to prepare a program for the Yom Kippur martyrology. She selected a group of Yiddish poems which she read to the congregation, in Yiddish, on Yom Kippur afternoon. After the congregation's favorable reaction to her presentation, we, along with several other congregants, decided to start a Yiddish program at the synagogue. We booked an all-star roster of Yiddish writers—Isaac Bashevis Singer, Jacob Glatstein, Chaim Grade, Avrom Sutzkever, and others—to read and perform, and also showed a series of Yiddish films. A famous quote was from I. B. Singer: "We must believe in free will. We have no choice." The SAJ Yiddish Film Program morphed into the New York Yiddish Film Festival.

I organized the first New York Yiddish Film Festival in 1972, and the second in 1973. I put together a conglomerate of sponsors: the 92nd Street Y, the Workman's Circle, the American Jewish Congress, the Brandeis Yiddish Film group, and the Society for the Advancement of Judaism. We all cooperated successfully, which was quite an accomplishment, as Jews are well-known for being contentious. I learned a lot about bringing in groups together—experience I've put to work in arranging symposiums.

We were very much influenced by an article in the *Village Voice*, written by J. Hoberman, about Yiddish cinema. Arlene read that article and wanted to see some of the films. We got the films from Eric Goldman or from Brandeis

At the time we were organizing the first festival, Hillel Halkin, who had married Arlene's cousin, visited us from Israel. Hillel, the author of *Letters to America from a Jewish Friend about Zionism*, didn't think the festival would arouse much interest. "You'll probably have an audience of ten Jewish men," he said—just enough for a minyan, in other words.

For more than one film, we filled the Y's Kaufman auditorium. Capacity: nine hundred.

* * *

I often quip that I am connected with two lost causes: Yiddish and psychoanalysis. The two are connected.

Psychoanalysis is quintessentially a Galician enterprise—it's been that way since its beginning. The first forty patients and analysts in Freud's group were either Galicians or the children of Galicians. How do you account for that? In my opinion, Freud's whole life and work played out in the context of Jewish Europe and European anti-Semitism.

Anti-Semitism was very much part of Freud's life and experience, certainly from 1880 on. He was, on the one hand, a prominent figure in Vienna's academia, but it was impossible to become a full professor at the university because of anti-Semitism. Freud joined the B'nai B'rith in Vienna, but he, and analysts who came later, disconnected themselves from being Jewish. When I was a psychoanalytic candidate, we had classes on Yom Kippur; even though almost all of the students were Jewish, I was one of only a handful who insisted we should not. My fellow candidates were trying to assimilate, rather than recognize their own identity. How does such hiding of the truth affect an analysis? An example is Heinz Kohut, who would not tell his colleagues that he was Jewish and that he'd had a bar mitzvah. If he went to a kosher restaurant, he'd order a ham sandwich, as if he didn't known it was off-limits. He was a deceiver.

An important part of being Jewish is a commitment to humanistic values, the values of the Enlightenment, respect for the mind and the intellect. Humanism and the intellect were central aspects of Freud's Jewish identity. The same outlook forms a key part of my identity as a psychoanalyst, and, I believe, should be part of any analyst's identity.

In 1873 Vienna there was a big bank failure; of course, people blamed it on the Jews. Beneath the blame was envy, envy of the Jews' success. Gentiles in Austria and Germany—and not just there—experienced the Jews as a threat. But Freud and other Jews thought the cause of anti-Semitism was the presence in Vienna of large numbers of unwashed, unkempt shtetl Jews, who had come from Galicia. I think that was a rationalization. I am convinced that Freud was embarrassed and ashamed by his shtetl Galician origins—hence his claim at one point that his family was from Cologne. On the other hand, he was proud of being a Jew on his own terms. He would repeat: "I am a German, but a German by culture and language." But anti-Semitism made him Jewish rather than German.

Then came the pogroms, mostly in parts of the Russian Empire within the Pale of Settlement. In the 1880s, anti-Semitism was on the rise in Europe. The Jews in Vienna moved from a hopeful attitude about assimilation in the larger society toward a recognition that assimilation was not going to work. My question is: What was the impact on Freud? His whole generation had a problem with identification with their fathers. Freud and his contemporaries desired to join the larger society and to participate in the Enlightenment. Less so their fathers. In my opinion, this conflict made Freud and his peers extremely introspective and self-aware about what was going on. An interesting thing is that during that period there were two sciences established by Jews: psychoanalysis and sociology. The two fields have much in common: The people who started sociology, like those who started psychoanalysis, were all Galician Jews. And both disciplines seek to promote understanding of oneself, and the impact of culture on science.

When Freud left Vienna and disbanded The Vienna Psychoanalytic Society, he said he was reminded of what the Jews did after the destruction of the Second Temple. Rabbi Yohanan ben Zakkai, after the Temple's sacking in 70 CE, went to *Yavneh* and founded an academy. What did he study at the academy? Torah. So here is Freud, the godless Jew, celebrating Yohanan ben Zakkai, the anything-but-godless Jew. Today I find that the analysts who are anti-Zionists also happen to be Jews—there are not that many who fit this description, but their existence is unfortunate. Most of these people had no Jewish affiliation growing up. They didn't go to Hebrew school, didn't belong to a synagogue, didn't have bar- or bat mitzvah, didn't learn any of the prayers, and so forth. Most of them have never been to Israel. All over the world the left has made anti-Zionism a cause. Mistakes by the Israeli political leadership are a good reason to oppose much of what the State of Israel does. I certainly don't count myself as an unqualified fan of the Israeli government—I place myself in the middle of American Jews on the subject of Israel, to the left of AIPAC, to the right of J Street. But you can disagree with their policies, particularly with those of Bibi Netanyahu, and still believe Israel has a right to exist. That is the question: Do the Jewish people have the right to their own state?

Today I am not Orthodox. I consider myself Reconstructionist. It's said that Kaplan, the founder of Reconstructionism, started SAJ because the Orthodox synagogue to which he belonged wouldn't give his daughters bat mitzvahs. I have more of an affinity with Mordecai Kaplan's Judaism, which he defines as an evolving religious civilization, than any other form of Judaism. I do not believe in a supernatural God. It's been said about Reconstructionism that you eat kosher, and you think treyf—although I personally do not eat kosher.

We belonged to a synagogue as long as our children were young; we don't now. My son's wife is sort of Orthodox—she keeps kosher—and they go to synagogue on High Holidays. I am sad that we did not teach our children Yiddish. Life was so hectic then—we didn't pay attention to this gift we might have given them. My great-grandfather's first language was Yiddish, my grandfather knew Yiddish, my mother understood some Yiddish, and Arlene grew up with Yiddish. I identify myself as a psychoanalyst who is Jewish and American. A Jewish-American psychoanalyst. I read the Siddur regularly, I read books and articles about Judaism, and I attend synagogue on the High Holidays, although we don't belong to a shul here in Palm Beach. I may join a synagogue eventually.

My favorite Yiddish song goes, "*Vas mir zeinen, zeinen mir. Ober Yidin zeinen mir.*"

"What we are we are. But we are Jews."

CHAPTER 5

A NEW PSYCHIATRIST
Kansas and Virginia

I was hardly a star in medical school, but my special standing was reestablished during my residency at the Menninger School of Psychiatry, in Topeka, Kansas, by the approval of the faculty and my fellow residents. I began there in July 1960.

The way it worked then was, upon finishing med school, a new doctor did a year-long internship, then went on to a longer residency. After I graduated medical school, in June 1958. I did my internship at the Public Health Service Marine Hospital Psychiatry Service, in Baltimore, with Larry Deutch, an analytic candidate at Downstate, and Steve Firestein, an analytic candidate at Columbia. Larry was in analysis with Melitta Sperling and was infected with analytic zeal. Analysis, Larry thought, could cure everything, including ulcerative colitis.

Halfway through my time in Baltimore I needed to make two decisions about my residency: What specialty? And where?

I briefly considered internal medicine but realized I was not serious about that area. What I'd always had my mind set on was to become a psychiatrist and then a psychoanalyst. The obvious choice for my residency was Albert Einstein, on Morris Park Avenue in the Bronx. For one thing, it was local. Second, Einstein ran a well-regarded, psychoanalytically-oriented psychiatry program. And third, some of my friends were going there—Marty Willick from Erasmus, Lester Schwartz from medical school. I was interviewed by

José Barchilon and Milton Rosenbaum. I must have made a good impression because I was one of eight applicants accepted. It made a lot of sense to go there, but I decided not to. Arlene and I had two children at the time. We did not want to live in a Bronx basement on a meager salary. Living expenses were much less in Kansas, and the salary was greater. During the second and third years I had a Public Health Service stipend. Going to Kansas turned out to make a big difference financially.

I applied to several other psychiatric residencies, as well. One was Mass Mental Health, in Boston, where I was interviewed by Sam Bogoch and Elvin Semrad. Mass Mental turned me down—a puzzling decision. Was the rejection due to my not having attended an Ivy League medical school? Was it because I was Jewish? I met Sam several years later when his wife was the only woman in my analytic class. I asked him about his interviewing me and turning me down; he insisted that he had no recollection of the fact. I couldn't get to Semrad for a discussion.

I also briefly considered several second-rate residences, but not for long. Topeka was the one.

I chose the Menninger Foundation sight unseen—well, I did see photographs in Menninger's brochure, which was impressive, very inviting, and described the scope of the training. Somehow, I was accepted without an interview, even though Menninger not only interviewed most other applicants but also gave them in-depth psychological tests. I don't know why they decided to skip those steps with me.

"At the time," recalls Arlene, "we already had our second child, Rebecca. We had been living on my very small teacher's salary for five years while Arnie was in school, and it seemed like the right time to be making a choice that would support us. Menninger's was paying $7,500 a year, which to us at the time was absolute luxury. And so, Arnie decided he would go there. It was also a superb residency. Very prestigious. And without having gone there to check it out—we didn't even talk to anyone who had been there—we just decided we would go. And we did."

Before I let Einstein know my decision to go to Topeka, I got a call from José. "Richards, are you coming?" I had to tell him no. Several years later I met him in Denver. He told me I'd made a mistake by not coming to Einstein.

I hadn't.

* * *

How did a world-renowned psychiatric study institute, treatment facility, and training institute wind up in Topeka, Kansas, of all places? It got there because an Indiana native, Charles F. Menninger, after finishing medical school in Chicago in 1889, moved to Topeka to continue his clinical education, specializing in internal medicine as he worked with doctors associated with the Kansas Medical College. C. F. Menninger had two sons. Envious of Dr. Charlie Mayo, whose sons worked in their father's Mayo Clinic in Minnesota, Charles Menninger sent his sons to medical school at Harvard, hoping they, too, would come back to the Midwest to join their father's medical practice. The Menninger sons did, indeed, team with their father, but together the three doctors turned the family focus toward a different branch of medicine: the study and treatment of mental illness.

Karl Menninger finished training at the Boston Psychopathic Hospital in 1919 then returned to Topeka where he and his father opened the Menninger Clinic. Six years later, William Menninger, a newly minted psychiatrist, joined his brother and father in what the three doctors now called Menninger Sanitarium, reflecting the institution's new focus on disorders of the mind.

Karl Menninger, starting with the publication in 1930 of his first book, *The Human Mind*, quickly became one of the country's leading authorities on psychiatry, both with books and articles aimed at specialists, and a regular advice column in the *Ladies' Home Journal*. Will Menninger's career was no less illustrious: During World War II he was appointed Director of the Psychiatry Consultants Division in the office of the Surgeon General of the United States Army. He chaired the committee that produced a substantial revision of America's system of classifying psychiatric disorders.

In 1946, with the war over, Karl persuaded the federal government to convert a former army hospital in Topeka into a Veterans Administration facility that would serve as the clinical heart of the Menningers' new training program, christened the Menninger School of Psychiatry. MSP quickly became the largest psychiatric training center in the world.

Menninger had a strong psychoanalytic tradition. To teach at the new school, Karl recruited prominent psychoanalysts from across North America and Europe. One great find was David Rappaport, who was working at Osawatomie State Hospital in Kansas. A host of other important analysts came to Topeka, including Robert Knight, Merton Gill, Margaret Brennan Gibson, Roy Schafer, Robert Holt, George Klein. From abroad came Nelly Tibout, Otto Fleischmann, Gertrude and Ernst Ticho, William Tarnower, and Ishak Ramsey. Robert Wallerstein was there, as well as Lois and Gardner Murphy. Paul Pruyser, a clinical psychologist, not a physician, became a key academic influence on Karl, co-authoring one of his books.

* * *

"We left the kids with my parents in New York and drove out to Kansas," says Arlene. "Found a place to live. And then I flew back, picked up the kids and then came back to Topeka."

We arrived in Topeka in our Chevrolet station wagon, at the end of June, driving from Baltimore to Topeka. I will never forget that sinking feeling I had when we drove up Kansas Avenue. As I looked around at what seemed to me to be a wasteland, I said to myself, "What are we doing here?" But that anxiety dissipated rapidly when we arrived at our destination and were met by Harvey

Bezahler, a third-year resident who had been assigned by the foundation to meet and greet me. We became good friends with Harvey and his wife, Debbie, and have remained so to this day. Harvey also became a psychoanalyst. He practices in New York City.

"Topeka was real fun," says Arlene, "because at the time, it was a one-horse town. Every Saturday there would be a cattle drive from the Blue Hills, which was where they would feed up the cattle that had come from Texas, on their way to Kansas City. The animals would go through the main street of town. There were cowboys and all kinds of excitement.

"By then our son was three and a half and seeing all those horses and cows and cowboys—he loved it. He made friends quickly there—all the kids loved it. For what a studio apartment in New York would cost, we found a nice three-bedroom house, with a nice yard and a creek in the backyard, which the kids found very exciting. It was right across the road from a great big cornfield, and about five minutes from where Arnie was working. It was lovely."

"My best friend in Kansas," recalls Stephen, "was Steve Bremner, who was the older of two sons of Dr. Jim Bremner, a psychiatrist and colleague of my father's at the clinic. He was my best friend there for three years. Steve and I used to run around—there's a creek there, the *Shunganunga* Creek, and there was a rise, almost just across the street from our house, called Burnett's Mound. Our dog, Jiggsy, a beagle, would run with us, too. There was one incident when my sister Rebecca was with us. She fell into the creek, which was quite shallow—nothing to be drowned in. But we left her sitting in the creek and ran away. I must have caught hell at home afterward for that, but I don't remember. I didn't have an abusive childhood, although I do remember my parents using spanking occasionally. But not with objects or anything like that. Later, when I went to school in Virginia, at the Bollingbrook School, there was actually corporal punishment with rulers. I told my parents about that later—they were shocked to learn of it."

The long and short of it is that the residency program was a warm, welcoming, friendly place. The sense of strangeness soon lifted as I realized that all of us in the program felt part of a close community, with good relationships among the residents, among the faculty, and between those two groups. Interpersonal conflicts that existed were between the staff and "Dr. Karl," as we called the boss. Many on the foundation hospital staff resented his presence and after several years—after I'd left—asked him to leave the hospital and never return. The story goes that after that request was made Karl turned to his closest colleague, Don Neher and said "Sigmund Freud was right. The Oedipus conflict triumphs again." I think Otto Kernberg and Gertrude and Ernst Ticho were the leaders of this palace coup but other staff members participated, as well. Otto had graduated and risen to a position of leadership and authority. (Otto's wife, Paulina Kernberg, was a resident at Kansas State Hospital.) The Menninger family had put Otto in charge, but after he took over they became unhappy with him. It was said that the foundation either had to become the Kernberg Foundation or Otto had to leave. He left. Karl stayed.

MSP boasted an embarrassment of psychoanalytic talent on staff, even though there had been an exodus of some talented people before I arrived: Robert Night Burton, Gail Margaret, Greg Mahon, and Roy Schaffer had left for New Haven. Holt and Klein had decamped to New York. But those who remained were my mentors, supervisors, role models, and ego ideals. I can't think of another psychiatric program in the United States with the caliber of this faculty. Herbert Schlesinger was my thesis adviser for my third-year paper. Additionally, there was the Alfred P. Sloan Visiting Professors Program that invited people both from psychoanalysis and the larger academic world. I remember seeing Max Gittelson, Judge David Bazelon, S. I. Hayakawa, Jean Piaget, Aldous Huxley, Fred Hacker, Peter Kuiper, Konrad Lorenz, and Margaret Mead. They all passed through, they all contributed.

"There was a regular schedule of these people," says Arlene. "Aldous Huxley, at the time, was pushing LSD. At Meninger they were investigating it as a method of treatment.

"There were no decent restaurants in town, because Kansas was a dry state at the time. These distinguished visitors got tired of eating in the hospital, so they loved coming to people's homes and having real dinners. I always signed up to host these people for dinner. I signed up maybe six months in advance for Huxley.

"Well, a little later on, I noticed that the night I'd signed up for dinner with Huxley was the first night of Passover. We decided to go ahead with the Seder and have him there. By this time we had two children and a third on the way—I was quite pregnant. Good friends who lived down the block—a resident and his wife and their three children—also came that evening, because we liked having a big Seder and having fun with a lot of kids. And so Huxley came, and I had prepared what I thought was as close to a Seder meal as I could manage with what was available in Topeka, Kansas. I made gefilte fish out of frozen cod—as you can imagine, not the world's best gefilte fish. But I did it. And the rest of the traditional meal.

"When Huxley arrived, it became clear that he was practically blind. And he was talking about children: 'There are so many children around; what the world needs is birth control.' And I'm sitting there five months' pregnant, although he didn't notice.

"So we get to the table and went through the Seder and he doesn't say a thing the entire time, as if this is a normal, ordinary dinner that he's used to. Our son, by that time was almost five, had learned the Four Questions in Hebrew, and was all excited. He recites them. Huxley says nothing. Finally we serve the egg; still, he doesn't say anything, as if this is an ordinary, everyday first course. Then comes the gefilte fish, and suddenly he says, 'Ah, *cannelle de brochette.*'

"And then he starts talking. And he's talking again about the world population explosion and the need for fewer children. Of course, like most upper-class British at the time, he was an anti-Semite.

"Not that he responded to the Jewish theme of the evening. Our friends, who were not Jewish, were very interested in the Seder, and they kept asking questions about it. Why we do this, why we do that. What does it all mean? Huxley just pretended it wasn't happening. The only thing that was happening was *cannelle de brochette.* He was enjoying a delicious fish dish.

"Another time, Margaret Mead gave a very interesting talk to the wives. There was a wives' group called the Winter Wives because in the Winter, the VA hospital was the facility where all the medical people worked. Mead talked about how we were all too young to be having children, and that it was disgusting that we had so many of them. She said that the one-child family was a huge improvement over all these tribes of children. Women would never accomplish anything, she said, if they had children while they were young. You had to have your career first. Which of course, was what she did. And she was quite right in predicting that was the wave of the future. But we were fifties wifies. Her talk was not exactly well received.

"And then there was Konrad Lorenz—Papa Duck, he was called, because he trained ducks. He was the first ethno-anthropologist. What he did was, he didn't let the newly-fledged ducks see their parents. He presented himself as the model for them, setting the example for them to walk around rather than fly. And they followed him for the rest of their lives. This was a theory of imprinting, which led much later to infant observation and much more emphasis on infancy as the most important stage of life, rather than the Oedipal stage, which Freud advocated.

"He was a fun guy, as you would imagine. It was such a ridiculous experiment, but it was so important."

It was a thrilling intellectual environment that broadened the horizons of all MSP's residents, making them aware of the larger academic world outside of the world of psychiatry. When I was there, we got a visit from Alexander Luria, who had started out as a psychoanalyst in Russia, and then, after Stalin banned psychoanalysis the same year, he banned the Yiddish theater, became a cognitive psychologist at the Bechterev Institute in St. Petersburg. Luria arrived on a Russian jet, which landed at nearby Forbes Air Force Base. He gave two lectures then returned to the Soviet Union.

"During the Second World War," says Arlene, "Luria was really the world's foremost neurologist. He had all these battlefield head wounds to diagnose, and he was brilliant. He figured out that people who were bilingual had each language on a different side of the brain. Therefore, some people whose brains got shot had one language, some had another. It had been thought, up to that point, that all language was on the left side of the brain. But no, if you have two languages, the second language goes to the right side of the brain. Luria was the pioneer of brain mapping.

"So Dr. Karl, through a contact in Washington known to Dr. Will—Karl's brother, Will Menninger—got permission from the Strategic Air Command (SAC) Air Force base in Topeka to have a Russian plane land and stay for forty-eight hours, while Luria gave a lecture. To have a SAC Air Force base have a Russian plane there—you can't imagine what that was like during the cold war. Karl arranged it all. An amazing coup.

"But when Luria was about a third of the way through the lecture—which he gave in beautiful English—Karl walked out. He was bored. To me, that really typified Karl. His brilliance, his nerves, his entitlement, and his disregard for any kind of propriety."

I think that my three years at the Menninger School of Psychiatry were probably the most important stage of my professional development, perhaps even more important than the five years I spent at the New York Psychoanalytic Institute. MSP broadened my reach and expanded my relationships to include some of the best and brightest thinkers in psychoanalysis from Europe and in the US. The approach to psychoanalysis and psychotherapy in Topeka was intended to broaden our thinking. It was a much better fit for me than Einstein, where the focus was narrow. Psychoanalytically provincial, you might say.

Overall, the clinical experience in the MSP residency program was excellent and the supervision superb. My supervisors were Bill Tarnower, Harold Voth, and Lawrence Stross. The first year of residency at MSP was spent at the Topeka VA Hospital. The patients there were not the best psychotherapy patients (they mostly were chronic patients and not very psychologically minded) nor were the outpatients in the VA clinic, which was a separate entity. I had more interesting patients at the community mental health clinic, which was not part of the VA.

The foundation was famous for treating celebrities. There was one actress who was a patient—she eventually got training and became a therapist. Celebrities paid well for their treatment, and they weren't the only ones who made Menninger a lucrative enterprise. After I left, a number of patients arrived from Saudi Arabia—they could certainly afford high fees. But the foundation's monetary success did not last. Gradually, Menninger began to lose money and was forced to relocate to Houston, Texas, where they got an offer of sponsorship from Baylor University, and where the foundation remains to this day. Glen Gabbard, who was my associate editor at *JAPA* (the *Journal of the American Psychoanalytic Association*) for several years, was in charge for a while but he left, and he was followed by another friend of mine, Talaat Mohamed, a colleague in the China program (which I describe in chapter 14).

* * *

The benefits of the Menninger program went beyond the professional training to encompass a rich cultural experience.

Topeka, Kansas, by itself, was a cultural desert—quite a change for this New Yorker. But the staff and residents of the foundation developed culture on their own. A group of people started a Chamber Music Society, which booked concerts by world-class musicians.

At the apex of our cultural life was the Menninger School Film Society, which was run by Leon Levin during my first year and then by me the next two. The Society showed the best foreign films, past and present. I was able to present the first screening in the United States of the movie of *The Three-penny Opera*. Other films that I remember were *400 Blows* (and a few others by Truffaut), *Zero for Conduct*, *The Two of us*, *L'Avventura*, *Hiroshima Mon Amour*, and a number of works of Bergman. We did show the occasional American film—*Seven Brides for Seven Brothers* was one, because my classmate Charlie Wellshear loved it. I was especially pleased with the shorts I found to accompany every feature. We showed one movie with a gay theme: *Fireworks*, by Stan Brakhage. Sometime after we showed that one there was an article in *Playboy* about the film which said that it was being shown at the Menninger Foundation as part of diagnostic testing. Of course, that wasn't true; we had just ordered it for the film series. (When Karl heard about the film and the article he became upset with the Film Society and with me.) We showed the films in the school auditorium, usually to a full house. The Society became an important event in the cultural life of the Menninger community. After I left Topeka, Otto Kernberg took over the Society's reins.

We didn't just *exhibit* cultural works; we performed them, too. We had a small recorder-playing ensemble—it was the only musical instrument I could play. We organized a poetry-reading group. Our play-reading group performed *The World of Sholom Aleichem*. Elisa Shevrin played the mother. Otto Kernberg played Bunche Shweig from the Peretz story included in the play. There was an annual Freudian Follies in which we spoofed the staff. Otto Kernberg, on staff at this time, played himself as a rabbit with a Prussian helmet and a habit of running around the stage shouting, "I'm late, I'm late, for a very important date."

Forbes Air Force Base was in the Strategic Air Command; "strategic" meaning they flew nuclear bombs around. Every day bombers would fly toward Russia and turn back before they were told to drop a bomb. Karl told us about one pilot who wanted to continue to Russia—the story may have been apocryphal, but true or not, it was terrifying for us at the time. I'm not sure how the Menninger staff got called into the situation—if, in fact, it did.

"We belonged to the officers' club at Forbes Air Force Base the second two years that we were there," Arlene recalls, "because one of the things Karl arranged was for residents to work for the Public Health Service, which was a branch of the Coast Guard, in exchange for being paid a decent wage—about $15,000 a year then—and serving for two years in a federal prison. Karl was very interested in crime and prisons and that sort of thing. So Arnie did that, which made him an officer in the Coast Guard, which meant that we could belong to the club at the base, which meant that I could take the children out there every day in the summer to swim in this giant pool. We had this country club life.

"It was one of the last big bases built in the US, and it was gorgeous. They had a golf course. It really was a country club. And the flyers—the pilots and the navigators and all that—were hot shot pilots. The base gave them a hot shot life.

"So we had this amazing life after having been really dirt poor for five years. Fifteen thousand dollars was big money then—it meant luxury living. We had had to save up to go on the subway in New York, so this was a tremendous contrast. We could go to the movies any time we wanted. It was sumptuous."

* * *

Everyone in the program, in order to graduate, had to write a paper. My mentor for my paper, which I titled, "Attitude and Drug Acceptance," was Herb Schlesinger. Published in the *British Journal of Psychiatry*, the paper had studied medication refusers by giving them the Forest Test (a urine test for tranquilizers) to determine whether they were taking their prescribed drugs. It was a great study but not a great paper—I think Herb deemed it of higher quality than I did. My relationship with Herb has continued since then. He is alive at the age of 100 and living in New York. He was my main proponent for the editorship of *JAPA*, and I am grateful to him for that.

What strikes me to this day is that there was a minimum of rivalry among the residents, reflecting the overall egalitarian atmosphere of the residency. The residents came from a variety of backgrounds and places. I remember many of their names: Donald Newman was also Jewish, as was his cousin Stanley Goodman (who was not a resident), who became chair of the Board of Professional Standards of the American Psychoanalytic Association and had been a member of the American Communist Party. Stanley is still alive at 101. Jim Bremner was from Bellingham, Washington; he became a fine psychiatrist. Arlene and I became friends with him and his wife, Lornelle, who died at a young age. Jim died more recently. Their son, who became a psychiatrist, and our son Stephen were friends in Topeka. Charlie Wellshear was from Wichita, Kansas. Ronald Earkin was from Missouri. I think there was one woman—I've forgotten her name. I think she was from Poland. Noel Williams, Art Larson, and Julian Toski were also in the program.

I'm sad to say that things didn't turn out well for some classmates: Frank Broadshire died of pancreatic cancer several years ago.

I also had important relationships with some of the staff, particularly Elisa and Howard Shevrin, with whom I shared many interests including Yiddish. "There were a lot of Jewish residents in Topeka—maybe three or four in Arnie's class," Arlene recalls. "About a third of the people there were Jews. Dr. Karl was very smart. He hired a lot of refugees—for relatively low salaries, compared to what they could make in New York. He paid the residents well, drawing really good students. And he was an autocrat. Everything had to be the way he wanted it to be."

We attended a synagogue in Topeka, *Ansche Emet*. "It was supported by a family called Posey," says Arlene. "The Poseys were an interesting family. They had come to Topeka in the 1880s or 1890s. The man of the family was a shoemaker from Russia. He noticed the cattle drives into Kansas City, so he contracted with the cowboys to buy some skins before they drove the cattle into Kansas City. He got a very good price, because the cowboys wanted some money to spend in Kansas City before they sold their cattle. He set up a shoe factory, and got other immigrants to come and make shoes.

"He made western boots and these beautiful shoes for women. I actually had a pair of them. They were beautiful, hand-tooled in the western style, like they do with the boots. Then after the war, there were very few people who wanted to be shoemakers in the US., and the shoe business mostly got exported to other countries. So this Mr. Posey developed a business with some people in Japan and started a shoe chain called Payless, which became a giant business. The family became extremely rich, but still lived in Topeka and still supported the synagogue. The ladies of the Posey family would go into Dallas to shop for their hats for Friday night. Every Friday night they had to have a new hat.

"That was how the synagogue was. It was a sweet little place. Another Meninger resident, a good friend of ours, was teaching Sunday school there, so I said, 'Okay. I know how to teach. I'll teach Sunday school too.' And I did. He and I would go every Sunday morning and teach Sunday school. And even though it was an Orthodox synagogue, the cantor was the local Catholic priest, because he knew Hebrew and had a beautiful singing voice. He loved doing it, and got paid handsomely. Everything there was done handsomely."

We all had an ongoing personal relationship with Dr. Karl, who met with us every Saturday morning. Arlene got a teaching job, which added to our income. "I worked at the local university," she recalls, "teaching reading and study skills to kids who had come from one-room schoolhouses to study agriculture at the university and had never seen a library. They had never seen any of the tools they could use as students; they didn't even know how to go about reading a book on their own. All the teaching I had done in New York was of kids who were disadvantaged and deprived; these kids needed the same things, but on a college level. So I taught there for two years. When I would teach, I'd bring my kids over to play with the kids of the people we invited to the Seder. And then that mother would come on Saturday mornings and drop her kids off, so I could take them to the cattle drive while she worked in a dress store, a fancy store that catered mainly to patients, because they could afford fancy clothes. They were Hollywood patients and Texas patients—people who could afford to pay the enormous fees in those days."

Art Larson was, I think, from Florida—that makes sense, since he owned a sailboat. Some of the residents were part owners—we each contributed $100 to its purchase—and we sailed on Lake Shawnee. Art once invited a group of us to go pheasant hunting.

"Well," says Arlene, "all the residents were good friends with each other, and everyone was trying to be as Kansan as possible, to fit in with the local culture. And that was Arnie—he was just trying to fit in, because he's very social. He was with the people he was with, this was what they did, and he tried to do it. One of the residents, Art Larson, was a hunter. He had grown up on a farm where he would hunt for pheasants every fall. He convinced the other guys to go. We also had a dog at the time, Jiggsy, a sweet dog—the kids loved him. Jiggsy was a hunting dog, so Arnie decided that it would be a good thing for this hunting dog to go hunt.

"This friend, who had plenty of guns, lent guns to Arnie and the others. They went out to western Kansas, maybe 100 to 150 miles from where we were, and went pheasant hunting."

I remember getting up early in the morning with Art's hound dogs, which were used for hunting. I had never gone hunting before. I shot one pheasant, that is, I *think* I did, but it may have been Art who brought it down. I brought it home.

"Arnie came home with a pheasant," says Arlene, "which made me cry, of course. So beautiful. So beautiful. He shouldn't have killed it. But I was willing. I had a cookbook, and the cookbook had recipes for pheasants. You're supposed to hang it on a clothesline for a couple of days. Somehow that made it less tough. And then you're supposed to pluck the feathers. I sort of had an idea of how to do the whole thing, because I had gone with my grandmother to buy a chicken every Friday morning. We would buy a live chicken, and then see it slaughtered and plucked and all that. So I knew how to do it, and so I did it. Then I roasted it and filled it with chestnuts, and this whole fancy recipe from a gourmet cookbook, and then none of us could eat it. We all cried. We all just cried. We had cornflakes for supper.

"Just the thought of this wild, living, beautiful bird—it was too much."

Arlene thought it was tough and horrible; I thought it tasted okay. When Dr. Karl found out about our escapade he was horrified. He was an ardent anti-vivisectionist. Everyone who went on the hunting trip was worried he would expel us from the program.

"Dr. Karl got hysterical," says Arlene. "He was in such a rage. He was anti-hunting and anti-guns. He yelled at the participants; he gave them a lecture. And that was the end of their hunting expeditions. It was certainly the end for Arnie."

The diversity among the residents provided a real contrast to what my experience would have been at Einstein, where most everyone was a Jewish New Yorker and on track to apply to the New York Psychoanalytic Institute.

I think Menninger gave me a wider perspective on psychiatry and on life. When I turned Einstein down, my place was given to Sandy Glassman, who pursued a different professional trajectory from mine. He did research on addiction, particularly cigarette smoking; sadly, he died prematurely, but not from smoking.

That I trained at Menninger in Topeka rather than at Einstein in New York made a big difference in regard to my practice when I returned to New York from Petersburg, Virginia (where I lived for a couple of years after Meninger). There were three of us New Yorkers who had trained at Menninger—Harvey Bezahler, Dick Simons, and Stanley Portnow—and we received referrals from the foundation. I was sent several patients, including one who was seriously disturbed and had been hospitalized in Topeka. She was a self-mutilator, and I wrote up the treatment into a paper on self-mutilation and father-daughter incest. I developed a well-deserved reputation among my peers for treating seriously ill patients, but that reputation diminished my reputation as a psycho-analyst because you were supposed to treat only neurotic patients.

The referrals were helpful to me, but a more important benefit from my Topeka training was its impact on my psychiatric thinking. What was central to Topeka and Karl Menninger's thinking was his anti-nosological approach. Nosology is defined as the branch of medicine dealing with classification of diseases. Karl argued that people are people, not confined to their classification in the *Diagnostic and Statistical Manual of Mental Disorders*. This outlook was very much in sympathy with Thomas Szasz and his statements about "the myth of mental illness." Karl was a big influence on such thinking, as he stressed the interconnections between biology, psychology, and social and environmental factors. While I was in Topeka, he was writing *The Vital Balance: The Life Process in Mental Health and Illness*, his principal anti-nosological tome. To Karl, diagnosis was not as important as the evolution of each human being. He opposed name-calling, and would go ballistic if you referred to a patient as schizophrenic. He took a highly dynamic view of psychopathology; this focus could be characterized as a biopsychosocial attitude and approach. The training was very much psychoanalytically oriented, but Karl's approach to psychoanalysis was not dogmatic, rigid, or rulebound.

Key to the residency program in Topeka was context—social, cultural, historical—and a distinct openness to other points of view, including other treatment modalities. What was central was Karl himself; his attitude toward psychotherapy, psychoanalysis, and psychopathology; and his broad range of interests, which included religion, morality, and criminality. One of the high points of the residency was the Saturday morning colloquium with Karl. He shared the chapters of his book-in-progress with the residents, giving us a unique opportunity to be engaged with his mind at work. The richness of my training in Topeka set me off from my peers in New York, particularly my peers at the New York Psychoanalytic Institute.

Dr. Karl was deeply involved in studying criminality. He would consult at the largest prison in Missouri, and the Foundation was involved in the evaluation of the murderers of the Clutter family—the Kansas case Truman Capote wrote about it in *In Cold Blood.* Dr. Karl's interest in prison reform became important for me because, with Jim Bennett, the head of the US Prison Service, he set up a program that enlisted psychiatrists in the United States Public Health Service. And so MSP turned out to be a serendipitous financial choice for me and Arlene because I was able to obtain a commission in the USPHS, with the salary, rank, and uniform of a Lieutenant Commander in the Navy, by agreeing to serve for two years as a resident in Topeka. The Public Health Service had money but a shortage of psychiatrists to work in prisons, so the deal, which included the perk of membership in the officers' club at the air base, fulfilled my military obligation, thus keeping me far away from Vietnam. Several of the Menninger faculty were interested in criminality and prison reform. Joe Satten is one who comes to mind.

After a year and a half at the Winter Veterans Administration Hospital, I spent the last six months of my residency at the Boys Industrial School working with adolescent juvenile offenders. The Boys Industrial School was one of the best adolescent treatment centers in the country, with the lowest recidivism rate of any place I knew of. What made it wonderful was the staff. The treatment mode was group therapy. I ran several groups, including one centered on reading books—I called the method "bibliotherapy."

That work led to my next job, in Petersburg, Virginia.

* * *

My clinical experience began at the Petersburg Federal Reformatory, where from 1962 to 1964 I was the chief medical officer and chief psychiatrist. I am not sure how qualified I was to be the chief medical officer but it was understood that I could call on physicians in town for backup. My job included conducting post-conviction psychiatric evaluation of the inmates. While my preference would have been to avoid definitive diagnoses, in accord with the position Dr. Karl had advocated, the courts demanded such evaluations on which to base the disposition of the cases. The diagnoses ranged from cognitively impaired, to psychopathic, to psychotic. All patients were male, age 18 to 25; they were sent to us for pre-sentencing evaluation. We would interview them and write a report. This was the time of the Durham rule, created in 1954 by Judge David L. Bazelon in the case *Durham v. United States*, stating that "an accused is not criminally responsible if his unlawful act was the product of mental disease." Since then, the rule has fallen into disrepute with the judicial system. People felt it was used to help defendants avoid responsibility and punishment. After my evaluation, a court would make its decision as to the inmate's fate. Some were released, some remained, sentenced to as long as five years confinement.

I did not treat the inmates one on one, but rather helped the staff with disciplinary problems on the job, particularly in dealing with the more difficult offenders. The main approach for an offender that made trouble was punitive.

Such inmates were put in what was called whole isolation—more bluntly known as solitary confinement or "the hole." I discouraged this practice.

I considered working with the staff the most important part of my job.

"Moving to Virginia was another adventure," Arlene says. "I was excited. I had loved being in Topeka, and a lot of good things happened there. We had our third child there, and I had a nice part-time job at the local university. But Topeka was a limited place. It was like living on a college campus."

When I arrived at this southern reformatory in 1962, it was segregated by race but, at the beginning of my second year, it was integrated. Robert F. Kennedy, in charge of the Federal Bureau of Prisons as US attorney general, decreed that all federal prisons be integrated. I met with the staff members in small groups to help them deal with the change. This was during a time of high tension in America, and not just because of the civil rights struggle. The Cuban missile crisis happened while we were in Petersburg; what I remember is the sound of army trucks going by. So what was remarkable to me was how smoothly integration occurred. We accomplished the transition in a single day, even though the move was not popular with the staff or, especially, the inmates, both of which groups included many redneck southerners. I was at Petersburg on November 22, 1963, when John F. Kennedy was assassinated. I was horrified that both inmates and staff expressed approval of the murder. The inmate who worked in my office openly celebrated. These people hated both Jack and Bobby because of their push for integration.

Arlene remembers her shock at the realities of life in the Jim Crow South. "I used to have a way of dealing with moving," she says. "I'd get a babysitter for a whole day, go down to a department store, and buy all the things one needs for a new place. Curtains, curtain rods, picture hooks, all kinds of things. Do it all in one day. So I went to the department store in Petersburg—it had all the stuff I needed. About halfway through the day, I needed to use the ladies' room. So I got to the front and saw a sign that said 'Women.' But as I went toward it, a saleslady pulled me by the back of my neck and said, 'That's not for you. You have to go to the third floor where it says 'Ladies.' This one's for the colored.'

"So they didn't have to say 'Colored' and 'White,' they said 'Ladies' and 'Women.' And then I noticed there were separate drinking fountains, which did say 'Colored' and "White.' There were all kinds of segregated facilities throughout Petersburg.

"We were both disgusted with this, but we had to be there for two years. It was the least bad possibility of all the choices we had. I mean, Arnie could have been a conscientious objector and gone to jail. That wouldn't have been too fun. He could have gone to Vietnam and not be with the three kids at home, and that wouldn't have been fun either. Neither of us believed in the Vietnam War, so that would have been very uncomfortable. This was the best possibility. To stay in the public health service and to stay at the prison."

We had a nice little house, on prison grounds, in a lovely setting with an alley of dogwoods. The prisoners were adolescents, not older hardened criminals. And this was a desirable place to be for them—at least by comparison. The idea was, if you steal a car, you take it across state lines, so instead of going to a state prison, where conditions were horrible, you go to a federal prison where you get three meals a day and learn to recap tires and finish furniture. The federal prisons were, relative to the state institutions, country clubs.

Still, the environment presented issues for our young family. "Living on prison grounds," says Arlene, "we were near a big tower, with guns, a big fence, and a very active little boy who always wanted to climb the fence. But it was electrified, so I was scared *all the time.*

"Occasionally one of the prisoners would escape. They'd have the dogs out, a lockdown, all the sirens going, and the guards with guns on the top of the tower. It was all scary as hell. The two girls were not really in any danger, because they would cling to me whenever there was danger; they were very little and very girly. But Steven would run out and want to see what was going on. To him it was exciting and fun."

"Absolutely," says Stephen, "I was definitely into adventure. War, shooting—all that sort of stuff. I would have found it exciting, not scary.

"I remember one time some prisoners escaped. The Appomattox River was directly behind our house—not more than several hundred feet. Supposedly, these inmates escaped and then somehow got a boat and were caught later. That's what I remember, although my memory may be faulty."

"I remember at least one day when our mom said a prisoner escaped so we have to stay in the house all day," recalls Rebecca. "I think she did a very good job at keeping us sheltered. I never felt like somebody was going to come in and get me. I just thought this was inconvenient: Why do we have to stay inside? I didn't really think a prisoner was going to come and shoot us.

"And there was the fact that my dad was working with them. I have vague memories of his talking about the prisoners and how he was helping them. And how they needed help. He said that some of them had committed a crime because they felt they had a better life in prison. They got fed and they got housed. My dad worked there and I thought, 'Well, he's fine. He comes home every day and he's fine.' My visualization was, these were not bad people in prison, because my dad somehow conveyed that. I mean, if he was a psychiatrist and he was there to help them, it implied to me that there was something good in them that could be helped."

"The warden was a neighbor," says Arlene, "and the assistant warden, and the psychologist, and a few of the senior guards. One of the guards had young children—our kids played with those children, and that was quite uncomfortable, because they were ardent segregationists. Very southern, very white, very Christian, and they always tried to convert. Especially, Rebecca. They were suspicious of us Jews from the North. They thought we were masquerading as Americans."

"The warden had the biggest house," says Stephen. "We had the next biggest house. Then there were a number of other smaller houses for soldiers from Fort Lee. Along with the children of these men, we used to play soldiers incessantly. We had our own platoon; I had the rank of Corporal. We played two sorts of games. One was war games, pretending to be soldiers—US soldiers, Korean soldiers. Also, we'd re-create Civil War battles with toy soldiers, with elaborate settings that we'd make out of mud and whatever. From that period onward I was interested in the Civil War.

"There were a lot of political discussions around the dinner table. In Virginia, I began to read on my own. I'd read late at night. Because I was put to bed at nine o'clock, and I didn't like to go to sleep so early, I would read by dim light whatever book I had. My parents gave me *The Complete Sherlock Homes* at age eight. My mother was very good at reading to us. At a later point, she read the entire *Lord of the Rings* to us, all three volumes."

Stephen remembers some of the perks of my position. "My dad was the chief psychiatrist at the penitentiary," he says, "which made him an officer in the Public Health Service, which is part of the Coast Guard. The Public Health Service is part of the Coast Guard because, originally, its major task was to prevent infectious diseases from coming in from overseas. I also remember going to the officers' club at Fort Lee. My parents never kept kosher, so we could eat there. We'd go for breakfast or Sunday brunch. I thought the food was sensational, the best food ever in the world: sausage links, eggs, pancakes, etc., etc. And as chief medical officer, my dad had certain privileges, one of which was to mandate the uniform for all medical officers. For the summer he mandated shorts, which apparently a lot of the other officers were upset about. They thought it was too informal.

"At this point in his life my father was quieter than he is now. He was very self-contained and very quiet. I think his personality in later life—he's incredibly talkative and social—was not his personality when I was growing up. I'd say he was more quiet, reclusive. Even so, he was also always very active,

UNORTHODOX: MY LIFE IN AND OUTSIDE PSYCHOANALYSIS

often a leader in different activities. He started movie clubs in both Kansas and Virginia."

I must say that on the whole, Petersburg was very pleasant for us. We made friends with the warden and the associate warden. And I even started the Petersburg Hopewell Film Society, so we had a film series. Stephen remembers the clubs in both Kansas and Virinia.

"He established this club," he says, "whereby they would get movies sent that otherwise wouldn't be available in Kansas or Virginia. Among the ones I remember seeing was a famous short film, *An Occurrence at Owl Creek*, based on an Ambrose Bierce story: A soldier is about to be hanged and then he escapes. But then it turns out at the end that it's a dream of escaping, and you see the man hanged. Another movie that I saw was *The Train*, with Burt Lancaster, set in France during World War II, about Nazi art theft."

I even developed a small private practice. I was approached by someone from Virginia Union University, a local Black institution, as to whether I would be interested in seeing some of its students. These young people were experiencing problems both in school performance and in relationships, particularly with their families, who expected too much of them. In the segregated South, many of these students carried a massive burden, representing their entire family's hope that they would succeed and help everyone advance. I saw the students at our home.

This was the time of SNCC (the Student Nonviolent Coordinating Committee) and CORE (the Congress of Racial Equality), a time of sit-ins and demonstrations as Black Americans fought for their civil rights. When Arlene and I first got to Petersburg we, along with Edna and Bill Kossick, organized an art show at the local teachers college, in which the paintings of White artists and Black artists hung side-by-side. "We rented a store in town," Arlene says, "and had an art show with Black painters and White painters, a Black ceramicist, and Edna, who was a White weaver. The show was a scandal because it was integrated."

We tried to invite Harry Golden, the editor of the *Carolina Israelite* and well known as an anti-segregationist, to give a talk at our local synagogue. "Harry Golden was a really good Jewish columnist, who wrote the *Carolina Israelite*, a newsletter that went out to Jews of the South. The newsletter was pro-integration. I went to our rabbi and said, 'We want to invite Harry Golden. He will speak, and we will, of course, pay for his accommodations and his travel. But we need a venue, and we would like to use the synagogue for the venue.' And the rabbi said, 'As long as you don't bring any of your *nigger* friends.'

"I was aghast. And we never did get a place. He never came."

Added to the bigotry was fear. The rabbi and members of the congregation were afraid that inviting Golden to speak might cause local White gentiles to boycott Jewish-owned stores.

"There was really a split in the Jewish community over this issue," says Arlene. We belonged to the Southern Christian Leadership Conference (SCLC) and met Ralph Abernathy, Martin Luther King Jr.'s right-hand man.

That's what those two years were about. The fight against segregation. The assassination of John F. Kennedy. The desegregation of the prisons by Robert F. Kennedy. A lot of change.

Arlene worked at Richard Bland College, a local junior college, teaching reading and study skills. "It was part of William and Mary University. I did essentially the same thing I had done in Kansas. By then I had a curriculum, because I'd been doing it already for two years, and I had a very nice group of students. It was all fine."

The morning of August 28, 1963, Arlene got up early and went to the Gillfield Baptist Church, whose pastor, Wyatt Tee Walker, was a founder of SCLC and MLK's chief of staff. Arlene and Sheldon Elster, the Fort Lee Virginia Jewish chaplain, were the only white people on the bus to D.C. for the March on Washington. "The Black people on the bus," she recalls, "were extremely suspicious of why this white lady and white man were getting on the bus." Arlene explained that she and Sheldon were Jewish and that, considering what had happened to their people in Europe, they she had to stand up for people suffering here in America. So she was on the Mall and heard Martin Luther King. I wish I could have been there, but members of uniformed services aren't allowed to participate in political gatherings.

"There was a feeling of exhilaration by the end of the day," says Arlene. "And the ride home was great fun. Everyone was exhausted, but singing, and having a good time. The whole day felt historic. Every moment of it felt like something new was being born. And it was. Something new was happening."

Arlene also had one private pupil, a boy named Jobo Riddle whom Arlene was able to help with his trouble learning and reading. Jobo belonged to a family listed in what were called the First Families of Virginia, the White Virginia social elite.

"I had volunteer-tutored at the Bolingbrook Country Day School, where our kids went" Arlene recalls. "There was a little boy there in the third grade, Jobo Riddle, and Jobo couldn't read. His father was a doctor and the family were business people. They all had advanced degrees and everything, and here they had this child who by third grade still hadn't learned to read. And they were very worried about him. (He's now a surgeon.) I volunteered to teach him to read. And after about a year, he was reading on grade level and beyond, and he was starting to read newspapers (most newspapers are written on a fourth-grade level). His grandmother, the matriarch of the family and the grand lady of the town, invited me to tea as a thank you for having done this wonder for her grandson. I had to say, 'I'm so sorry Mrs. Riddle, but that's the day I'm marching on Washington.' And she did not bat an eyelash. She said, 'Oh, I'm so sorry dear. Would the following Wednesday do?' So I went to tea at Mrs. Riddle's house. You have to know, tea in the South is the most intimate thing: You could have a business lunch and you could have a political dinner, but tea is where you invite your sister or your sister-in-law, your daughter-in-law, your second cousin—but no one more distant than that. Tea is really a time for the closest people in your life. It was a very elegant tea and I was totally overwhelmed. She asked me about the March on Washington, and I told her. And she was fine with it, unlike my rabbi. I guess she was not afraid. She had nothing to lose."

In Petersburg we connected with members of the Jewish community, such as the Kossicks, our partners in the integrated art exhibit. Ebba was a student, Bill was in the army at Ft. Lee. Ebba learned to weave; they later left Petersburg and moved to Maine, opening the Weave Shop in the town of North Deer Isle. We would visit them in Maine and buy a house nearby. We met many community physicians in Petersburg. These doctors were anxious that we stay in Petersburg so that I could practice psychiatry there. The medical community in general was concerned that segregation discouraged competent physicians from moving to Petersburg.

"We were trying to make life as normal as possible," says Arlene. "So we found a synagogue at Fort Lee, Virginia, and we went there. They didn't have a Sunday school. So I found a Sunday school in Petersburg and took our son, Steven, there on Sunday mornings, so that he should know that there were other Jewish children in the world. Because there weren't any in the place where we lived, and there weren't many in town altogether—I think there was one other Jewish child in his elementary school. I taught for two years at the little Sunday school. It wasn't really a Hebrew school. They did the Bible and stuff, but they didn't teach the language. And the kids just loved my class, because I was by then a professional teacher, and I knew how to make things fun for kids and how to make them want to learn. They'd always go home with projects they'd done in school, so the parents were pleased."

While we were in Petersburg, the public schools had been shut down before because of integration. In response, a group of residents, professional people, started a private school which they called the Bolingbrook Country Day School. "Only white kids were allowed to go there," recalls Arlene. "And we were in a dilemma, because we knew we weren't going to stay in Petersburg forever, but our kids would have to go to school somewhere that year. Otherwise Steven, who was a very lively, not to say hyperactive, child, would be home with me all day. How could I entertain him?"

With no place else to send our son Stephen and daughter Rebecca, we sent them to this segregated private school—third grade for Stephen, first for Rebecca, who was born in Baltimore in 1958. I was elected the chair of the Parent Teachers Association for the entire school and chaired the meetings. Why I was chosen for this honor was a mystery, given that the school was formed, in part, to isolate children from integration, which Arlene and I so deeply believed in. I suppose they selected me because I was a physician.

"The other interesting thing about our time in Virginia was," says Arlene, "the second summer we were there, we sent Steven to a camp in Ashville, North Carolina, called Blue Star. With a white flag featuring a six-pointed blue star as its emblem, it was a camp for all the Jewish kids in the South to meet each other, so that they could know other Jewish kids. They were in so many small towns in the South. There were department stores run by people who had been peddlers and settled down in these towns, often becoming quite wealthy, Nieman Marcus being the prime example. Lots of such stores in lots of such places. When we went to the camp to visit Stephen, he asked us not to park in the parking lot, because we were the only ones who didn't drive a Cadillac.

"Still, he got along well and liked the camp, and they liked him. It was a really good experience for him. And it was a very good experience for me, because then I didn't have to worry about his climbing the electric fence."

So, in numerous ways I did become involved in the Petersburg community and did, briefly, consider remaining there. Members of the Jewish community wanted me to stay. But I decided that my professional career path needed to be pursued elsewhere.

"We were determined to go back to the North," says Arlene. "Arnie applied to an analytic institute in Washington, and two in New York City. I was really interested in moving to Washington, because I wanted to go to graduate school by then. I still just had a bachelor's degree. I was going to study reading and study skills, because by then I had a career in that field. I had two years of teaching that subject in Topeka, and two years in Virginia, but I had no formal credentials. I had made up these courses myself, using my experience of teaching elementary school in New York as a basis. I wanted to go to either American University, which had a good psychology department, or George-town. Neither of them accepted me; they said I was too old. In those days that's the kind of excuse that they would have. The problem was that I had children. Maiden ladies might get away with it, but certainly not mothers of children.

"We had already picked out a house in Washington, a beautiful house in the park, which we could afford at the time. Prices in Washington were still low. Under a hundred thousand. Maybe eighty. It was gorgeous. A beautiful three-story house.

"But that fell through, because Arnie got accepted by New York Psycho-analytic. That was the high church of psychoanalysis at the time, so he wanted to go there. As a result, we didn't go to Washington. I wound up at Teachers College at Columbia, in New York, which was better than what I would have had in Washington, anyway.

"I'd read a story in *The New Yorker* about a woman named Anne McKillop, at Teacher's College, who was a professor of educational psychology and was *the* expert in reading and study skills at the time. It was a whole new field. So I wrote to her and I said, 'I would like to apply to be your student.' I got an appointment, and I was going to take the bus overnight from Petersburg to New York, where I had a ten a.m. job interview scheduled the next day. The plan was that I would then take the bus back to Petersburg. Arnie was set to babysit for the day. The bus was to leave Petersburg at ten p.m. We went to the bus stop, got there before ten, and no bus came. And no bus came. And no bus came. Finally, it was clear the bus wasn't coming. So Arnie said, 'I'll drive you.' We were at the bus stop, with the children sleeping in the back of the car. So we drove all night. The kids eventually woke up in the back seat—we stopped for food on the way and bought the kids some fresh clothes after we got to New York. I had *my* clothes—an interview outfit. I went into the ladies' room in a gas station, washed up and changed, and went to the interview. Anne McKillop was so impressed by how I had gotten there that she said, 'Of course we accept you!' With the motivation I'd shown, she said, 'You come.'

"And that was how I got to Teacher's College."

When Arlene was admitted I was sure I was going back to New York. She and I would always be like Crick's DNA, two strands of a double helix. My aim was that she would always belong in everything I did,

"Arnie was always supportive," says Arlene.

CHAPTER 6

BACK IN NEW YORK
Training at the New York Psychoanalytic Institute

In the spring of 1964, we got in the car and drove to New York City. Our first apartment was at 380 Riverside, Drive, at 110th Street. Teacher's College, where Arlene was enrolled, was at Broadway and 120th. One benefit of our new circumstances was that the kids could attend the Agnes Russell School, a grade school run by the College as a laboratory for educational innovation.

For the next phase of my training, I applied to the New York Psychoanalytic Society and Institute (NYPSI). The New York Psychoanalytic Society had been founded by A.A. Brill in 1911, and the New York Psychoanalytic Institute, an outgrowth of the Society, was established in 1931, again under Brill. But he was more involved with the Society than the Institute. The first director of the Institute was Sandor Rado, who had trained at the Berlin Psychoanalytic Institute.

After an Eastern European childhood spent in poverty—in *Kanczuca, Galicia, Austria-Hungary*—Abraham Arden Brill immigrated to the United States at age fifteen with two dollars in his pocket. Determined to make a place for himself in society, He thrived in his new country, becoming a successful physician and psychiatrist. Brill established the medical identity of psychoanalysis, defining the field in a way that excluded people who might have added a dimension many physicians were not capable of contributing. To be a good psychoanalyst, you have to be humanistic. This aspect was essential to Freud's work, influenced by his interest in archaeology, literature, and other studies in the humanities, and also to his Judaism, centered, as it was, on humanism and the Enlightenment. In essence, the conflict was this: Can a psychoanalyst be a *lay* analyst, without medical training, or is medical training necessary to practice the profession? Therein hangs a tale—in fact, a pivotal historical conflict in the history of psychoanalysis and in my own life, as you will see later.

Institutional psychoanalysis has always had an ambivalent relationship at best with democracy. The field was conceived and informed by an autocratic genius, Sigmund Freud, who did not willingly relinquish authority. Yet this same genius welcomed anyone into his tent—as long as they followed his rules. Psychoanalysis in America has been less ambivalent toward democracy in the profession but, at least in the foremost psychoanalytic organization in the country, democracy has sometimes been given short shrift, as will be seen later.

When I applied to NYPSI, I sat for three interviews. The first was with Bernard Fine, who I believe was a recently appointed Training Analyst. (A Training Analyst is one who can supervise and analyze candidates.) In order to graduate you had to be analyzed by a Training Analyst. The second, on the following day, was with Andrew Peto. I told Peto that in a dream I'd had the night before, someone had said, "That's fine," a play on words (referring to Bernard Fine), although I don't recall having heard those words before the dream, which contradicted Otto Isakower's idea that spoken words in dreams are always words heard recently in waking life. My third interviewer was Lilly Bussell, a child analyst, who, at the end of the interview, said, "Now I understand your case," which I thought meant she decided I was analyzable and would be admitted. If the institute decides you are not analyzable they will not admit you. There are no criteria for who is analyzable or not. It is a matter of the judgment of whoever is interviewing the applicants—and each interview might come to a different conclusion.

Evidently, I was analyzable, because I was admitted, one of thirteen accepted out of thirty-five applicants. I started as an analytic candidate in July1964. This was a halcyon time for the New York Psychoanalytic Institute and for American psychoanalysis in general. Membership in the American

Psychoanalytic Association (APsaA), the mother church of psychoanalysis in the United States—the organization that includes all the societies and institutes nationwide—was growing. Most hospital departments of psychiatry were chaired by psychoanalysts. Psychoanalysis carried a lot of prestige, enabling psychoanalysts to command high fees. There were plenty of patients and plenty of candidates. The numbers of candidates promoted conformity and compliance to rules and practices set by those in charge, because trainees were aware that if they did not comply, there were many other interested applicants waiting to take their place. It was also a time of a burgeoning psychoanalytic literature by important contributors within the perhaps too narrow classical Freudian clinical approach. It was a medical profession at this point—Brill had prevailed over Freud, who indeed was an advocate for non-medical analysis. But there were important research efforts underway by psychologists who were not allured by clinical training, for example those at the New York University Research Center for Mental Health, including George Klein, Bob Holt, Leo Goldberger, Fred Pine, Sheldon Bach, and David Wolitzky. Wolitzky entered my class at NYPSI as a CORST (Committee on Research and Special Training) candidate, the only nonphysician among us.

We thought those days would never end, but they did. Due to reasons such as alternative treatments, psychopharmacology, limited insurance reimbursement, and a change in prevailing cultural and societal attitudes, the place of psychoanalysis in the mental health universe has dramatically changed. I don't know of a single chair of a psychiatry department who is a psychoanalyst now. Indeed, psychiatry itself is now in trouble. There has not been a single graduating medical student from Albert Einstein Medical School who opted for psychiatry in recent times. There was one about ten years ago, but I don't have the current statistics.

Of the thirteen in my class, there were twelve psychiatrists and one psychologist (Wolitzky, the CORST candidate); twelve men and one woman. I was fortunate in the teachers I had: among them. Robert Bak, Nicholas Young,

Edith Jacobson, Phyllis Greenacre, Margaret Mahler, Ruth Eissler, Charles Brenner, and Jack Arlow.

My supervisors were David Beres, Ted Lipin, and George Gero, each with his own approach. Beres was an ego psychologist, following Freud's structural model of the mind, with its divisions of ego, id, and superego, to understand and deal with the personality's interaction with the external world. Lipin followed the Paul Gray "close process monitoring" approach in the practice of psychotherapy, focusing attention on the ego-directed resistance to psychoanalytic treatment and how it could be overcome. Gero adhered to the topographical model, which postulates a conflict of the unconscious versus the conscious mind. Beres, Lipin, and Gero were different men. For example: George Gero, a wonderful European, conveyed a big picture of the unconscious fantasy and the Oedipus complex, while Ted Lipin, a down-to-earth American, although German-born, attended more to the minute-by-minute material of interactions between analysis and analysand.

My first case was a person who had hypochondriacal delusions; I was able to analyze him, and he has done quite well. The Europeans would say that certain patients were schizophrenic and unanalyzable. The Americans, like Charlie Brenner and Jack Arlow, saw the matter differently, believing that every patient had conflicts you could try to understand, whether your understanding helped them or not. I believe that the concept of analyzability does not get you very far, that you should try to help every patient you can, even if they are discovered to not be analyzable in the classic Freudian sense. I have seen patients who supposedly were psychotic, but when you got to know them you discovered they were hungry for a connection with someone dedicated to understanding and helping them, rather than using or misusing them in some prescribed or doctrinal way. My patients changed me. I now see them in a much less rigid, open fashion. Above all, I was fortunate, as the years went by, that each of my cases responded to the approach I offered.

I graduated in 1969 after finishing only four years of classes; that timetable was hardly the norm, but not unheard of. I think my below-average time to graduation was indicative of the high regard in which I was held in by my supervisors and instructors. I had excellent relationships with most of the Institute's faculty and with most of the general non-student Society membership. Looking back on my class of thirteen, two dropped out, three died, and eight graduated. Three of the graduates are still practicing psychoanalysis.

As a group, we were mostly unquestioning. Remember, this was the heyday of American psychoanalysis; we were sitting at the feet of the masters. When I graduated, I finished my analysis, after four times a week for five years. My analyst, Henry Lowenfeld, had analyzed the great artist Louise Bourgeois for thirty years, as she once wrote about. Leonard Bernstein, and Marilyn Monroe, and Kurt Vonnegut were all seeing analysts at the time. George Gershwin's analysis had a tragic outcome: His analyst, Larry Kubie, had said that Gershwin's severe headaches were psychological in origin, but the cause turned out to be a brain tumor. This correct diagnosis came just weeks before the cancer killed him.

Political crosscurrents affected our lives at the Institute, despite efforts to insulate ourselves. Before emigrating to the US in 1938, Dr. Lowenfeld had trained in Berlin with Otto Fenichel and been associated with Wilhelm Reich, both analysts known for their pairing of Marx and Freud. Even though Lowenfeld was aware, during the analysis, of my father's Bolshevik background, he did not share his own history with me.

Thomas Müller recounted Lowenfeld's history in detail in his PhD thesis about Henry, *From Charlottenburg to Central Park West: Henry Lowenfeld, in Psychoanalysis in Berlin, Prague, and New York*. Born in Berlin, Lowenfeld recognized the Nazi menace early on, moving to Prague in the early thirties. There, he and his wife became members of the Freudian left. In New York, he became a prominent member of the New York Psychoanalytic Institute, with involvement in the treatment center. In the sixties, Alexander Mitscherlich suggested that Lowenfeld relocate to take over the Frankfurt Psychoanalytic Institute. He turned the offer down, refusing to return to Germany. That's when I started my analysis with him.

During the student revolutions of 1968, I had the sense that Lowenfeld was not sympathetic to the students; he seemed to share with Bruno Bettelheim a concern, based on their experiences in Nazi Germany, that the uprising would go too far. I told him about Marty Willick's analytic patient who, while taking part in the student strike that year at Columbia, would climb out of a window—in Butler Hall or the president's office, perhaps—to go to his analysis and then return to the sit-in via the same route. One of my patients at the time was also at Columbia, so the conflict was front and center in my office.

Four years of class, three cases—that was the sum total of my formal analytic training. But my informal experience, through my connections with colleagues and teachers, was much more extensive. Indeed, some of those connections continue to this day.

My fellow candidates had many different paths to the profession. I knew a couple of them from earlier—Bennett Simon from Erasmus and Howard Kremen from the University of Chicago. Howard had the misfortune of being assigned to Leo Loomie, an analyst who was not very good, so he dropped out of the institute and was then treated by Edith Jacobson, who helped him. He went on to have a successful career as a psychiatrist. Bennett became an analyst, as did classmates Stuart Feder and Scott Nininger. Eleanor Bogoch took fifteen years to graduate. Her husband, Sam, was on staff at Mass Mental Health when I applied for residency there; he interviewed me and turned me down. Herb Pardes graduated with me but did not become an Institute member because he refused to write up his cases. He felt that being forced to write up the cases to become a member was an imposition. He went on to become one of the most important psychiatrists in the United States, serving as dean of Columbia's medical school and president and CEO of New York-Presbyterian Hospital. The building of the New York Psychiatric Institute, which he headed, is named for him—in fact, he is the only person I know of who had a building named for him while still alive. For years, he was a very good friend to me. It is unfortunate that the New York Psychoanalytic Society and Institute did not find a way for him to remain a member. His departure was a great loss for NYPSI.

NYPSI has had problems with inclusion, excluding people not only because they are psychologists but also for more personal reasons. When Bob Waller-stein applied for training—I guess it was in the 1940s—he was rejected because he was told he was too confident. The admissions committee felt he wouldn't make a good candidate because he had already achieved too much and knew too much, with little left to learn. Bob went on to an enormously distinguished career, conducting groundbreaking research and authoring twenty books. I know of others who, after being rejected, also went on to distinguished careers in psychoanalysis. These facts raise the question of what the Institute was looking for. I think the main thing was conformity. NYPSI wasn't looking for candidates who would rock the boat. I went on to rock the boat but I must've kept my nature hidden during my application and training. I had no problem graduating.

I did, however, rock the boat just a bit during my first year of training. After Mortimer Ostow and I learned that classes were scheduled for Yom Kippur, we complained. Those in charge relented, agreeing to move the classes. I guess this initial scheduling was indicative of the attitude held by the people running the New York Psychoanalytic Institute, as well as by many of its members, about religion in general and Judaism in particular.

After graduating from the New York Psychoanalytic Institute, I became certified in 1972 after writing up two cases and submitting them to the certification committee. A dozen years later, after Joan Erle interviewed me, I became a Training Analyst. My standing at the New York Psychoanalytic Institute advanced in the years following my graduation. I was appointed Secretary of the Society—the Secretary is Chairman of the Program Committee and reports on Society meetings to the membership.

I continued my post-graduate analytic training at the Madison Avenue Delicatessen, at 86th Street and Madison Avenue, just three blocks south of where Arlene, the kids, and I were then living. A group of us would go for lunch—Charlie Brenner, Bernie Brodsky, Ernest Kafka, Sandy Abend, Mervyn Peskin, Arthur Schwartz, Arlene, and I. It was around 1972 that Charlie said to me, "Do you know this fellow Kohut has written a book? Maybe you can read it and let me know if there's anything in it worth thinking about." So I read Heinz Kohut's *The Analysis of the Self* and basically agreed with his approach of not dismissing narcissism out of hand as pejorative.

Nevertheless, nine years later I started my career as an essayist—which made my fortune, so to speak—disagreeing with Kohut when I wrote a paper called "Self Theory, Conflict Theory, and the Problem of Hypochondriasis," which was published in *The Psychoanalytic Study of the Child* (Richards, A. D., (1981). I used the example of my hypochondriacal former patient to show that conflict theory could explain narcissistic conflicts as well as self-psychology. I felt that current psychoanalytic theory could also account for the psychopathology of the self. It became a theme of my writing to criticize what I called "false dichotomies"; for example, to say either unconscious conflict or the psychology of the self is the way to explain a disorder. Both theories are equally valid. As I wrote in my paper:

> I do not argue against the usefulness of the concept of the self as it relates to the importance of certain broad identity themes which characterize each of us, themes by which we organize our experience. But I want to stress that these themes are inevitably the result of the outcome of the vicissitudes of the important childhood conflicts and are related to the expressions of these conflicts in adult life. And at the root of these conflicts are indeed the core calamities of childhood—loss of object, loss of love, castration anxiety, and guilt. Evidence of the importance of all four could be found in my patient.

Charlie liked the paper, but I am not sure he ever got around to reading Kohut.

This paper set me on a new course of writing a series of reviews of the work of Kohut, Arnold Goldberg, George Gero, and Robert Stolorow. I became known as the Mac the Knife of psychoanalysis, because in each review I brought in my own critical conflict theory. I also wrote critical papers about the work of the young psychologists Steve Mitchell and Jay Greenberg. I did not win friends or influence people in their group, who were known as "relationalists." I think what I had to say was quite accurate, but they did not appreciate it.

After Mitchell and Greenberg published *Object Relations in Psychoanalytic Theory* in 1983, they became known as relationalists for their postulating a relational theory in opposition to classic Freudian "drive" theory, in which unconscious fantasies organize childhood memory and experience. In subsequent writings, Mitchell, more than Greenberg, portrayed contemporary psychoanalysis as dominated by two competing perspectives: Freud's drive theory and the cluster of theories Mitchell favored—theories he depicted as relationally based. Mitchell described "the relational matrix" as an organizing positive principle, which is "a counterpart of drive" and contended that drive and relational thinking cannot work together "in a smooth and consistent manner which is mutually enhancing." (Greenberg, J.R. & Mitchell, S.A., *Object Relations in Psychoanalytic Theory*, (Cambridge: Harvard University Press, 1983)

For Greenberg and Mitchell, as I wrote (with Janet Bachant) in my review, "relations with others shape and color psychic life," and the mind is dominated by the interactive and the interpersonal connections in the world. They argued that psychoanalytic metapsychology was based either on the orthodox view of instinctual drives or the radical alternative of real or imagined relations with others. But Janet and I argued that Freud's theory of drives already accounted for such object relations: "Freud thought in continuums and dualities, not dichotomies." To sum up, "the fundamental concepts of psychoanalysis, including an *integration* of drive and relational considerations, are supported by generations of clinical experience. This is not to say that there have been no changes, but there has not been the radical shift that Mitchell suggests." The relationalists certainly enriched psychoanalytic dialogue with their focus on the dynamics of the interpersonal field within psychoanalysis, especially in the interaction between psychoanalyst and patient, but Mitchell presents us with a dichotomy which I asserted was false in a later (1993) issue of *Psychoanalytic Psychology*.

There were plenty of issues with critiques of Greenberg and Mitchell's book—reviews were written by Alan Sugarman and Arnold Wilson, as well as by Janet and me. Some referred to our reaction as "the empire strikes back." I would argue that Mitchell and Greenberg's purpose was political: to establish a movement with a set of principles disjunctive from contemporary Freudian psychoanalysis, to be, in Martin Bergmann's term, a modifier rather than an extender—perhaps something closer to a heretic. Mitchell and Greenberg both left the psychoanalytic mainstream. But with regard to their relationship to psychoanalytic theory, Greenberg's later writings were less different from the mainstream than Mitchell's. Also, organizationally, Greenberg accepted an honorary membership in APsaA and Mitchell did not. Greenberg jumped ship from Mitchell's cause and stayed with the mainstream. Greenberg felt that relational ideas offered by Steve and him were helpful in our effort to refine psychoanalytic process and psychoanalytic interaction, and the role of the analyst in the dyad, but did not qualify as a paradigmatic theoretical shift.

Mitchell and Greenberg might have been young rebels at this point in their lives, but they were just as dogmatic and authoritarian as everyone else. We had some fights. I believe that unconscious drive-related conflict and developmental deficit—an arrest or a mental insufficiency requiring empathic and reparative techniques—are interactive variables: Conflict leads to deficit, and deficit affects the way conflict is experienced. Again, to bring up my frequent *bête noire,* I am against dichotomies, and that was my problem with Mitchell and Greenberg. I think the reason Freud has survived as well as he has is that he never came down on one side of dichotomies. He was always for nature *and* nurture, conflict *and* deficit. He always embraced a complex, even dialectical, view of human mental functioning.

My review, and the turmoil it provoked, served to sharpen my "Mac the Knife" blade, which was all to the good. I would certainly need it in the personal and professional conflicts to come—conflicts that would be, perhaps, the most significant in my life.

CHAPTER 7

IN-GROUP, OUT-GROUP

Conflicts and Politics in the Psychoanalytic Community

The shadow of the founder falls over an institute. A.A. Brill and his shadow featured the politics of exclusion and his disagreement with Freud about lay analysis—Freud for, Brill against—affecting the medical identity of both the New York Psychoanalytic Institute and the American Psychoanalytic Association (APsaA). These two organizations marched in lockstep, although APsaA followed NYPSI more than NYPSI followed APsaA. Questions of status and inclusion that determined Brill's outlook, which included his commitment to medical psychoanalysis, can still be found in how the issues of certification and membership are framed in APsaA today.

After emigrating in the late 1880s as a teenager from Eastern Europe, A.A. Brill studied medicine at Columbia at the dawn of the twentieth century, then trained as a psychiatrist for four years at Central Islip State Hospital on Long Island. On a trip to Europe, intended to broaden his knowledge of international trends in psychiatry, Brill was captivated by Freud and his theories. He pursued additional training at the psychoanalytically informed *Burghölzli* Mental Hospital in Switzerland, and paid a visit to Freud himself, in Vienna. Freud selected Brill to translate his works into English.

Thus did Brill become the first American psychoanalyst. He was the first American to travel to Vienna to meet with Freud. Distinction and status were important to Brill, and also the need to protect the new psychoanalytic discipline from accusations of quackery. And so he laid down the requirement of a medical degree for membership in the organization he founded, the New York Psychoanalytic Society. This restriction, which meant the exclusion of lay analysts, determined the earliest practices of what eventually became APsaA.

Until the 1920s, Freud seemed to agree that a psychoanalyst had to have medical training. But he then altered his view, arguing that a medical degree was not a requirement. I always felt that Freud's educational background, his gymnasium training—which ensured that he would be versed in history, archaeology, philosophy, literature, and other humanistic disciplines—his *Bildung*, accounts for his support of lay analysis.

In New York, however, Brill's view prevailed—he was the founder of the New York Psychoanalytic Institute, after all. Indeed, there were few dissenting voices on the issue of lay analysis when I trained, and even up until the settlement of a lawsuit in 1985. Although my wife was a psychologist, and felt that psychologists should be admitted for training, until the mid-eighties I sided *with* The Powers That Be in supporting the physician requirement. Almost everyone I knew did as well. But their support of the medical requirement did not prevent some members of Institute faculty from teaching psychologists and social workers.

Exclusion extended to theory as well as discipline. I think there was more openness to unorthodox Freudian views in the early thirties than there was after the Europeans came a few years later. The rescue of the psychoanalysts from Europe before the war, mounted by Lawrence Kubie and Bettina Warburg, was an important achievement. They encountered some resistance initially, a fear of competition perhaps. When William Langer approached Burt Lewin, the president of NYPSI, about the rescue, Lewin was lukewarm, saying, "Don't we have enough analysts?" But Kubie, who would succeed Lewin as president, saw that question for the callous and ignorant comment that it was. He recognized the extreme danger and the dire circumstances faced by the Jewish analysts in Europe, and he was able to marshal the resources of the psychoanalytic community, obtaining visas, raising funds, and finding positions in New York and elsewhere.

However, there was an unintended consequence: The émigrés came and they conquered. Replacing the American-born psychoanalysts (Kubie, Brill, et al.), they became the ruling class. Their advantage was their closeness to Freud. I believe they brought with them a rigidity in theory and practice. Some feel that the image of the silent analyst developed in part because the émigrés had difficulty with English, making it more comfortable for them to say less.

The Association was dealing in the late thirties with several intertwined issues: the absorption of the refugee psychoanalysts, the enduring question of lay analysis, and the controversial proposal to establish a psychoanalytic credential and subspecialty within the American Psychiatric Association. Brill kept pushing to make psychoanalysis a medical profession and create a board certification in psychoanalysis.

The acrimonious debates that ensued would greatly influence the course of American psychiatry and its relationship with the European founders. These arguments continued until 1938, when an agreement was reached between the International Psychiatric Association (IPA) and APsaA to allow APsaA to exclude lay analysts—or, better put, for the IPA to look the other way as the restriction was implemented by APsaA. As part of the agreement, the IPA had to agree that, except for an elite handful of individuals, nonphysicians training in Europe who became members of IPA could not ask for membership in APsaA if they came to the United States. You could practice without APsaA membership, but it was a matter of prestige and of belonging to the analytic community. The issue was a particularly sticky one at the time because of the forced emigration of Jewish analysts from Central Europe after the rise of Hitler and then the Anschluss. APsaA did agree to include as members lay analysts of substantial reputation, such as Theodor Reik, Erich Fromm, and Ernst Kris, presumably members of the IPA, but granted them only a kind of second-class membership status. Going forward, the 1938 agreement established the autonomy of APsaA and limited entry into psychoanalysis to psychiatric physicians. A 1946 agreement (which I refer to as APsaA's Versailles Treaty, since it brought to APsaA disruptive consequences like those the 1919 post-World War I pact caused in interwar Europe) basically renovated APsaA, creating its Board of Professional Standards (BoPS), which would handle an additional requirement for membership: undergoing a medical-specialty-like certification process. Certification involved candidates' submitting papers for review in order to determine the post-graduate competence of those individuals. This problem, however, is that assessing competence is not that easy; indeed, some feel it cannot be done at all.

Brill succeeded in establishing the M.D. degree as a requirement for membership, and further excluding nonphysicians, first from the New York Psychoanalytic Society, then from the APsaA. Even though Brill was prominent in the structure of both entities—president of NYPSI, founding member of APsaA—his ability to impose the medical requirement had more to do with his influence than with his organizational positions. Before 1946, the Committee on Psychoanalytic Training, part of APsaA, had been the advisory organ on educational issues in American psychoanalysis. Functioning as a consulting body, this committee could not issue binding decrees on matters of training without the unanimous consent of all the APsaA affiliated institutes—the major psychoanalytic institutes across the country, of which there are now thirty-four. But in 1946 the committee was replaced by BoPS, which could act without the unanimous support of the institutes. BoPS could promulgate whatever training standards it chose as long as a simple majority of the institutes agreed to them. And so, the Training Analysts of BoPS determined membership in the national organization

Arlene explains some of the rationale behind the medical requirement: "The idea behind that was that up until the late nineteenth or even early twentieth century, anyone who was a barber could do medical procedures. And the medical schools were totally corrupt. Then organized medicine, the American

Medical Association, gradually raised its standards for who could be a doctor, who could be a surgeon, who could be a specialist in various fields. And among these fields was psychiatry. And within psychiatry was the field of psychoanalysis. Those making the rules weren't bad people. They just thought that if the field accepted psychologists, then it would be quackery, the same as barbers doing surgery.

"Established psychiatrists also felt they were going to be undercut, that the psychologists would work for lower fees, because psychologists mostly worked in universities or in mental health centers, where they received much lower salaries than psychiatrists. So if psychologists were just as good as psychiatrists, the psychiatrists would lose business. It was the same argument with women. Women will work for less. So if you had a woman psychologist, she was *definitely* going to work for less. Which would make the established psychiatrists economically vulnerable.

"That was the theory. However, remember that all over the world, psychoanalysis is a non-medical profession. Why should it be medical in the US? Freud wanted it non-medical. We no longer have the quackery. We no longer have the corrupt medical schools that would give you an MD degree in a year. This was not a current issue, and it was a restraint of trade: You don't want us to be as well trained as you are. We'd make just as much money if we were."

From the very beginning, the handwriting was on the wall for non-medical and noncertified candidates. From 1946 on you had to be certified to become a member of APsaA and that didn't change until the 1990s. I describe this structure because this is the world I found myself in, and this is the world that I disrupted. BoPS was more interested in narrowing the boundaries of psychoanalysis than expanding them. What particularly bothers me, given my excellent experience in Topeka, was that in 1946, the year of the reorganization, William Menninger was President of APsaA. He had recruited a legion of physicians to work as psychiatrists in World War II, and in so doing probably did more for the advancement of psychoanalysis in America than did any other individual before or since. After discharge, hundreds of these physicians applied for psychiatric residencies all over the country, and then for analytic training at APsaA institutes—in New York, Boston, Chicago, Baltimore, Philadelphia, and Los Angeles. Topeka enrolled more than one hundred psychiatrists in its first post-World War II class.

As APsaA was undergoing this reorganization, Menninger made a strong plea to APsaA to admit non-APsaA-trained scholars and psychotherapists, contending that doing so would enrich psychoanalysis, but his proposal was rejected by the "loyalists," who included many of the émigrés. These APsaA members had standing because of their connection to Freud and because of their theoretical contributions. In truth, Menninger advocated more for the Menninger Institute than for the other APsaA institutes. My openness to non-medical psychoanalysis came in part from my experience in Topeka where many of my instructors and supervisors were not physicians. Menninger allowed non-physicians, such as Herb Schlesinger, to become Training Analysts—it was as though the Menninger analysts were an exception, as members and as Training Analysts. Still, APsaA, maintained its restrictions. Not only did it feel that it had to limit membership to graduates of APsaA analytic institutes in order to maintain its "pure" analytic identity; the association even looked askance at its own people. Even APsaA-trained graduates—and not everyone who trained graduated—had to provide examples of their clinical work and be certified by a BoPS committee before applying for membership.

The result of BoPS's guardianship of psychoanalytic education was that over the next several decades, as many as seven hundred APsaA-trained graduates did not become members of APsaA; among these were eminent psychoanalysts who went on to achieve important academic psychiatric positions. (Herb Pardes comes to mind.) What does that say about BoPS's much vaunted educational standards? And what does it say about how much APsaA lost by not allowing non-certified as well as non-medically trained analysts to become members? The so-called question of lay analysis became a burning issue, but there were other things going on, too. There was the general issue of standards of psychoanalysis and how close the treatment came to the rigid Freudian model and followed Freudian dogma. BoPS saw itself as keeper of the flame. I saw myself as pouring water on that flame, and moving in the direction of more inclusion and less exclusion. Prior to 1946, training and membership had been open to non-physicians, but after 1946 this possibility was never even discussed. In fact, APsaA specifically excluded IPA members who came to the United States before and after the war who were not physicians.

Attempts were made to abrogate this rule, particularly on the West Coast, and particularly with regard to lay psychoanalysts of considerable stature. But these efforts went nowhere except in Topeka, where thankfully (given my own course of study) Karl Menninger was able to get special treatment for his cadre of psychologist-psychoanalysts, some of whom, like Roy Schafer and Herb Schlesinger, in subsequent decades became members of the Association for Psychoanalytic Medicine (APM), which was a components society of APsaA and connected with the Columbia Center for Psychoanalytic Training.

An unfortunate consequence, therefore, of the hegemony of the Board on Professional Standards was the secondary status of the larger membership, part of the politics of exclusion. Certification was central to becoming a member, running for office, and for voting on bylaw amendments, all of which are requirements that have since been undone. But certification for Training Analyst appointments remains a requirement to this day.

* * *

Despite its medical orientation and Brill's unbending opposition to lay analysis, NYPSI did not want to be absorbed into the larger world of psychiatrists, specifically, the American Psychiatric Association. NYPSI wanted to remain autonomous.

The politics of the NYPSI during the late forties and through the fifties were thus fascinating and rife with controversy. Exclusion from the New York Psychoanalytic Institute was not only a matter of the degree one happened to hold. It was also a matter of ideology. The process of ideological exclusion had begun when Karen Horney and several other analysts, all physicians, walked out of a NYPSI meeting in 1941 after she had been denied training status because of her neo-Freudian ideology. The story, perhaps apocryphal, is that Horney and her supporters left the hall and marched toward the local tavern singing "Let My People Go." They drank to their solidarity in a local bar, and then went on to establish the American Institute for Psychoanalysis. AIP was interested in the work of Horney, and in interpersonal social psychoanalysis and the role of culture.

But APsaA and BoPS, post-reorganization, learned little from this debacle. When APsaA was reorganized in 1946, Horney applied for membership for her institute, but APsaA, taking several years to make its decision, denied the request. The ostensible reason was that her institute's training standard was three times per week instead of four to five times. Merton Gill, on the committee making the determination, told me that the real reason her application was denied was not frequency but theory. Specifically, the committee could not abide her sociocultural psychoanalytic orientation, one of the roots of the relational theory that would cause so much controversy later.

APsaA and BOPS had clearly learned nothing about how costly the enforcement of unnatural boundaries can be to the strength of an organization. The issue was dogma and inclusion and being open to different theoretical points within the Freudian framework. As time went on, I myself became less dogmatic and more open to different points of view. For example, Karen Horney has some key insights into female psychology. The exclusion of lay analysts from the New York Society in the 1940s, and the exclusion of one lay analyst in particular, had a profound impact on the trajectory of psychoanalysis in New York City and anticipated the erosion of APsaA's reach, a falloff with which we struggle today. That lay analyst was Theodor Reik. Reik's prosecution for non-medical practice in Vienna had provided the occasion for Freud's 1926 polemic in favor of lay analysis. But since the days when Freud was making his case in Europe, Americans, especially A.A. Brill, had been fighting to medicalize the field. They had largely succeeded, although they were not successful in making psychoanalysis a subspecialty of psychiatry.

If Reik and other non-physicians had found a welcome at NYPSI, they would have become part of the APsaA psychoanalytic establishment. But they had not, and they did not. Excluded from the big tent, in 1948 they formed a tent of their own. The founding of the National Psychological Association for Psychoanalysis (NPAP) was the beginning of the Balkanization of American psychoanalysis. Similar breaks led to the forming of other new societies, many of which are still part of the non-APsaA psychoanalytic landscape in New York.

In such a divisive context, two groups naturally formed, the ins and outs, at NYPSI. The two groups were defined by personalities more than issues. The dividing line was power: Who was in charge? The ins ran the place, and were mostly Europeans like Otto Isakower, Kurt and Ruth Eissler, Nick Stein, and Roby Bak. The three émigrés most important to psychoanalytic theory, Heinz Hartmann, Ernst Kris, and Rudolph Loewenstein, essentially supported the side of the other émigrés, but I think their interests were more in theory than in Society politics and administration. These three analysts were central to the development of the structural model after 1946 as well as to child analysis; they had prestige, power and authority at NYPSI. The two most important American-born psychoanalysts there, Phyllis Greenacre and Martin Stein, allied consistently with the Europeans in charge. Greenacre and Stein, although they did not train in Berlin, came out of the Berlin model where the tradition was the centrality of Training Analysts within authoritarian structures that were fundamentally anti-democratic and self-perpetuating.

On the other side were Jacob Arlow, Charles Brenner, David Beres, Kenneth Calder, Betty Joseph, Edward Joseph, Victor Rosen, and Martin Wangh. These were the Americans outside of the hierarchy at the New York Psychoanalytic Institute, excluded from the Education Committee and the ruling group.

People are amazed when I tell them that Jack Arlow was never on the Education Committee. Both Jack and Charlie, but especially Jack, had problems with the Institute curriculum. Jack thought it was not up-to-date, that too much Freud was taught. Jack was asked, or perhaps he requested, to prepare a report outlining a new contemporary curriculum, which he did. He submitted it to the EC, which rejected it. Jack was not pleased, and decreased his involvement in NYPSI, teaching more at Columbia and Downstate. Charlie, on the other hand, connected with the younger members and eventually had more influence at the Institute, although his political clout was still limited—I don't think he was ever elected to the Education Committee. His influence also increased as some of the émigré analysts passed on.

There were seven women at NYPSI, including Phyllis Greenacre, Ruth Eissler, and Annie Reich. Someone asked Otto what it was like to be chairman of the Education Committee, whose other seven members were women. Otto, who was short, replied, "Seven Snow Whites and one dwarf." Otto was an interesting man. Although he published widely, it was a single paper, twenty-nine pages in length, that made him a phenomenon. During his reign on the Education Committee, no Training Analysts were appointed. This became known as the "other Isakower phenomenon," besides the Isakower phenomenon on the couch: the unusual set of physical sensations experienced by his patients. He moved from Berlin to Liverpool, England, before he came to the United States. He loved the Beatles and owned an incredible collection of their records.

Arlow and his group instead became very important in the American Psychoanalytic Association, with several of them—Arlow, Beres, Victor Rosen, Brenner, Edward Joseph, and Calder—assuming its presidency. If these analysts couldn't have power at the Institute, they would have it at the Association. Their influence in turn had an important impact on who became president of the

IPA in 1969. Anna Freud and Ruth Eisner were concerned that Jack wanted to become President of the IPA, but Jack assured me that that was never true.

Leo Rangell was chosen to be IPA president by Anna Freud without an election. Anna Freud decided who would occupy that office, even though Heinz Kohut was the sole nominee to become president and had already selected his secretary, Frances Hannet, Max Gittelson's wife. This was in 1969, before Kohut had written *The Analysis of the Self*, which came out in 1972. In that book he developed the form of psychoanalysis called "self psychology." Leo Rangell insisted that Kohut became a self psychologist as a form of breaking away from Anna Freud after he did not become the president of the IPA. Holding that position had been Kohut's dream, and he very much wanted to be connected to Anna Freud, but she told him that he had to withdraw in favor of Leo Rangell because the Europeans did not want him. They feared that Arlow would run against Kohut and be elected. In other words, the implication was that Leo Rangell would be the lesser of the two evils, Arlow being the greater evil. Of course, Leo denies this story and believes that Anna Freud selected him because she preferred him on his own merit. Some of this information I learned from letters in the Library of Congress that passed among Anna Freud, Marianne Kris, and Ruth Eissler.

Jack Arlow says he actually had no intention of running for the president of the IPA, partly because he was afraid to leave the country for meetings of that international body. Unaware of Arlow's non-interest in the position, Ruth Eissler feared that Arlow would become president, and that his group, including Charles Brenner, would then have more political clout that would affect the balance of power at the NYPSI.

Ruth Eissler had spoken to Marianne Kris, who was an analyst of Marilyn Monroe and Jacqueline Kennedy Onassis. Ruth and Marianne wrote to Anna Freud about the fear that Arlow would be elected. Anna did not like Arlow because he was from the American Board of Psychiatry and favored excluding lay analysts, which Sigmund Freud had been in favor of including. Anna also was concerned about Arlow because he favored excluding child analysts. Another reason Anna was so influenced by Ruth Eissler and Marianne Kris was because it was through Kris and Ralph Prince that she got the desperately needed funds for the Anna Freud Centre, a children's mental health facility in London. Douglas Kirsner has written a lot about this relationship, the money, and how Marilyn Monroe supported the Anna Freud Centre, with Ralph Greenson in the middle of it all.

* * *

By the 1970s, BoPS totally controlled the certification process. As the number of applicants increased dramatically, the membership process became more and more arduous. In response, growing numbers of graduates of approved institutes chose not to apply for membership certification, while others made the attempt and were denied. The exclusionary policy, which I would later contend had been with the APsaA since its inception, engendered a great deal of bitterness and hostility.

It was not one of APsaA's finest hours, and it was taking place during a period of decline for the discipline as a whole. Nineteen-sixty-nine, the year I graduated, may have been the highwater mark for psychoanalysis in the United States; the profession's fortunes receded from that point on. By 1976, Anton Kris wrote that approximately 800 eligible psychoanalysts, graduates of Association-approved institutes, had decided not to apply for membership in APsaA because of the Draconian requirements and second-class status experienced by the large group of fully trained but noncertified psychoanalysts.

The first modification made by BoPS, and put into effect in 1973, was the creation of a dues-paying, nonvoting, time-limited "associate member" category open to all graduates of approved institutes. The modification was made to allow graduates to become members for a limited time until they got certified. This measure was intended to entice noncertified graduates into applying for fully certified membership. But by the early 1980s, few people had applied to be associate members, so another category, "extended associate member," with no voting rights or right to hold office, was proposed in a 1983 bylaw amendment, and was adopted by an overwhelming vote of the members, 661 to 44. The "extended associate member" category was not time-limited, unlike the "associate member" classification.

In the 1980s, therefore, as new classes of nonvoting membership in APsaA were created that did not require certification, certification effectively became a prerequisite for voting, for holding office, for being a member of committees or of the Board on Professional Standards, and for being appointed a Training Analyst. This was when I began to be swept up in these matters.

Where did I fall in all these political currents—the in-group and the out-group? I started, in the early 1970s, after my graduation from the Institute, as a member of the in-group. In the early eighties, I was invited to a seminar in Ruth Eissler's living room, where aspiring young members were vetted by Ruth and her acolytes to determine if they could become Training Analysts. (I was open to being considered for appointment as a Training Analyst; I would become one in 1984.) I remember well those meetings with Ruth in her living room. There were the older members, including Maurice Edelman, Irwin Solomon, and the generation behind them, George Gross and Bill Grossman, who were all in attendance. I remember a meeting in which Ruth announced that George and Bill would become Training Analysts. The problem was that they were not certified, and not members of APsaA. Of course, APsaA and BoPS ran the certification committee, but that was not an insurmountable problem because a BoPS member, Irwin Solomon, was also the head of the certification/membership committee so it was expected that certifications would come easy. There was somewhat of a brouhaha when Irwin's wife, Rebecca Solomon, was appointed as a Training Analyst, as there was when Mimi Young, Nick Young's wife, was likewise appointed. Brenner and his close colleagues accused the Training Analyst system of nepotism.

The New York Psychoanalytic Institute decided who was a "real" analyst, appointing the Training Analysts whom the American Psychoanalytic Association would later certify. Phyllis Greenacre opposed APsaA's maintaining a roster of members because it would make it seem as though non-members were not real psychoanalysts, and because people would think the people listed *were* real analysts—that they had finished the process—when they were not and had not. This reminds me of the story of when D. W. Winnicott, who started out as a pediatrician and never became a psychiatrist before becoming a psychoanalyst, was giving a paper and put a revolver on the lectern. "That's for the person who says I am not a psychoanalyst," he said. That's how controversial an issue it had become at the time. Winnicott, whose approach to psychanalytic technique was less orthodox and more innovative, had come in from London and landed at the airport in the rain, but no one came to pick him up. He got pneumonia and ended up in the hospital—Milton Jacoby paid the hospital bill out of his own pocket. Winnicott died not long after that.

As secretary and chair of the program committee of NYPSI, I was most proud of the fact that Milton Jucovy and I removed the red cord in the auditorium that separated members from non-members at programs. This was one of the early indications of a rebellious streak when I was a candidate for Training Analysis. I arranged terrific meetings. The NYPSI program committee invited Paul Gray to give a paper about his work; I think the title was Developmental Lag and Technique. I worked hard to edit the paper. In 2000, Paul and I both got a Sigourney Award, an annual honor for achievement in psychoanalysis, for our general work in advancing psychoanalytic thought, and he gave me credit for my work editing his paper. Another accomplishment I had in the Society was organizing the extension division with Chuck Ruston and Ernie Kafka—the extension division was very successful in offering courses to people outside of the institute.

All this activity led the Institute's president, Milton Jucovy, with the approval of the Board of Directors, to appoint me as Secretary of the Society and, especially because I had developed a reputation as a psychoanalytic scholar, Chair of the Program Committee.

But that all would change in 1995 after I gave the A. A. Brill Memorial Lecture at entitled "A.A, Brill and the Politics of Exclusion." To trace the evolution of my thinking with regard to lay analysis and the politics of NYPSI in general, it is first necessary to consider the Brenner amendment.

CHAPTER 8

AN AMENDMENT AND
AN INSURRECTION

Personalities, Politics, and the Fight Over Power

My thesis is that personal relationships determine politics and are affected by politics. A good example is the political battle between the in-group and out-group at NYPSI, a battle that would become visible, public, and acrimonious during the introduction of the Brenner Amendment in the early 1980s. This battle was fought after a member of the out-group, Herb Waldhorn, was turned down for a Training Analyst appointment by the Instructors Advisory Committee. Charles Brenner and others in the out-group felt that the committee was stacked against them, so they proposed that the bylaws be amended to allow members to be nominated to the Instructors Advisory Committee (and thus potentially chosen) from the floor—that is, by general vote of the membership, with all members eligible to be nominated. In addition, members of the Training Analyst Nominating Committee could be nominated from the floor, and not just by the Executive Committee. I don't quite understand how I became involved in this Brenner Amendment on the Brenner side, given my connections to the in-group. But I did go to several meetings organized by Eugene Goldberg, Eleanor Galenson, Martin Wang, Milton Jucovy, Lou Linn, and others to support the Brenner Amendment.

I have a vivid memory of a general meeting, attended by all sides, at which the Brenner Amendment was discussed and voted on. Kurt Eissler spoke, saying that when it comes to national politics, he was a radical, but within Institute politics, he was a conservative, opposing the amendment. Victor Rosen spoke next. He said, "I can detect the fine Machiavellian hand of Robert Bak," whom Rosen saw as the mastermind behind the scenes.

As I'd mentioned before, this brouhaha was taking place against an overall decline of the profession—for example, by this time there were no chairs of departments of psychiatry in universities who were psychoanalysts. In the fifties and sixties, psychoanalysis had been in a healthy state with what I call "psychoanalysis-aplenty": plenty of patients, plenty of candidates, plenty of prestige, and plenty of money. Leo Rangell could practice in Los Angeles and all the stars flocked to him. But then when I was a candidate, there was a controversial campaign to destroy Melanie Klein and her contingent. Klein was anathema in both New York, where Anna Freud and Ruth Eissler led the effort, and in California, where Ralph "Romy" Greenson spearheaded the opposition. Basically, there had been a major conflict between Anna Freud and Melanie Klein in Europe, repeated in America with Greenson allied with Anna Freud. The issue had been the Oedipal complex: Anna Freud believed it set in at the ages of three and four, Melanie Klein felt it occurred earlier. As a result of this schism, we weren't encouraged to read Klein by the NYPSI. I, for one, thought it was an incredibly dogmatic position that restricted my ability as a student to be exposed to a variety of psychoanalytic theories. Plus, all the *tsuris* of this internal dissension had an impact on our profession's ability to present a sensible picture to the world at large. What's more, in the fifties we promised more than we could deliver, so there were disappointments in people who expected to be magically altered by psychoanalysis.

To reiterate, my thesis is that politics determines personal relationships and personal relationships are affected by politics. My saga and history at the New York Psychoanalytic Society and Institute illustrates the second half of that formulation, and accounts for my up-and-down, in-then-out status at NYPSI. After I graduated in 1969 after five years as a candidate, I enjoyed excellent relationships with most of the faculty and most of the members. I identified and was accepted by the in-group and concurred with their commitment to orthodox Freudian theory and technique. I was not aware that there was an out-group led by Arlow and Brenner, who were less "Freudian" and had a problem with the system of Training Analyst appointments and the control of the Executive Committee and curriculum by the in-group. I was not aware of the issues that divided the in-group and the out-group until the Brenner Amendment, which challenged the political power of the status quo.

The political structure of the Institute involved three committees: the Education Committee, which was the power center; the committee that selected Training Analysts, the Instructors Advisory Committee; and the Instructors Executive Committee, which nominated members to these other two committees.

Members of all these committees had to be Training Analysts. I believe they were voted on by all the members but nominated by a committee of Training Analysts. No nominees were allowed from the floor.

It was in Ruth Eissler's "perversion" seminar that I first became aware of the in-group / out-group divide, because Ruth and others routinely bad-mouthed Jack Arlow and Charlie Brenner, whom they derided as "political." It was a fact that the Arlow/Brenner out-group was excluded from the Educational Committee by the in-group Training Analysts who were in charge of the committee and by the rest of the in-group. This ruling group would decide who should be elected to all three committees I think the Board of Trustees and Board of Directors were a separate matter, not needing the same election effort because the power was in the EC and Instructors' Committees, not in the Board's.

The in-group would decide on the slate, from their side, they wanted elected. They organized telephone trees to ensure the outcome. I was aware of all this because I was told to make phone calls to let the members know whom to vote for.

The political battle with the AB^2C group—Arlow, Brenner, Beres, and Calder—bubbled over with the introduction of the Brenner amendment. I will list some of the amendment's supporters who made up the out-group. In addition to Jack Arlow, Charlie Brenner, David Beres, and Ken Calder, there were Victor Rosen, Eleanor Galenson, Milton Jucovy, Buddy Meyers, Larry Roose, Phil Wiesman, and Arthur Root. Some of them shared a far-left political outlook and had been or were members of the Communist Party—including Jack, Charlie, Eleanor, and Milton, with Victor Rosen, Larry Roose, Buddy Meyers, and, perhaps, David Beres as fellow travelers. I have not been able to decide about Leo Stone—for the most part he kept above the political fray but one of his analysands told me that he had copies of *The Nation* in his waiting room, suggesting that he was, if not Communist, at least left-leaning. Eleanor Galenson was a part of the American Communist Party during her residency at NYU in the forties. Nat Ross was connected with the party. Bluma Swerlow and Stella Chess also belonged. Jack's wife, Alice, was also a member.

I do not know how the political affiliations of the out-group affected their situation in NYPSI. The in-group émigrés included some Austro-Marxists and all were socialists I am sure, but not Stalinists. But I do believe that the leftist politics of many members of the out-group formed a basis for solidarity. Some lived on the Upper West Side and sent their children to the Little Red School-house and Elisabeth Irwin High School, the progressive schools in Greenwich Village. However, outside the group, their leftist politics were not very public. Charlie did write a letter about the Vietnam War to the *New York Times*, which published it. This letter upset Phyllis Greenacre, who said transference would be destroyed if patients were aware of the political views of their analysts. But Charlie, Buddy Mayer, and some others did come out of the political closet when they raised money for a full-page ad in the *New York Times* opposing the Gulf of Tonkin resolution. The ad had more than 100 signers, mostly psycho-analysts, many from NYPSI.

Requiring a two-thirds majority to pass, the Brenner Amendment failed by one vote. The out-group, unable to crack the power structure at NYPSI, shifted their involvement from NYPSI to APsaA, becoming presidents in this order: Brenner, Arlow, Beres, Calder, Rosen. The in-group, on the other hand, had had very little interest in, and very little use for, APsaA except for their involvement with BoPS. They were interested in BoPS because BoPS was concerned with institutes and training but not membership. In any case, some of my favored status with the in-group survived my support of the Brenner Amendment, because I did agree with them on other matters, such as psychoanalytic theory and technique.

* * *

The next major political event was the so-called Gross Insurrection of the early 1980s. George Gross, as president of the Institute, also chaired the Board of Trustees. The Board presumably had the final say on all educational matters, including the appointment of Training Analysts and instructors. The Education Committee proposed Bob Kabcenell for a Training Analyst appointment. Ruth Eissler, who had included Bob in her "perversion" seminar, supported the appointment. But George and the board refused to give their approval, which led to a confrontation between the board and the committee. George insisted on a secret ballot on the nomination—he thought that with an open ballot, people would be afraid to support him in opposition to those in charge. I supported an open ballot—Bob Kabcenell was a very close friend of mine, so I was on the side of the Education Committee. Hoping to change the voting balance on the Board of Trustees, the in-group nominated two candidates to it: Mike Porder and me.

George vigorously opposed our candidacy; it was no surprise that we lost. George had the nonfaculty Society members on his side as well as the faculty out-group. The in-group was composed of the members of the Educational

Committee and not the Board of Trustees. This affair was called the "Gross Insurrection" because George did not go along with the Educational Committee and the Instructors Advisory Committee, which appointed Training Analysts. But the Gross Insurrection did bring into focus the problem with the TA appointment procedures: The appointments were arbitrary and based not on merit but on the arbitrary opinions of a committee. Basically, Ruth Eissler decided who would become a Training Analyst and she was for Bob Kabcenell. The Board appointed a committee to make recommendations to change the procedure for selecting Training Analysts. The committee, which included Bill Grossman, Sandy Abend, and Marty Willick, recommended a new procedure, involving self-nomination, case presentation, and a review. The Executive Council adopted this recommendation.

At that time, I was asked by members of the Education Committee to apply for a Training Analyst appointment. After I presented two cases to Joan Erle, I was approved in 1984. At that time I was active in the Institute as well as the Society. I taught courses, supervised, and served as a faculty adviser. So I was fully invested in the NYPSI when the next big challenge came, for both NYPSI and APsaA, a challenge that would subject the exclusionary policies of not just APsaA and NYPSI, but also IPA and Columbia to a lawsuit.

CHAPTER 9

CALL OFF YOUR HUSBAND
My Involvement in the Struggle Deepens

On March 1, 1985, three psychologists, Helen Desmond, Arnold Schneider, and Tony Bernays, filed a lawsuit on behalf of the American Psychological Association's Division 39, the division on psychoanalysis, against the American Psychoanalytic Association. The suit charged that APsaA had monopolized high-quality psychoanalytic training in this country in violation of the Sherman Antitrust Act. The action named three organizations as codefendants: the International Psychoanalytical Association, the Columbia University Center for Psychoanalytic Training and Research, and the New York Psychoanalytic Institute.

I became involved in not just the whole issue of lay analysts in the NYPSI in general but also this particular legal battle waged by the American Psychological Association's Division 39, the division on psychoanalysis, to force APsaA to train nonphysicians. I had a personal interest in the matter because my wife, Arlene, is a psychologist. She had applied in the early seventies for admission to NYPSI as a Committee on Research and Special Training candidate—CORST allows non-physicians to get training in order to do research but not to practice—but was turned down because she refused to agree not to practice. She was one of the prime movers of the Division 39 effort, which culminated in the lawsuit, raising money to support the legal action.

Arlene recalls:

"I wanted to become a member of the International Psychoanalytic Association, the IPA. At the time, only medical societies and medical institutes and medical doctors in the US could belong to the IPA. But non-medical colleagues all over the rest of the world belonged to the IPA. So I myself, and a group of other people, who had started a division of psychoanalysis at the American Psychological Association, sued the IPA, New York Psychoanalytic, and the American Psychoanalytic for restraint of trade, because they wouldn't let us join this organization, which was very helpful: in referrals, in learning the latest ideas, and in meeting colleagues in other parts of the world. We couldn't do any of that, because the IPA had this arrangement with APsaA, which was all medical then. So we sued.

"Now, I was not a party to the suit. The reason was that the lawsuit was about restraint of trade. And at that point, I had a practice going and it was very successful; I was making as much money at my trade as the psychiatrists were. So I couldn't say, 'I'm hurt by the restraint of trade,' because personally I wasn't, not financially. I had a very good reputation among other psychologists, and even among psychiatrists, some of whom sent me patients, too.

"Luckily, we had been in Topeka with the then-president of APsaA, Dick Simons, and the then-president of the IPA, Bob Wallerstein. We knew them from back when. And we knew they were on the side of having psychologists become full psychoanalysts, because that was Dr. Karl's idea.

"Simons had been a bachelor in Topeka when we were there, and we would have him over for dinner. We were very close and we really, really liked each other. And the same thing with the Wallersteins. Their kids went to nursery school with our kids. We were in a small social group, and really liked and cared about each other. And among that group also were psychologists who didn't have high positions but were close to these people who were now presidents of these organizations. So Simons and Wallerstein knew we weren't carpetbaggers or people who were trying to do things on the cheap.

"They had both worked side-by-side with psychologists who were analysts, and who were even Training Analysts, and they thought that this should happen, and they were going to make it happen. They personally believed it was the right thing to do but wanted to be sued into doing it. So we were suing people who wanted to be sued. The people at New York Psychoanalytic, however, not so much. They wanted to keep the field medical.

The details of the suit have been written up by Bob Wallerstein and Dick Simons. I was close to both of them and played some role in the negotiations, including the eventual replacement of the law firm Paul Weiss by Joel Klein as representative of APsaA, the IPA, NYPSI, and Columbia. In supporting the psychologists despite my previously favored position at NYPSI, I was opposing almost everybody there, in both the in-group and the out-group. I also published Dick Simons's account of the lawsuit against APsaA in *JAPA*, the *Journal of the American Psychoanalytic Association*. Bryant Welch, the lawyer for Division 39, had said that the four organizations were guilty not of an antitrust violation but of arrogance. Simons, in the touching conclusion of his account, concurred.

With a lawsuit threatened, the two sides met for negotiations in D.C., hoping to avert legal action. The psychologists were represented by Janet Spence, then president of the American Psychological Association, as well as Nathan Stockhamer and Welch, two of the central planners of the pending lawsuit within Division 39. The American Psychoanalytic Association was represented by its president and chief spokesman, Edward Joseph; its president-elect, Richard Simons; and its chairman of the board, Homer Curtis.

The psychologists ultimately felt that representatives of the APsaA were "obdurate," for which they held Joseph responsible. The psychologists also stated that they were told that the training matter was a "pocket book problem" (business practice revenue) for the members of the APsaA—for some on the psychologists' side, that comment amounted to a smoking gun. There was also information in a comment to the effect that Joseph had actually submitted a bill to Division 39 for the Washington trip to cover not only his own expenses but those of his wife for the Washington trip. That was the immediate provocation for starting the lawsuit. The infuriating arrogance of that bill seemed a deal-breaker. As I understand it, Joseph claimed that his secretary had sent the bill by mistake and that it was withdrawn when it elicited such an angry response from the Psychological Association.

"The American Psychological Association," notes Arlene, "had invited Joseph to Washington to discuss the feasibility of having psychologists get full training and full recognition as psychoanalysts. And he came down to Washington to discuss this, and sent his hotel bill to the American Psychological Association—including his wife's transportation fare, his wife's hotel bill, and the bill for their laundry. The laundry was what did it. Such arrogance: In order for him to talk to us, we have to pay for his laundry?"

There was another wrinkle to the suit. On January 14, 1986, I called Helen Fischer, the executive director of APsaA. Helen, a bureaucrat who was larger than life and a very nice person, summarized this call in a memo sent that day to Joseph, Shelley Orgel (the Chair of the Board on Professional Standards since May 1985), and Lewis A. Kaplan of the firm Paul Weiss, their main litigator at the time. I had learned that the plaintiffs in the lawsuit were pursuing an additional angle: They had requested that the Federal Trade Commission investigate whether APsaA had committed federal trade infractions in addition to possible violations of antitrust law. Kaplan did not seem terribly concerned about the threat of FTC action, even though the threat of bankruptcy loomed as the Association would have struggled to compete against all the resources available to the FTC and could not afford the rapidly escalating legal bills submitted by Kaplan.

Once the lawsuit was filed, on March 1, 1985, Kaplan, and other attorneys representing the New York and Columbia Institutes, quickly filed a motion requesting the court to render a summary judgment dismissing the suit as without merit and in violation of the defendants' First Amendment rights to free speech and academic freedom.

When summary judgment was denied, the plaintiffs wisely replaced Kaplan with Joel Klein, who was not only tough and smart but would work harder than Kaplan to achieve a fair and honorable settlement. Jack Arlow had read Kaplan's request for summary judgment and said that it was neither well written nor well argued. Kaplan negotiated a settlement that resulted in the FTC's taking no action involving possible restraint of trade by APsaA.

Otherwise, the terms of the settlement favored Division 39. Nonphysicians were admitted for training, and three non-APsaA institutes were admitted into the IPA. This settlement abrogated one of the most cherished restrictions enshrined in the 1946 reorganization, the one dictating who could and could not be trained. But the long and bitter battle over the suit, and the ugly nature of the suit's resolution, was as much a consequence of what I call our "Versailles" in 1946 as World War II was a consequence of Versailles 1919. Like that ill-fated treaty, the creation of BoPS was an effort to establish peace among uneasy factions, but it did so by enforcing unnatural, undemocratic, and ultimately untenable barriers.

Following the inability of APsaA to move forward on the issue of non-medical training in San Diego in May 1984, where there was a meeting of Division 39, the lawsuit was inevitable. Would APsaA have eventually changed its bylaws regarding non-medical training without the lawsuit? Possibly, but it might have taken thirty years instead of the twelve it did take, from 1977 when the issue was first raised at an APsaA meeting in Puerto Rico to 1989 when it was settled. And by that time, any number of institutes might have disaffiliated with APsaA and gone ahead on their own to train qualified non-medical candidates and join IPA, which, for the most part, opposed the medical requirement. If APsaA did allow non-medical people, those institutes might have grown even closer to the American Psychiatric Association, instead of APsaA, and in turn disaffiliated from the International. The American psychoanalytic community, for the most part in favor of non-medical treatment, might truly have become balkanized, hopelessly splintered between medical and non-medical analysts. I believe Herb Schlesinger was right when he said the lawsuit saved APsaA. Maybe it saved even more than APsaA. Wallerstein believes, and I agree, that the suit clarified, permanently defined, and thereby saved the identity of the profession of psychoanalysis.

After the settlement of the lawsuit, and after its discussion in *The American Psychoanalyst (TAP)*, a task force was formed in 1990 to resolve the membership issue and the certification requirement for full voting membership. In 1992, the task force proposed that the bylaws be changed to allow all graduates of APsaA institutes to become APsaA members with the right to vote for officers, but without the standing to run for office, serve on BoPS, or be appointed a Training Analyst. The task force further proposed to confer permanent "Active Membership" on noncertified graduates, but created a new kind of division within the category of "Active Members" based on the member's certification status. Non-certified Active Members would be granted limited voting rights (such as voting for officers) but were barred from voting on bylaw amendments. Finally, a new provision, titled "Certification Requirement" was added to the bylaws as part of the compromise with the explicit intention of "protecting" the Board on Professional Standards, a seeming accommodation, but more an "Empire Strikes Back" move. This provision stated that only a certified Active Member could become an officer, an Executive Councilor, or a Training or Supervising Analyst; furthermore, only a certified Active Member could serve as a Fellow of the Board or could be appointed a member of any committee of the Board. (In retrospect, this was probably an illegal arrangement under state law. It created classes of voting members with different voting rights, but without the necessary formalities required under corporation law to assure the preservation of the rights of each such membership class.).

This compromise proposal received the two-thirds majority necessary for passage, and the bylaws were amended in 1992. As a result, the Associate and Extended Associate membership categories were abolished, rendering all such members unofficially second-class full members instead. This process of democratization had taken about forty-five years. But the remaining restrictions on participation still stood.

Still, the change represented a momentous step forward. The settlement of the lawsuit meant that members of the IPA who did not train at APsaA institutes (including those trained at the New York Freudian Society or IPTAR, the Institute for Psychoanalytic Training and Research) were now eligible to apply for APsaA membership. Two new APsaA members, who applied and were admitted after the lawsuit, Gail Reed and my wife, Arlene Kramer Richards, also applied for certification. Reed's application was accepted but my wife's was deferred.

I encouraged Arlene to apply for certification, because I was trying to show that APsaA welcomes the new members who were able to apply because of the settlement of the lawsuit. She went to Toronto, where APsaA was meeting, to be interviewed by the committee and present her cases. The interviewer made no eye contact, and at the end of the meeting said, "Now, I have what I need." We thought those words signified that she had been accepted. No, she was rejected. Keep in mind that at that time she was a Training Analyst at two institutes, and several of her analysands had become Training Analysts as well. I felt guilty that I had put her through this ordeal, believing that her rejection called into question both the reliability and validity of the certification process as a test of psychoanalytic competence.

"I applied," Arlene recalls, "and you were supposed to give your credentials. By then I had good credentials: I had written analytic papers, which had been published in the most prestigious journal. So I thought this would just be a fun thing, to talk to colleagues about my work. I had a case of which I was particularly proud, which was of a woman who had Lupus. At the time of her analysis—as a result of her analysis, her doctor thought—her symptoms decreased dramatically. So he thought that there must be a psychological component in her misery and insisted she stay in analysis. And this doctor was a big deal in the Lupus world, people listened to him. The case was also interesting, because she was a creative person from a wealthy and accomplished family. In her field, she was a leader: She was a dancer, of all things, and Lupus is hard on dancers. She was a member of an international troupe, and they would go on these trips to Europe and do concerts in different cities. She was a star. And her symptoms were in remission during her entire analysis. Eventually, she became the first person with that degree of Lupus to be become pregnant and deliver a healthy baby. So all of this was very gratifying to her Lupus doctor, and I had a whole theory of how this worked for her.

"So I presented the case, and the guy I presented it to was ice cold to me. He was so unfriendly and so unaccepting. I couldn't figure out what was going on. I finished presenting the case and was about to start another—you're supposed to present two cases—and he said, 'That's all I need. I have enough.' Meaning, I have enough to sink you. In fact, there was a junior guy with him, someone I had known. We had spent four days together discussing cases in a small group. When I came to the interview, he shook my hand and said, 'I'm Doctor So-and-So, who are you?' What?! What do you mean, Who are you? That's the degree of coldness there was.

"This guy didn't want the senior guy to think he was on my side. The result was predetermined.

"Afterward they said, 'Well, you probably won't want to apply again, it was so humiliating.' And I said, 'No, I'm going to apply again.' I didn't feel humiliated. I felt they acted like assholes.

"The simple reason is that they rejected me because I was a psychologist. I don't think it was anything personal. And I was the psychologist who had sued them. They didn't think that was nice."

Why was she rejected? The committee claimed that her presentation was not good enough. Really, though, they evidently didn't feel she was their kind of psychoanalyst—she didn't walk the walk or talk the talk. But I think the decision was more political, in that she didn't train at an institute of APsaA. Now, Reed didn't either, but people who ran the Certification Committee saw her as more conservative than Arlene, with values consistent with their own.

"By bringing that lawsuit," Arlene says, "I was doing them a favor. The lawsuit saved their asses. Because the lawsuit allowed psychologists to be trained at their institute. And just at that time, psychiatrists stopped wanting analytic training, because they couldn't make as much money doing analysis as they could dispensing drugs. They became drug lords. That's what they do. Psychiatrists give you drugs. And they make a thousand dollars an hour doing it. You can't charge those fees as an analyst. You can't.

"So a year later I reapplied. And this time the patient in the first case was really amazing. Sometimes you have a patient who has wonderful dreams and talks about them, and has interesting ideas about himself, and who learns something in the course of an hour. The last session before I presented this case, he gave me the perfect analytic hour. Perfect. So I presented the case, and I presented the hour (for which I had stenographic notes). It was a great, great case. And the second case I presented was very good, too.

"At the end of it, the senior person in that interview said to me, 'All right, you passed. Now will you call off your husband?' It was clear, the whole thing was just a political issue.

"Arnie had been giving papers, and leading discussions against the certification system, which was an unscientific thing. The whole process was totally unscientific. You can't conduct an objective test that's all about seeing if you liked a person or not.

"The second time, they didn't like me any better. They just didn't want my husband making any trouble for them. Arnie and I were troublemakers everywhere we went. We were troublemakers in Virginia."

Arlene's experience with this process heightened my awareness of how the certification test does and does not work, so I decided to moderate a discussion on the subject on *Openline,* an APsaA members' listserv—this was just as email communication was becoming available. A lively and spirited discussion ensued, with many participants from the pro- and anti-certification camps weighing in. It appeared that although views differed on the validity, reliability, and relevance of the test, there was widespread agreement that making certification a requirement for voting for educational bylaws or for running for Association office was neither rational nor adaptive for APsaA.

And here again I will offer a personal narrative to illustrate how the democratic process gained traction with the help of the new communications technology, and how vital the new political landscape it enabled has proven to be to the threatened well-being of American psychoanalysis. In 1989 I became the editor of the *Bulletin* of APsaA which I named *The American Psychoanalyst,* and in 1994, I was appointed editor of *JAPA,* an even more prestigious position. Both Arlene and I worked hard to get IPA members to join APsaA. It was not an easy task both because of the years of exclusion and the lingering conviction held by many IPA members that people like Arlene were not "real" analysts. But uncertified IPA members slowly did join and, in time, there were many more uncertified APsaA members looking at the anomalies of APsaA governance with a jaundiced eye. With these advances in communications, there was now a medium for discussion unconstrained by geography or time zone.

* * *

In the wake of the lawsuit's settlement, I became very much involved in the whole issue of certification. I started the whole certification discussion in 1993, after the lawsuit had settled membership but not certification. My wife, Arlene, had become a member of the Institute for Psychoanalytic Training and Research (IPTAR). When IPTAR joined the International Psychoanalytic Association (IPA), IPTAR members became members of the American Psychoanalytic Association as well. I was pleased to see that because it had always been my ambition that Arlene would be able to join all the organizations of which I was a member. I always did my best to empower Arlene.

The New York Psychoanalytic Institute was an exception because they did not accept anyone not trained within their Institute. Andre Green, from France and trained there, could not become a member, and certainly not Moises Lemlij, from Peru, who had trained in London. (I also fought for decades to get NYPSI to agree to train social workers; about ten years ago, they finally agreed to, but only after fifteen years of advocacy by Manny Furer and me.)

After Arlene's certification, I began raising questions about the whole certification process through my editorial position at *The American Psychoanalyst (TAP)*. For example, I explored the question of how difficult it was for BoPS to enforce its will on individual institutes. Expelling an institute required a majority of all the voting members of ApsaA plus a two-thirds vote of the Executive Council and BoPS—clearly impossible to achieve. The only leverage BoPS had on noncompliant institutes was its power to withhold certification from their members. Both Martin Stein and Stanley Goodman, who served as Chairs of BoPS, acknowledged this to be the case in the special issue of *TAP* that came to be known, because of the color of the cover, as the "white issue." I was the editor at the time, and devoted the entire issue to the question of "delinkage"—what we called the separation of membership from certification. I invited twenty pro-certification members and twenty con to argue their positions.

I also published, in *JAPA*, Bob Michels's plenary "A Psychoanalytic Case Study," which argued that the purposes of the Certification Committee and the purposes of the Committee on Scientific Activities were mutually incompatible. He argued that the certification test had no scientific standing because it lacked reliability and validity.

After the committee first rejected Arlene, the Chair told her, "We would understand if you decide not to reapply." Arlene's first thought was to go to the judge from the lawsuit, who still had an oversight role, to ensure compliance with the settlement's terms. I argued against that step, telling her I would start a discussion on the APsaA listserv about certification, which I did. I began the discussion by quoting Bob Michels's APsaA plenary. Many on the members list made the case that the process had no validity and no reliability. Certification remains a requirement for Training Analyst appointment so I have continued my efforts on the members list to remove that requirement.

There was now an opportunity to make the certification process public, whereas, there had been minimal public discussion before. Successful applicants usually heaved a sigh of relief and went about their business. The unsuccessful—either angry, frustrated, mystified, or ashamed—were not inclined to share much of the experience. But Arlene, whom I have dubbed the Rosa Parks of APsaA, not only persevered after her rejection, and then won certification, but in 2000 recounted her experience in a paper written for the Psychoanalysis Estates General in Paris. It took a second amendment to the bylaws, later that year, before the certification requirements for voting for bylaws and running for office were removed.

Pressure was thus mounting to dispense with the membership-certification link altogether, and to grant some kind of permanent Active Membership to noncertified institute graduates. At this point people who were not certified could be members of the American Psychoanalytic Association but could not vote, hold office, or become Training Analysts.

After an active discussion back and forth, vital amendments finally passed to implement "delinkages." The first delinkage was that if you were not certified you could nonetheless become a member, but not a voting member; the second delinkage, which quickly followed, built on the first, saying not only that you could become a member but that you could also become a voting member and run for office. These measures marked a very important change in the American Psychoanalytic Association.

I think my involvement in this issue accounts for my being moved from the in-group to the out-group at my institute. Sandy Abend, from New York, whom I knew quite well, said to me, "Arnie, I will never forgive you for what you did."

"What did I do?"

"What did you do? You provided a voice, a platform for people who should not be talking about education." He meant that members who were not Training Analysts and not part of the Board of Professional Standards were able to talk about the pros and cons of certification on the listserv that I'd fostered in the early 1990s. And then my other best friend besides Sandy, Leon Hoffman said that he also would never forgive me because he thought that I'd destroyed psychoanalytic education, meaning the hierarchical system run by the Board, the system that included certification and the subjective decisions about who could get certified and who could become a Training Analyst. I had committed the sin of providing a platform (on the members' listserv) in which noneducators (none of them Training Analysts) could discuss "educational matters." Another colleague later told me that I had destroyed psychoanalytic education by advocating for appointing non-certified members as TAs. One of the chairs, Myrna White, of the Board, declared that an uncertified person would become a Training Analyst over her dead body.

The Board was convinced that out there were the barbarians—like me, Paul Mosher, and Judith Schachter. We were the bad guys trying to destroy psychoanalysis. I am not sure to what extent this attitude was a conviction or a rationalization. I think it was mostly political; that is, it had to do with power and staying in charge. The Board of Professional Standards wanted to run things by staying in charge of overseeing psychoanalytic education, including certifying graduates at every institute, all thirty-two around the country. The members of BoPS were convinced that if they were not in charge, psycho-analysis would suffer. Every now and then when there was change, these BoPs members would threaten to leave the organization. They'd say they were going to take their marbles and run. But they had no place to go.

* * *

How could the grassroots voices in American psychoanalysis, for so long silenced or, worse, excluded, make themselves heard in the interests of a more truly democratic system? A new technology—specifically email listservs—proved to be a potent force in organizational change, and the one that finally required the guardians of the Treaty of 1946 to pay attention to the realities of the new world that had developed over fifty years. In 1995, Bob Galatzer-Levy started the first APsaA email bulletin board. In 1996, Paul Mosher started a members' list and the "Open Line"—discussion groups that go to the members of APsaA, and are opt-in. Members can join either listserv, or both. Changes began to occur, slowly at first—glacially, it sometimes seemed—but less slowly than they would have if the fundamentally democratic communications machinery of the Internet had not been developed. For the first time, the citizens of the territories occupied by BoPS and APsaA could organize.

These events provide the backdrop for what we have called the "third delinkage": removing certification as a requirement for training and supervising analysts. This requirement, unique to the APsaA in world psychoanalysis, is based on the conviction among some analysts that a "national test of clinical competence" is essential to ensure the best training for candidates as well as the overall integrity of psychoanalysis as a discipline. I always felt this requirement was exclusionary.

Now at last there is a new system with two tracks. An institute (and there are many around the country) can decide whether or not to require certification to be a Training Analyst.

This system is termed "institute choice." In some institutes you have to be certified, in others not.

Although "certification" now plays no role in most activities within APsaA, the fact that the Association requires certification for a Training Analyst appointment, for fellowship on the Board of Professional Standards, or for membership on any Board committee means that certification continues, via remaining bylaw provisions, to be the basis of a two-tiered membership structure in APsaA.

Over the years, the changing ways in which certification in APsaA has been employed, or rationalized, seem to indicate that certification in psychoanalysis, aside from what intrinsic value it may have in principle, has served mostly a changing set of discriminatory and exclusionary goals. Such an exclusionary attitude is deeply embedded in the history of American psychoanalysis, beginning with A. A. Brill's ironclad conviction that only medically trained psychoanalysts should be allowed to treat patients in the United States. (Mosher, P. W. & Richards, A. (2005) The History of Membership and Certification in the APsaA: Old Demons, New Debates. *Psychoanalytic Review* 92:865–894.)

My experience with these conflicts sharpened my opinions about APsaA's exclusionary arrogance, about its whole structure of training and membership, as that structure was molded after the reorganization in 1948 and the creation of the Board of Professional Standards. The latter became a self-perpetuating group that never changed, with the same people, year in, and year out, deciding who was and was not a good analyst, and who could become a member. This attitude was not consistent with development of the science or the profession. If you look at the minutes of meetings of the Board of Professional Standards and the Association over the years, the general effect was always the same: not what we can do to advance psychoanalysis, but what we can do to keep people out, make rules, set standards. One of my major efforts as a psychoanalyst and psychoanalytic political activist has been to change that overbearing system.

There were analysts in New York who were also working in hospitals and therefore could not become Training Analysts, because, so it was felt, they were not committed enough to the private practice of psychoanalysis. One of my classmates was Herbert Pardes. When he was excluded because he wouldn't apply for certification he resigned from the New York

Psychoanalytic Institute and did not become a member of APsaA. and went on to become one of the most important psychiatrists in the United States. What did his case say about the state of the psychoanalysis as a profession?

These were good people who were being excluded. So it's especially the case that I do not know how we can understand the psychology of the people who run the organization and maintain it in that kind of hierarchical, authoritarian direction, except to say it is about power.

All of which would feed into one of my most important papers, my 1999 Brill lecture titled *A. A. Brill and the Politics of Exclusion.*

CHAPTER 10

AT GREAT COST

The Price Paid for Exclusion

My reasons for writing this paper on the theme of "exclusion" were not just professional but deeply personal, going back to my childhood and my memories of the 13th Avenue Retail Market, in Borough Park, where Mayor Fiorello LaGuardia spoke in 1939. The market's construction, a Public Works Administration project, as part of the New Deal, was a huge event, because before then vendors could only sell their wares off pushcarts—I still remember going with my mother to buy from the butter-and-egg man. But not everyone got a stand in the new market. There was an old lady who sold lemons who couldn't get a stand, and this treatment of her affected me deeply, because she reminded me of my grandmother who had just passed away.

It seemed to show everything that was wrong with "exclusion." That old memory combined with my desire to make sure Arlene was at my side professionally every step of the way and could belong to every organization that I did. I was deeply gratified to see Arlene progress over the years from teaching in the public schools to teaching in graduate schools to becoming what Freud called a lay analyst, i.e., one not necessarily trained as a physician. In fact, despite my medical degree, I consider myself a lay analyst rather than a medical analyst. I entered the medical profession primarily as a first step toward becoming a psychoanalyst not a physician, as Martin Bergmann defines the process.

To summarize and excerpt my thoughts as I presented them in this paper: Just as Freud originally conceived the mind as composed of conscious, preconscious, and unconscious systems, each with its own laws yet forming an inter-dependent whole, so the history of psychoanalysis can be said to unfold on three distinct levels—personal, intellectual, and institutional.

Freud (1926) argued that psychoanalysis requires less a medical education than "psychological instruction and a free human outlook." But when Brill brought psychoanalysis to America, he not only used his medical credentials to campaign for psychoanalysis, but also was convinced that psychoanalysis would not flourish in America unless it became a branch of the medical profession. He presented the medical requirement as an effort to protect people from quacks and impostors. However, he was also clearly trying to guard something for which he had fought so long and which had now become an integral part of his personality.

For better and for worse, the shadow cast by Brill's politics of exclusion lingers to the present day. It haunts us in the unabated fragmentation of psychoanalysis and in our lack of theoretical consensus. The deplorable penchant for dichotomous thinking, with the tendency on the part of orthodox practitioners to brand interpersonalists and others outside the institutional fold as "not analysts," can be laid at Brill's door. Yet, to his credit, Brill was indubitably a force for conservatism in the best sense. In a turbulent period, he "conserved" the science and profession of psychoanalysis

The idea of clinical common ground was introduced by Robert Wallerstein at the 1987 Montreal Congress (Wallerstein 1988). Arlene Kramer Richards and I (Richards & Richards, 1995) proposed a psychoanalytic thought experiment in which we presented a clinical case interpreted first from our own contemporary Freudian perspective and then from what we took to be the perspective of other psychoanalytic schools. Two Kleinian analysts, two self psychologists, an intersubjectivist, and an American object relations theorist were asked to respond. From this exercise we concluded that the relationship of modern Kleinian thought to contemporary Freudian theory indeed sustains

Wallerstein's claim of common ground, probably because both positions accept the centrality of the concepts of conflict and unconscious fantasy.

Drive-oriented and relational, two-person and one-person psychology are on common ground, as I have argued; the drive/relational antithesis can be explained historically as a reaction to Brill's politics of exclusion.

The refusal to train psychologists and social workers is what I call "external exclusion." But there also has been and continues to be *internal* exclusion. That has to do with an organizational structure which does not allow full participation of all graduates of APsaA institutes in the educational enterprises at both the local and national levels.

If our goal is indeed to advance psychoanalysis as a science, and not simply to defend our hegemony, the effort to represent our interests to other psychoanalysts—including self psychologists, relational psychoanalysts, and interpersonalists—must engage these colleagues constructively. If we want them to listen to us, we must be prepared to listen to them. Thus, to appropriate the positive aspect of Brill's legacy we must finally disavow its obverse—the politics of exclusion sustained by its enshrinement of dogma. We must acknowledge the inescapability of institutional pressures in the unfolding of any theory.

As we know all too well, there is a psychopathology of everyday psychoanalytic life. It is manifested in the power struggles and rivalries from which no analytic group is immune.

On one issue, of course, Freud did speak out unequivocally—that of lay analysis. In this matter, it is now beyond dispute, Freud was right and Brill was wrong. There is today a collective willingness to define psychoanalysis as an autonomous healing profession. By transforming an outworn legacy of exclusion into a new politics of inclusion, we will be able both to till common ground with our colleagues and to advocate a distinctive vision that is—in the most vital, enduring sense of the term—Freudian.

* * *

Of course, for politics to transform, structure must also be transformed.

When APsaA was reorganized in 1946, a Board of Professional Standards was set up which, through its Membership Committee (later through its Certification Committee) determined who could become a member, who could run for office, who could vote for bylaws, and who could become a Training Analyst. The first three strictures were removed after considerable effort because of a recognition that APsaA would not otherwise survive, but the last stricture remains in place. Certification is a mandatory requirement for a Training Analyst appointment by a local institute, and only analysands of Training Analysts can become candidates (students in the institute), and only candidates can become graduates and members. Although the leaders of BoPS asserted that educational and membership functions are separate, in this regard they are inextricably connected. These leaders insisted that APsaA certification is an examination for psychoanalytic competence on which the professional standing of psychoanalysis depends. But this is an example of APsaA hubris—a refusal to see that the world of psychoanalysis is larger than one organization so hung up on certification. BoPS's preoccupation with certification and exams is an investment not in professionalism, but in the defense of old hegemonies—the most dangerous remnant still with us from our 1946 Versailles treaty.

This system contributes to the self-perpetuating leadership situation in BoPS. Only certified members can become Training Analysts, only certified Training Analysts can become Fellows, and only Fellows can nominate and vote for the Board Chair. There was a recent change in a bylaw vote, saying that one didn't have to be a TA to be on BoPS. The conservative faction on BoPS disliked this reform, sensing that the more liberal faction might have a majority. The reorganization in 1946 set up APsaA with a bicameral leadership structure: a Board of Directors, which was responsible for membership issues rather than training issues. and a Board of Professional Standards with absolute authority in regard to educational matters. However, a recent change in the bylaws set the Board of Directors in charge of training as well as membership.

In the 1990s, many on the Board of Directors and the Executive Committee felt they needed to find a way to reduce the stranglehold BoPS had on membership and Training Analyst appointments. Three individuals, then-President Robert Pyles; a former president, Warren Procci; and Rich Pearlman, who did not train at an APsaA Institute, introduced what was called the PPP Proposal (after the proponents' last names) which asked BoPS to define objective and verifiable criteria for Training Analyst appointments. Members who met these criteria would be designated national Training Analysts and could be appointed Training Analysts by local institutes. The proposal passed the Board of Directors twenty-three to fourteen, creating a firestorm within APsaA because the Board felt the change to be a direct attack on the authority of the Board to certify Training Analysts.

BoPS did not respond to the request to define objective and verifiable criteria. The fact is that at the next meeting of BoPS, its members considered this request for only fifteen minutes. Their contention was that this proposal violated the APsaA bylaws passed in 1946, which as I indicated earlier, enshrined BoPS's absolute, final authority in regard to educational matters.

Seven leaders of BoPS would go to court to file an injunction to prevent APsaA's Board of Directors from implementing PPP. The seven filed a brief paid for out of their own personal funds—legal costs, it was estimated, totaled more than $250,000. The judge who heard the case ruled in favor of the BoPS seven. When APsaA's Board of Directors appealed the ruling, the higher court upheld the first judge. The court's recommendation was that APsaA rewrite its 1946 bylaws to end the bicameral structure. A committee appointed for this task recommended a bylaw amendment to confer upon the Board of Directors final authority on all educational matters, thus sunsetting BoPS.

The essential position of the seven was that ordinary members of APsaA could have no standing in regard to educational matters. The organization was at an impasse because passing bylaw amendments requires a two-thirds supermajority, and it was not clear that such a margin could be obtained given the position of the BoPS leaders.

It appeared that all was lost because the BoPS leaders' side was adamant. They could have satisfied the members and retained their own educational authority and autonomy by supporting what we call institute choice, allowing each institute to decide for itself whether or not to require certification five years after graduation. But BoPs would not allow the institutes this autonomy. I have referred to the stance of BoPS as an illustration of what Robert Michels has called the iron law of oligarchy, where the group at the top maintains its hegemony in the organization. Or, as I said, it all relates to our Treaty of Versailles, because it was unfair and led to later battles.

I was not involved in writing the amendment, but worked hard to get it passed, making many phone calls. The measure received just one more vote than the necessary two-thirds, so in a way I feel personally responsible for its passage.

Something like this development actually took place when the third delinkage, removing certification as a requirement for Training and Supervising Analysts, became unnecessary because a six-point plan was approved by the Board of Directors which sunsetted BoPS. This did not require a bylaw amendment. Our "Versailles" has now passed into history. The bylaw for the certification requirement is now a matter of local institute option except for those institutes that have joined another national body, the American Association for Psychoanalytic Education (AAPE), which is an externalized BoPS set up to maintain educational "standards" and avoid APsaA member oversight. It is significant that the NYPSI Educational Committee has voted not to join AAPE. I do not think the NYPSI Educational Committee will ever agree to appoint TAs who are not certified, but will probably agree to a waiver system which would allow a candidate to have a non-TA as a personal Training Analyst. This replaces the Training Analyst system with a Personal Analyst system. And then NYPSI joined AAPE which requires that in order to become a Training Analyst you have to be certified.

* * *

The settlement of the lawsuit, my fight on behalf of Arlene, and the delinkage battle had consequences for me personally. My (unsuccessful) nomination to for the Board of Trustees. back in the 1980s, during the time of the Gross Rebellion, was the last time that I was nominated for any office.

I am convinced that my advocacy on these issues, as well as the successful outcomes on the delinkages and the certification requirement for Training Analysts, contributed to my first becoming moved from the in- to the out-group, and then becoming *persona non grata*—shunned and excluded—from the institute and society of which I have been a member for forty-nine years.

There have been positive changes at NYPSI in a progressive direction, more in accord with my own views. But that progress has not done much to improve my standing. For example, my request to join the Website Committee and the Public Relations Committee were both rejected—twice—and unanimously by the members of the PR committee. And there are several members with whom I had long relationships who will not interact with me. I have also made a series of proposals for projects that have been rejected; in fact, I've been told that no project will fly if I'm the one proposing it. Those in charge of NYPSI have limited interest in, or tolerance of, dissent, dialogue, or the studying of our history. I am not optimistic that this text will be seriously considered by those in charge.

Recall that when Arlene finally received certification, the Committee Chair told her she would pass but added, "I hope now you will call off your husband." I guess I've been called off.

* * *

The very success of NYPSI's exclusionary structures—long protected by vested interests in APsaA as necessary for the organization's strength—now threaten the very survival of both APsaA and NYPSI. It is time to revise the psychoanalytic continent, and to rethink our "Versailles treaty."

APsaA members are, on average, in their early sixties; Training Analysts are mostly in their seventies. A financial crisis looms as more and more members age into the dues-free retirement years and few new members take their place. Candidate enrollment continues to fall, partly because of our unwelcoming caste system, and partly because the certification process is seen as arbitrary and unfair. And even if we attracted more candidates, we would likely not have enough patients to go around. APsaA, several years ago, hired a marketing consultant—an extraordinary development, and not a cheerful one—who found that while psychoanalysis as a theory was widely appreciated, the APsaA analysts who offer it were perceived as aloof, distant, and wedded to a rigid and outdated model—an orthodox Freudian approach as compared to one more interpersonal/relational. (Although our practice surveys show that fully half of the psychoanalyses now conducted by APsaA members are carried out at a frequency of three times per week, as Freud himself suggested for certain cases, the orthodox model is four or five times per week while the relational model is three times per week.) We are not seen as offering, within our theory or our practice, the other modalities informed by traditional psychoanalysis, such as less frequent sessions and family therapy.

As a result of recent conversations with some members who have read what I have written so far, I now have a better idea about the politics of NYPSI, present and past, and the key players. These colleagues point out that what is missing from my report is an account of the movement toward progressive change, a movement that is developing now. But such change depends, in large part, on the passing of the bylaw amendments, and such passage is uncertain.

The bylaws have to do with faculty membership of all graduates, the appointment of the Instructors Advisory Committee (IAC), which appoints

Training Analysts, and the allowing of non-TAs to run for the Educational Committee (EC) (as opposed to the present arrangement, which allows only one non-TA to be a member) The larger picture is that there is now, as there always has been, an in-group of TAs and their acolytes, and an out-group composed of faculty TAs, such as Jack Arlow, Charlie Brenner, and me, and non-TAs. The in-group is intent on maintaining a majority of the faculty and a majority on the EC. Appointment of TAs is important.

Although the system of appointment has changed to self-nomination and case presentation, the final decision belongs to EC. This despite the fact that it is and has been such a source of contention. The Brenner Amendment controversy came about because EC would not appoint a member of the Brenner out-group, Herb Waldhorn, TA. (He was eventually made a TA, even though the amendment failed by a single vote to gain a two-thirds majority.) Brenner's aim was to change the makeup of EC by allowing nominations from the floor—presumably nominations of TAs who belonged to the Brenner out-group. The Gross insurrection occurred when a TA proposed by the in-group, Bob Kabcenell, was turned down by the Board of Trustees, chaired by the President of the Institute, George Gross. Over the decades the in-group has organized to ensure that their candidates are elected when there is an election in which the entire membership or the faculty votes. The in-group uses peer pressure and the promise of faculty appointments, patient referrals, and the "ultimate," TA appointments, to achieve compliance. There does now exist a group of eight members (TAs) who seem to be supporting a progressive change. And six women and one man, whom I call the gang of seven, who oppose change.

It has been traditional at NYPSI for many decades for women to line up on the in-group, anti-progressive side—such women have included Phyllis Greenacre, Lillian Malcove, Ruth Loveland, Ruth Eissler, Joan Erle and Lilly Bussell. The male in-group members have included Martin Stein, Robert Bak, and Manny Furer (although Manny became more liberal toward the end of his life). Prominently included in the next generation of the in-group were

Lester Schwartz and Bill Grossman. Bill opposed the certification requirement for Training Analyst appointment because he thought it was a slippery slope toward the end of the TA system itself.

APsaA has come a long way from the politics of exclusion enshrined in 1946 and defended at great cost to psychoanalysis as a profession. I hope APsaA is on its way to becoming a fully democratic and participatory organization. The decisions that the newly vested members of the Association make in the next years will determine whether APsaA can be renewed as a vibrant and forward-looking professional organization, or whether it will wither away as new and more flexible organizations of younger psychoanalysts develop and come to dominate the profession.

CHAPTER 11

THE BEST OF EVERYTHING

A Manhattan Family

Arlene did it all.

You might say we followed the shtetl model: The husband studies and the wife runs the family. Except that Arlene did everything. She made three meals a day, seven days a week—as well as everything else. At the same time, she was pursuing her career and graduate school. My ambition was that Arlene would belong to all the same organizations that I did. Of course, Arlene's a Training Analyst and a substantial professional person. she made it all on her own. She didn't go to an institute.

She began her New York training at Teacher's College. "The first step was the educational psychology division there," she recalls. "I was working there one-on-one with kids who had learning disabilities, which had just then become diagnosable. Such children used to be called 'stupid' or 'retarded' or 'slow learners.' But some of them were very smart kids, which I knew because of my tutoring of Jobo Riddle in Virginia.

"I went to the Teacher's College the first summer we were in New York and the following year; by June, I had my Master's, and it was time to think about my next step: Did I want to go into practice, or did I want to continue to pursue studies in psychology? Stephen, our son, said 'You know, Mom, I'm only in fourth grade and I've been in four schools. Could we stay here another year?' He was able to attend the Agnes Russell school, the lab school of Columbia, only because I was a graduate student. I thought, 'This poor kid has really

155

been shlepped around the world. Why don't I do this for him?' There was an intermediate, two-year degree called a Professional Diploma, so I decided to go for that.

"However, psychology courses at Teacher's College became unpleasant for me, because the psychology department there was anti-analytic, anti-internal. It was all about training rats. The only courses I could bear were those in statistics and research. I'd always liked math and algebra and geometry—those courses were fun. Most of the students hated those subjects, taking them only because they were required. So if you were in these courses because you liked them, oh my God, the teachers were so happy.

"A woman named Rosedith Sitgreaves was one of those professors. The statistics editor of *Science* magazine, she was open-minded and creative and thoughtful. I loved her, I loved her courses, and I took everything. There was no baloney there, no politicking, no 'we're *against* this and we're *for* that.' None of that. So I wound up being an expert in research.

"Stephen then said, 'Can I stay another year?' Yes, he could stay another year—sixth grade—because I enrolled on a doctoral path. I eventually earned a doctorate in psychology, mainly because of my research credentials. And then I got a job working at the Center for Research and Education in American Liberties, which was a joint project of the Columbia Law School and the Teacher's College Psychology Department. For two years, I designed the research for them. We made movies, we wrote a book, and we were featured in a front-page article in the *New York Times*. It was a very exciting and fun thing to do.

"We were researching how kids in high school could be gotten to refrain from protesting. It was the height of Vietnam, and the colleges were in revolt. There was a fear in education circles that the high schools would blow up next; we were trying to figure out how to prevent that. And we succeeded. We succeeded by creating ways of asking high school students what they wanted, getting them to be part of the discussion of whether, for example, there should be ROTC on campus or whether there should be courses in various kinds of social and political issues and the law, rather than just the standard courses in their schools at the time. It was the opposite of repression, it was *expression*. I used a method of research called 'critical incident theory,' which asks kids, 'Tell me one time when you had a problem in democracy in your school, and explain it.' They could write down whatever they wanted. It was totally anonymous, so they could be as honest as they wanted to be. I devised a scale for measuring by an inductive method. It was very innovative at the time; all of these ideas were adopted eventually in high schools. Yes, we were in the forefront.

"I also worked a lot with the computer science department of the engineering school. We had this computer that was less powerful than a standard smartphone is now. It took one whole floor of the engineering building, which is a block long on the Columbia campus. One whole floor for a computer with 64 bytes. Not megabytes, not kilobytes. Bytes. Sixty-four bytes. In a big, refrigerated room.

"The work was wonderful, a lot of fun. But it was limited. I had to think about whether I wanted to go back to teaching. Did I want to teach reading and study skills in some college? I got offers from universities, but they were mostly out West. Arnie didn't want to move, because he was where he wanted to be, so *I* wasn't going to move. I finally decided that what I really liked doing was working one-on-one with kids, so I started a practice teaching reading and study skills to kids with learning disabilities.

"As I worked with those kids, it gradually became clear to me that most of the difficulty was not intellectual, but emotional. Meanwhile, in pursuing my doctorate I had gone into analysis myself. I was really quite involved in it, and much helped by it, because by that time I was quite depressed. I didn't know what to do. I suffered from writer's block—I couldn't write my dissertation. I realized that I had gotten around the problem by taking courses in mathematical fields—these courses required doing math, not writing papers. So I hadn't needed to do the kind of writing required for a dissertation.

"But with analysis, I was able to write my dissertation. That turned out to be a fun thing, too. I'd taken a lot of courses in languages, so I did my dissertation on the language development of a six-year-old. By then, our youngest child was six, and I felt I wasn't spending enough time with her, so I did the pilot project with her. And then I expanded it into a dissertation-size study.

"Noam Chomsky, a prominent linguist at the time, had the idea that language structures are inborn, not learned by imitation. There was guy named Roger Brown at Harvard, who did a book called *Words and Things: An Introduction to Language,* about how language structures are learned by imitation. Well, I knew enough from rearing my own children to know that children learn language instinctively. They *want* to know how you say things. They *want* to know what things mean and they ask you all the time. I knew that you could say to a two-year-old, 'Go in the next room and get your diaper—it's on the bottom shelf—and bring it to me.' And they would. Well, that involves a very complicated language structure. The words are easy, but the structure is technically difficult because it's one idea embedded in another. I knew that understanding wasn't learned by imitation, because a child at two could not *say* anything like that, could not imitate me. She knew what to do, but didn't know how to say it, couldn't have articulated it. So that structure was innate. It was coming from within the child, not from imitation of a parent or anybody else.

"So I did my dissertation on that idea. I finished my dissertation, then I wrote a book about the research project and also wrote a lot of papers on the topic. It was like opening up a faucet. Everything was flowing. So I got to feel that that was what I wanted to do. I wanted to be an analyst because I had gotten so much help from it.

"So I looked around. I applied to New York Psychoanalytic, which was accepting psychologists as research students. I brought my research with me—three shopping bags of published papers. These were my credentials as a researcher. And I was told that I could enter the program only if I promised that I then wouldn't practice.

THE BEST OF EVERYTHING

"Really? What was the point? What was the point of getting the training? They weren't going to teach me how to do research, I was cutting edge in that.

"That wasn't going to work, so I told them, 'I can't.' They said, 'You can go to London and study with Anna Freud.' I said, 'Would you tell your wife that? My husband lives in New York and so do my children.'

"But there was a friend of Arnie's who knew a psychologist, Martin Bergmann, who was teaching courses. So a group of psychologists, all of us in the same boat, got together and hired him—and, eventually, everyone else who was teaching at New York Psychoanalytic—to teach us the same courses being taught there.

"We had a wonderful time. We were the first people—our little group!—to read through the whole standard edition of Freud, which had just come out at this time, the late sixties. I received a superb education, with excellent supervisors, and so I was accepted as a member of the New York Freudian Society and the Institute for Psychoanalytic Training and Research (IPTAR)."

* * *

Our first apartment in New York, on Riverside Drive and 110th Street, was certainly a change from Petersburg, Virginia.

"We were on the first floor," recalls Tamar, "so it was very noisy, I wasn't used to the sound of cars in a city. But it was a nice apartment."

"At Christmas time. they had a tree in the lobby," remembers Rebecca, "with a train running around the base of it. We thought that was amazing."

After a few years we moved to 305 Riverside, at 103rd Street. "We were on the top floor, the twelfth," says Tamar, "and had beautiful views of the Hudson River. It was a lovely apartment with old-fashioned sconces on the walls."

"We had a telescope," says Rebecca, "and would look across the river—we would see Palisades Amusement Park. You looked down at the river and could watch the boats going back and forth. You looked north and saw the George

Washington Bridge. You saw the seasons change—in the winter you saw the ice on the river.

"It was a pre-war apartment with beautiful moldings at the ceiling, and then the square frame moldings on the walls. Original parquet floors. Rent-controlled—$320 a month. Although my mom redid the apartment a bit, it was still cramped and crowded. Three bedrooms and a maid's room, although the kitchen was very small. My parents had a small bedroom, my sister and I shared a room, and my brother had a room.

"My parents liked a well-decorated apartment. They loved art, buying and selling a fair amount of it over the years. There were two different Alexander Calder gouache paintings that they owned (and ended up selling later). My dad also owned a very important bronze sculpture: Aeneas Carrying His Father from Burning Troy, by Leonard Baskin.

"Also noteworthy—I don't know where my dad got the idea for this, maybe he saw it in a store—in living room we had a coffee table that was half of a sphere of lucite or plexiglass set into a metal rim. Like a giant bowl, covered by a plate glass circle. And inside was a saltwater fish tank. It was pretty incredible. My dad was really into saltwater fish.

"My parents liked to get the maximum out of life. I don't know if that came from the memory of their relatives who died in the Holocaust. My mom would say, 'Living well is the best revenge.' They both wanted to get the best of everything."

We led an active social life, which, interestingly, Stephen sees as supporting my transformation into an extrovert. "I think my father's talkative personality developed a lot in New York," he says. "He and my mother had parties, they had loads of friends, different connections. They definitely became very active and social once they got to New York. I think that was where the development happened—he was sort of quiet before. My parents had a lot of parties, which I would sometimes attend, if it was appropriate."

"My parents are very driven people and they're achievers," says Rebecca. "They would jog. For a while, in the late seventies; jogging was popular around the Reservoir in Central Park. My dad was never really an athlete, but when they lived on the forty-fifth floor at 200 East 89th Street, he would walk up the stairs, all forty-five flights, every day. And my mom? She just walked and walked and walked and walked—like four miles a day. That's one of the reasons she loved living in New York, because she would walk up and down Madison Avenue. She has a lot of nervous energy.

"My mom loves the city, and she loves fashion. She's a New York person. My parents always wanted to come back to New York. Their parents grew up poor in Brooklyn, and now their dream had come true. They lived in Manhattan. They do have a certain quality about them: They're not completely *'We think we're better than other people,'* but they were ambitious, and they wanted to get out of Brooklyn and into Manhattan. They were really happy to be there. And then my mom wanted to give her kids what she thought was the dream life.

"At an early age we went off to museums—the Museum of Modern Art, the Metropolitan. My mom would take us to ballets, and I studied music. It was a very cultural kind of upbringing. I thought it was fun. We three kids had each other for company. It was a good time."

Dinner was a vital element of our family life—thanks, of course, to Arlene. "My mother insisted on regular meals together," says Stephen. "Every meal, practically. Breakfast, lunch, dinner. And she cooked them all, even though I don't think she had a great interest in cooking. She was working, she was going to school, she was doing all those things. I think as time went on she resented being a homemaker more and more, and resented not getting kudos for it. So she lost interest in it."

"Dinner was late, I thought," says Rebecca, "usually at seven-thirty, because our parents worked until seven. But every night we had dinner together, except on weekends, when my parents would sometimes go out."

There was always conversation at dinner—I encouraged that.

"There would often be discussion of the news of the day," says Rebecca. "My father and my brother used to talk about politics. My mother and father didn't talk psychoanalysis at the table—thankfully. Sometimes if we were out to dinner with their friends, yes. But in the family, no, as I remember."

"There was very little discussion of psychoanalysis," says Steven. "I would say that, in line with just the general gestalt of the times, there was a lot of analyzing going on. Instead of accusing you of doing something bad, our parents would say you're doing that thing for such-and-such a reason. But I heard very few discussions between them of the actual content of psychoanalysis (although they may have talked about that between themselves). What they did talk about endlessly was the politics of psychoanalysis. The different associations, how one association didn't like my mother because she wasn't a medical doctor and how my father would stick up for her. The only thing I remember learning about was that my father is definitely an orthodox Freudian. So is my mother. And they both often talked about the rival or heretic forms of Freudianism—trends they pooh-poohed or disagreed with."

Tamar, however, remembers our conversations differently. She's the youngest, of course; perhaps Arlene and I changed over time. "My parents would talk about psychoanalysis at the dinner table," says Tamar, "because my mother was studying it after my father had. He would teach her stuff—a lot of different words and jargons and diagnoses. And then later on they would talk about patients. I grew up in the middle of that.

"My parents had a lot of friends who were colleagues. My mother and father would go to the Madison Delicatessen every day for lunch with Charles Brenner and Jack Arlow and Sandy Abend. When I was a teenager, I would go with them sometimes. That was a little strange for me, because they were usually talking about psychoanalysis the whole time."

* * *

"What I remember about the early days in Manhattan," says Rebecca, "was taking the bus to school with my sister. I was, what, seven? She was five, in kindergarten. We took the city bus by ourselves, to school and then back home. A lot of kids were doing that then—if you grew up on the West Side, that's what you did. You had a bus pass taped to your lunch box. We took the number 5 bus, on Riverside, or the 104, on Broadway, to Agnes Russell. I liked taking the bus to school."

"Because it was the lab school of Teacher's College," says Stephen, "Agnes Russell (which no longer exists) employed the most progressive methods of education: combined classrooms of different grades, open classrooms with no assigned seating. One of the things I liked best was those machines you used to read microfilm. There was lot of new math, a lot of experimental stuff."

"A very liberal school," says Tamar, "very liberal. It was easy. I didn't study math until sixth grade, and they had something called math modules. I went through all of them in one year. Although, earlier on, my parents gave me a little bit of money for learning the multiplication tables.

"It was very open. The last year I was there it was a little more structured. We had contracts, where you had to write down what you were going to do each week and then, at the end of the week, you had to turn it in. But before that, you could do whatever you wanted. You could go to the little library, where I read books of folk tales of different countries. I was in third grade in 1968 when the Prague Spring took place, and my teacher happened to be from Czechoslovakia. So we went to an exhibit about it. I had trouble making friends; my parents tried to encourage me by having sleepovers with girls and so on.

"Also, we volunteered for a few experiments at the school—we were asked to do small tasks, like moving plastic disks. We got M&M's as rewards."

For high school we sent the children to Fieldston, the Ethical Culture School, which is in the Riverdale section of the Bronx.

"In the beginning," says Tamar, "I took a car service to get to Fieldston from the Upper West Side, and then I took the subway. I was very shy and spent a lot of time on homework most of those years. The subway ride was a part of our lives. My sister took the subway the whole time, and so did my brother. The ride took about an hour on the number 1 train.

"When I was, was in ninth grade, we moved to East 89th Street and Madison. I had to take the crosstown 86th Street bus to transfer to the train on the West Side. My father encouraged me a lot, academically, during those years. Sometimes my mother helped me with my English papers. My sister was kind of glad to move away from the Upper West Side, because it was kind of dirty, with cockroaches and so on. I guess I was glad to move, too. It was nice on 89th Street."

* * *

"Some of the best memories of my father are of experiences we had on weekends and on vacations," Rebecca remembers. "Growing up in Manhattan in the late sixties and early seventies, we all had bikes—we would ride together as a family. I remember him teaching me to ride a two-wheeler in Riverside Park. We also rode in Central Park. It seemed like an adventure: We would ride through the city streets to get from our apartment on 103rd Street and Riverside Drive to Central Park West, and on into Central Park. We would sit in the park for a while and sometimes have lunch before returning home. I enjoyed living in New York City. I wasn't aware that I was missing out on nature."

Riding bikes was probably our main activity. Tamar, who was four when we moved to New York, remembers riding with me even before we got there. "I remember my father taking me on the back of his bicycle in Virginia," she says. "At one point, I wondered what would happen if I put my foot in the spokes. He had to take me to the hospital—I remember him carrying me on his shoulders. That's a nice memory, because he was very concerned."

"I spent a lot of time in Riverside Park," says Stephen, "riding a bike or just walking around, playing, walking the dog. We had another dog at this point, Ginger, a wire-haired fox terrier."

"We just loved Ginger," says Rebecca. "Later we learned that my sister was allergic, so we had to give the dog to my grandmother. And then—so the story goes—the dog ran away, so we never knew what happened to her. But that dog was the love of our lives as kids. We had her in the apartment on 103rd Street, and then up in Maine."

We had two houses in Maine. The first was in Deer Isle—we would spend at least a month there each summer. The kids would be there unless they were at camp. And then we had a house in Stonington. Our home ownership in Maine started because of our friends from Virgina.

"We took a trip to Maine," recalls Rebecca. "It might have been 1967. This was a total coincidence: We were driving through the town of Deer Isle and saw a sign that said, "The Weave Shop." And the woman who owns The Weave Shop was Ebba Costick, whom my parents had known in Petersburg, Virginia. So we stopped and they had this reunion with Ebba, a weaver, and her husband, a potter. Across the street from The Weave Shop was a house, which had what's called a Dutch roof. It was a Civil War-era house, and it was for sale. My parents decided to buy it.

"We spent several summers in that house," says Rebecca. "My mom and dad were always up for activities and adventures, like clam digging, lobster bakes, beach walks, and exploring. We climbed Mount Katahdin together and explored Acadia National Park. They liked to do projects like that. These are some of the best memories of my life.

"My dad was working, so he would drive back and forth to be with us on weekends. There was an attic—we set up a little den there. We took off some of the wallpaper there, and underneath it we found an old newspaper that described Lincoln's assassination. And there was also, from about the same era, a complete or almost complete set of the Encyclopedia Britannica, which we had in our house for many years. We found old things in that house. For us kids, that was really cool.

"Although my dad is a cerebral and intellectual person, he would enthusiastically join in activities such as renovating the house and refinishing furniture found in antique stores along the roadside. In Maine you would often find these antique pieces that were painted over. You would scrape off the paint, then refinish the piece so you could see the wood. We did that with a rocking chair and with a bureau dresser. That work brought out my mom's defining characteristic: persistence, grit. For instance, if there was a grating in the grill that had to be cleaned, I'd be cleaning, cleaning, cleaning. I couldn't clean it. But she would work on it until it was done. She has that kind of nervous energy where she just keeps going at something.

"My dad is a typical intellectual. He doesn't fix things around the house—nothing like that. So it was kind of surprising that when we were little he built us a toy barn. I was shocked, because he didn't build anything else. He was not a do-it-yourselfer.

"What he likes to do is to read, write, and talk. And he's so into his psychoanalytic theory—that's basically his whole life. Other than that, it's going to concerts and talking to people. Whenever he gets into a taxi he starts talking to the driver. 'Where are you from? What do you do? What's your story?' He likes to hear people's stories. He's a good listener. He's able to convey that interest in someone. He's focused on you, as though you're the most important person that ever was.

"His favorite thing, though, is talking to other Jewish people about family. 'Where are your people from? Russia? Poland? Tell me *more* about them.' He just lights up when he's talking about that."

* * *

"Judaism was important," says Tamar. "Our parents took us to synagogue all through our upbringing."

"We lit the candles every Friday night," says Stephen. "We kept Passover, including the kosher restrictions for that holiday. We went to synagogue every Saturday—we went religiously, so to speak. I don't think we missed a Shabbat for many years. Our shul was *B'nai Jeshurun,* on West 89th Street, which is the most beautiful synagogue in the world that I've ever seen, in terms of the decoration—it was originally a Sephardic congregation, so there's a kind of Middle Eastern feel to the décor. We went to Saturday services. I went to the separate children's services. I also went to Hebrew school two evenings a week. That lasted to thirteen, when I was bar mitzvahed there. I don't think there was ever a moment at which I didn't view myself as Jewish."

"At B'nai Jeshurun," says Tamar, "there was a lot of Hebrew, which I didn't understand, but it was a beautiful sanctuary. Then we started going to SAJ, the Society for the Advancement of Judaism, which is Reconstructionist—classically Jewish, with a lot of Hebrew, but the sermons were very liberal. The rabbi, Alan Miller, was very liberal, very intellectual, but kind of cranky. He would get very upset if a baby cried during the service. He used to talk about a lot of the same things my mother talked about, the sacrifices and the rituals. On holidays, my mother would read these historical passages about Judaism, about the sacrifices, about how Judaism was way back when. That was a little annoying—all that talk about the bloody sacrifices in the Temple. It didn't seem to have much relevance to today. But we celebrated the holidays. We celebrated Hanukah. We always had a Seder.

"After my brother had his bar mitzvah, he got a trip to Israel as a present. My sister and I were told that if we went to Hebrew school and had bat mitzvahs, we would get a trip to Israel, too. That sounded good to me. But then the first day of Hebrew school my sister said, 'We shouldn't do this.' So we both left and never went back. I was just following my older sister. We didn't go to Hebrew school and we didn't get bat mitzvahed."

* * *

"Although my father was usually busy with his work," says Rebecca, "he was a kind and steady presence in my life. One of my earliest memories was of him helping me fall asleep at the age of five, when we were living in Virginia. I told him I couldn't fall asleep; he said, 'Imagine that you are on a boat, and the boat is gently rocking, rocking you to sleep.' I'm not sure if he had training in hypnosis, but this was in 1963 before meditation and visualization techniques had entered the mainstream.

"To expand on this theme, I think one of my dad's defining characteristics is his interest in seeing other people's points of view. Growing up, I sensed that he was genuinely interested in my thoughts, perspectives, and opinions. As a father, he knew that children have a special wisdom, and he conveyed a respect for that wisdom. He made me feel as though I had something to teach him. This made me feel special, because I knew that he was an extremely intelligent and well-educated adult who cared deeply about ideas.

"It goes back to the focus and the listening. I got from him that kids have a special knowledge. For example, my dad likes to play around with the stock market. He would ask me, 'What do you think of this stock? What do you think of this company?' And he really seemed to think that whatever I said was a real, true insight. He also wanted to know about music. 'Do you like this music?' If he asked a question, or he said he wanted to hear about something, it really seemed that whatever I said, he was going to respect it and believe it. Part of it may be that my parents have wanted to be great. They are great. They think they're great, and they always thought their children were great. Sometimes that was true and sometimes it wasn't. But he made me feel like my thoughts, ideas, and opinions were special and valuable.

"I always wondered what was the secret to my parents' success. And I couldn't really understand it, because I still don't get the big deal about psycho-analytic theory, and the books and books that are written about it. But some of my dad's success has to do with the way he speaks—his voice and his tone of voice. He has charisma, so that people are attracted to him. He has a lot of attractive qualities.

"He's confident and secure in his own knowledge and in his desire to share it. Both my parents have that quality. My mom doesn't question herself and she doesn't apologize. She knows who she is and she makes decisions quickly. My dad is a little less rigid, or a little less self-involved. But he has his own way of being confident, especially now that he's getting older. His tone of voice conveys that confidence, that charisma, and of course he has a way with words. I did study philosophy, but I could never understand psychoanalytic theory. Of course, there was among many people a huge rejection of Freudianism—for a lot of reasons, among them that it's sexist and rigid. And everything had to go into this one paradigm. Later on, I came to see Freudianism as a cult, with the whole idea of the supervising and the analyst and the institutes. For me it was like: This stuff is really crazy.

"But for my parents, this was it. Don't question it. *And* it led them to such financial success, which none of their kids have achieved. That was hard for all of us. We've all adjusted in different ways.

* * *

"Growing up," says Rebecca, "I sometimes wondered what made my father so successful. While listening in—briefly—to some of his seminars, which would take place a few evenings a week at our apartment, I was able to hear my father speak to enraptured groups of trainees. I was aware that he was an expert in his field, although I didn't understand then the significance of his field of study. What I did notice was that he was able to write and speak at length on what seemed to be esoteric topics. What struck me the most was the way he spoke. His speech had a tone and cadence that conveyed authority. He seemed to have a rock-solid belief in every word he uttered. Witnessing these seminars,

I realized that a confident speaking voice was a key to success. Later in life, in my own career, I used this lesson to be able to collaborate with physicians when providing care as a labor and delivery nurse, as well as creating trust and confidence in my encounters with laboring women and their families.

"My father's confident speaking voice has a musicality to it. He has always loved music, especially folk, rock, and classical. In recent years our shared love of classical music has brought us closer together. He's also an enthusiastic singer who can definitely carry a tune. He loved to belt out Woody Guthrie songs and lead the family in songs at the Seder table."

"There was a lot of music in the house," Tamar recalls. "There was always WQXR on the radio in the evening before dinner—my dad played it pretty loud. We were always turning it down."

"My parents' love of music started when they were in college," says Rebecca. "They were a bit pre-Beat Generation. They were into the folk scene then— Woody Guthrie, Pete Seeger. That was what was hip back then. Then Joan Baez and Bob Dylan. I think my dad bought every Bob Dylan album. I was, like most kids, into rock music. We bought every Beatles album the day it came out. I definitely remember the day the White Album came out. I dragged my mom into the record store. She bought two copies, one for me, one to give as a gift to a friend. They were seven dollars each, which was a h-u-u-u-g-e amount of money. Fourteen dollars! Wow. It was a big deal.

"In 1968 or 1969, when my mom was doing a research project at Columbia, she threw a party in the apartment at 103rd and Riverside and invited all the people who had worked on it. A bunch of people came. I remember bongo drums. It was like a big, loud dance party in the living room. I remember being in my bedroom and thinking, 'Oh no. That's a party. I'm a kid. I can't join it.'

"We had a record player that was blue plastic—you lifted the cover and the turntable was there. We painted on it in DayGlo paint with this sort of psychedelic design. When the Sergeant Pepper album came out, we had people over to listen to it. There were other aspects of the sixties counterculture.

170

"Our parents weren't radicals, but even though my dad was a little older than the typical 'hippie,' he wanted to understand the counterculture and in some way, be a part of it. The sixties counterculture had to do with music, it had to do with politics, it had to do with protest. My parents were very antiwar. My dad was helping young men avoid Vietnam. He didn't have any shame about doing what he did. He would say, 'Yeah, I helped this kid not get drafted.' Was the kid really mentally ill? My dad didn't imply that he was. I thought, 'Wow. Whoever got to see my dad was lucky, because he didn't have to go to Vietnam.'

"My dad was dedicated to causes that he believed in. As a family, we went to several antiwar marches both in New York City and in Washington. I remember attending a rally in UN Plaza where we heard Dr. Martin Luther King Jr. speak against the war. I can remember my dad hoisting me up on his shoulders so that I would be able to see above the crowd. I was nine years old. We went to a peace march in Washington, too. There was a lot of political theatre there—they had a person on a stretcher, and there was a piece of meat on his abdomen looking like an open wound. As a kid, I thought that was pretty horrifying. I remember that we stayed at the home of a psychiatrist friend of my parents.

"New York is about style. It's about trends. My parents wanted to be in on the trends. They didn't get into it fully; for one thing, they didn't smoke pot. They actually went to the Fillmore to hear Janis Joplin. But they left before she came on stage, because the music was too loud.

"My dad let us know, without sharing any confidential details, that one of his patients was in the music business. This was around 1968. So he would bring home record albums that his patient recommended: Disraeli Gears by Cream, Aoxomoxoa by the Grateful Dead. He always wanted to know what my siblings and I thought of the music."

"We went to a Grateful Dead concert," Tamar recalls, "just my father and me. That was pretty strange. It was his idea. I don't know if we stayed the whole time. It was at Madison Square Garden, and I couldn't really see much."

That's right, we went to see the Grateful Dead. And we went to other concerts like that—Janis Joplin at the Filmore East, for example, which was, indeed, loud. Rock music formed a very important connection between myself and Tamar and Rebecca—the Beatles, the Dead. Music, getting records, playing them. I felt like I was on the same level with them, with a common interest. It was a way of connecting with my daughters.

We also encouraged Tamar and Rebecca to play instruments.

"My sister played the harp," says Tamar, "and I took up the harp, too. They were going to give me violin lessons, but I don't have a very good sense of pitch, so that might have been hard for me. With a harp, once it's tuned, it's tuned. With a violin, you have to know how to make it in tune with your hands as you go along. Then they got me a piano. I liked that. I started with easy pieces, and was learning to play, but I stopped at the Bach Inventions. When we moved from Riverside Drive to East 89th, my dad sold the piano. But he didn't sell the harp, so I kept playing it. My sister did, too. For most of high school, we were at a music camp every summer.

"We both went to Interlochen, and my sister went to Tanglewood, which is even more prestigious. Merrywood was before that. We were very much influenced by our harp teacher, who was strict but nice. She told us where to study and what to play. She lived in Larchmont. I started going to visit her in Larchmont toward the end of high school. Before that we studied at the Manhattan School of Music on the Upper West Side, where we also took theory and ear training. Ear training was impossible for me. I could not tell you, if you played a note, what note it was. My sister was better at it—she has a gift for music. I worked as hard as I could with it and did okay—I was first chair in the lower orchestra at Interlochen a lot of the time, and one year I got to be second chair in the even better World Youth Orchestra. My dad and mom both encouraged it. They both played the recorder, as did my brother."

"My parents were always very supportive and proud of our music," says Rebecca. "There was an event called the Irish Feis at Lehman College in the

Bronx. It was a festival of Irish dances and culture; because harps are Irish, there was a big harp competition. Both my sister and I took part in it, and our parents were there cheering us on. My dad would move the harp where it needed to be moved. They called them 'harp dads.' They're the ones who move the harps for the kids. You can start with a smaller harp as a young child, but once you get older you get the full-size instrument—you've seen them in the orchestra, the pedal harps. Very tall. He moved my harp up to the camp that I went to in Massachusetts, in the summer, because my teacher actually taught at Tanglewood. This was before I was old enough to go to Tanglewood—I went to a couple of different music camps in Berkshires. One was Belvoir Terrace in Lennox, Massachusetts. The main house of the camp looked like a castle. There was a turret room—what in San Francisco we'd call the witch's hat—with the cone on top of the turret and the round tower. My harp was in one of those circular rooms—he moved it up there.

"My dad faithfully supported my musical interest. And our shared love of classical music has brought us together. He loves all kinds of music, always has. He's very musical. My mom cannot carry a tune. But they're still both huge music fans. Whatever kind of concert they can go to, they go to, especially in Palm Beach, where they're living now."

* * *

"My father never talked about sports," says Stephen. "I think part of the issue might have been that he had been a rabid Brooklyn Dodgers fan when he was young—he had a Brooklyn Dodgers uniform. After the team moved, he entirely lost interest. We never had a discussion of professional sports, as I can remember."

"But my father and mother both doted on their grandchildren. And my father enthusiastically took them to baseball games, hockey games, basketball games. Never once did he take me to any sporting event. The only person who did was actually my uncle Donald, my mother's brother. He took me to the Yankees game at which Mickey Mantle hit his five-hundredth home run. He also to the game in 1969 when the Mets first went into first place—for the first time in the team's history! People were shouting, 'We're number one! We're number one!' That was a moment.

"I don't think I ever, at the time, thought anything of my father's not taking me to games or wondering about it or resenting it. It was just amusing when, in terms of grandchildren, he was all in."

I wasn't going to take him to a game—the Giants and the Yankees were the enemy. I was too traumatized from the departure of the Dodgers. And I never got interested in the Mets. Zero. I could name you the entire Dodger team when I was growing up. And I still can.

* * *

There was this family, the Gara family. They were Jews who had immigrated from Iraq. The father was a physician in Harlem or the Bronx; he had two sons, one of whom, James, was a friend of Stephen's at Fieldston. Their mother, in Israel, was ill, in a hospital long-term. Tragically, the father was murdered by someone who came into his hospital to steal drugs.

"I met James because he was a classmate of mine at Fieldston," says Stephen. "Like me, he had entered the school in a later grade. The core of the student body were kids who had attended from pre-kindergarten on; many had parents who were members of the Ethical Culture Society, which my parents weren't. James started in tenth or eleventh grade. We became friendly and then his father was murdered. He and his younger brother, Leslie, were in a very difficult situation, because their mother couldn't take care of them, and, being refugees, they didn't have any other family here, as far as I know, except for a sister who was already in college. They had no place to go.

174

"I said to him something like, 'Well, you can stay with us'—for a couple of days, I meant. James put me off, saying, 'No, it's not necessary.' But then, one time, I was doing something with him and my parents drove him home, and they conceived of the idea of taking him in as foster parents."

"James was about sixteen at this time," says Rebecca. "Leslie was about seven. These kids needed a family to live with."

We took them in, and they were with us for two years. We had to deal with the children's services agency—it was all very complicated.

"My parents asked us, 'Would it be okay if these kids came to live with us? Will you accept them into our family?'" Rebecca recalls. "At my age, I had no idea, so I said yes. My parents had a big heart and they wanted to help people. And that was that.

"James and I became friends, we'd take the subway together. It was a bit of an odd friendship—I was thirteen, he was sixteen—but we would spend a lot of time with one another. It was always just friends. It was always brother and sister. Our parents tried to make it seem like these boys were part of our family."

Tamar remembers an interesting change in my behavior once we had the two foster boys in our home: "My mother had read all the children's classics to us," she says. "Like *The Wind in the Willows*. My dad didn't do that until we had these two foster brothers, James and Leslie, for a couple of years. He read Isaac Bashevis Singer stories to me and Leslie. And that's when my mother said something to the effect of: that it's because of Leslie—your father really is more into the boy children. That's how I interpreted it anyway."

"Unfortunately, my parents didn't get along with James," says Stephen. "I had difficulty getting along with James sometimes—sometimes we got along, sometimes we didn't—partially because of his attitudes. I was a socialist, but he was an extreme radical, much more so than I was, and more culturally radical as well. I didn't know until the very end that he was actually Jewish. He claimed his father was Jewish and his mother was not, which was not true. He was very pro-Palestinian. He learned Arabic on his own and he came to graduation in full Arab regalia."

"The older boy, James, was starting to be more pro-Palestinian," says Tamar. "My mother didn't like that."

In fact, James's views bothered me more than they bothered Arlene. And that was a major, major problem, because he was pro-Palestinian. We had that ongoing fight. But that conflict didn't have anything to do with their leaving after two years—that was just the way the system worked.

"They went to a different foster home," says Rebecca. There was a home on Long Island where they had originally stayed while they were waiting to find a place closer to Fieldston. So they went back to live on Long Island, and had to commute back and forth to school. They went back to the original family they had been placed with."

Rebecca said to me, just recently, James was her best friend, that the two of them rode the subway together to Fieldston every day, and then suddenly he and his brother left. It was very traumatic for her.

The interesting follow-up is that James became the chief operating officer for the Museum of Modern Art. And his brother, Leslie, became a successful politician in Alaska.

CHAPTER 12

A CERTAIN KIND OF FREEDOM
TAP, JAPA, and IPBooks

I was editor of *JAPA* for a decade. For those ten years, *JAPA* was my life.

"One of the crowning glories of my father's career," says Stephen [accurately], "was that he was editor the *Journal of the American Psychoanalytic Association.* For the entire ten years he did that, he was absolutely devoted to it, body and soul. And from what I've heard—and this is not just from him, but from others—he transformed it, he reformed it, he made it bigger and better in every respect."

The fact is, once I became editor of *JAPA,* I did not need anything professionally from any organization. That position gave me a certain kind of personal, professional, and intellectual freedom, which I maintained even after I was no longer the journal's editor. I could be as heretical and as activistic as I needed to be in terms of psychoanalysis. To put it bluntly, I didn't need anything from anyone. I think that's it.

This is a very, very important story. It began by my being asked by Homer Curtis, the president of the American Psychoanalytic Association, to take over as editor of *TAP,* which at that point was called *The Bulletin of the American Psychoanalytic Association.* It was a house organ, and like all house organs, very uninteresting. So I took it on, and that was the beginning of my whole creative publishing career.

One of the first decisions I made was to give the publication a different name. We would call it *The American Psychoanalyst, TAP.* The "bulletin" of The

American Psychoanalytic Association doesn't have any substance. It's ordinary. *The American Psychoanalyst* gives it pizzazz. Identity. Identity as not just a house organ, but as a serious publication. The first issue commemorated the death of Freud. Under my leadership, the publication would include more historical and biographical content. We did features about every place APsaA had a meeting. I redesigned *TAP;* well, I had someone redesign it, and that design has remained the design of *TAP* to this day, which is remarkable. *TAP* has continued since then, with ups and downs. Most recently, Arlene and I were its book review editors.

TAP was a bulletin. It included articles, interviews, views. But *not* scientific papers, not peer reviewed papers. It was like a newsletter. But *JAPA* was a scientific journal, and the most prestigious psychoanalytic journal in the United States.

Here's how I started with *JAPA.* The first editor of *JAPA,* which started in 1954, was John Frosch. He served in the job for twenty years. He was followed by Harold Blum, a very good friend of mine, for ten years, and he was followed by Ted Shapiro, another friend of mine, for another ten years. And then they were looking for a new editor.

I was told the editor received a stipend of $25,000 per year—which was only fitting, since the job involved an enormous investment of time. My assumption was that the stipend would continue, so I applied, along with several other people, all of whom I knew: Warren Poland, Elise Snyder, Tony Kris, and Bennett Simon. But then the American decided that they couldn't afford the stipend, at which point Warren dropped out. But the rest of us continued to seek the job. Somehow Bennett Simon never got to the Search Committee, but they did interview Elise, Tony, and me. The committee was Herb Schlesinger, who had been my mentor in Topeka, Arnie Goldberg, Harry Trosman, whom I knew from Chicago, Otto Kernberg, Phyllis Tyson, and Jack Arlow, the chair. Now, Otto Kernberg was very much for Tony Kris. I'm not sure why, since Otto and I had known each other from Topeka. Otto didn't come to the meeting with me, but still Herb, Phyllis, Harry, and Arnie Goldberg did come. Arnie Goldberg was a self-psychologist, and I had written a series of very critical papers about Heinz Kohut and self-psychology and Arnie Goldberg.

Anyway, I came to the meeting and I did my thing. I told them more about *JAPA* than they knew themselves, and I was told that my presentation was incredible. They were overwhelmed by it. Arnie Goldberg told me this, as did Herb Schlesinger. The decision was unanimous in my favor, and that's how I became editor of *JAPA*.

So, there I was, editor of *JAPA* with no stipend. But then there was a meeting of the executive committee of APsaA and Ted Shapiro, the outgoing editor, got up and complained. "Look," he said, "*JAPA* will be on the shelves when you guys are no longer around. You need to restore the stipend." And I guess out of shame, they did. The other thing they did was give me a budget for a secretary. That was very important for me personally, because I could hire Tamar as my secretary and pay her. She certainly needed an income at that time. I'm not sure what she was doing and what her husband, Larry, was doing, but they did not have a regular source of income.

So I got the stipend. And I got the money to give Tamar work and income.

My time as editor may have seen the best-version of *JAPA*. I ran it as a collective. I assembled a superb group of associate editors—Glen Gabbard was the most important and hard-working of them. Warren Poland was the book review editor. It was a good journal; I made it better. When I took over it had about 2,400 subscribers. When I left, that number had grown to 5,400. That alone was a major accomplishment.

I also changed the mechanics of *JAPA*'s publication. When I started, *JAPA* was published by IUP, International University Press. But IUP stopped publishing it; it was then published by The Analytic Press, whose director was Paul Stepansky. But I soon proposed that we self-publish it, and that Tamar and Larry could be in charge of the process. Of course, there was a lot of ambivalence about it at the American. Judy Schacter established a committee and hired a consultant to review the matter; the consultant said, "No, not a good idea. Too difficult. Too expensive." But Judy decided it was worth a try. The change ended up increasing the journal's income by $100,000 each year, for nine years. The treasurer, Alvin Compton, publicly gave me credit for having done that. Again, it was a *major* accomplishment.

Why self-publish? First, I could get more work for Tamar. But also, this would be *my* journal. I'd have complete control over content and distribution and promotion. Over everything. When we were working with the Analytic Press, they were the publishers, I was just the editor. A worker. I wasn't in charge.

This goes back to my father, who always said, "Don't work for anyone else." I followed those words in my life.

We published many terrific issues. We did one on female sexuality. Another special issue appeared in 2000: "American Psychoanalysis in the New Millennium." What's more, as soon as I became editor, suddenly people sent me papers from IPTAR, from the Freudian Society, from all over. I opened up the journal to the rest of the analytic community, not just the American Psychoanalytic. After I left as editor, that opening closed.

Also, circulation dwindled. After my departure, the number of subscribers dropped to about two thousand, although it's hard to know for sure. *JAPA's* now published by Sage Publishing, and it's bundled, and distributed as part of a package—so no individual subscribers, other than members of the American. It's sold to libraries. After me the editor was Steve Levy, who made it more psychiatric. And then I got them to appoint Bonnie Litowitz, a friend. She ran it for five years, and then decided she didn't want to do it for another five years. Then it was taken over by someone named Mitchell Wilson, who I think has made a disaster of it. He published a paper on whiteness, by someone named Donald Moss. It was not peer-reviewed, and it somehow took an extremely paranoid view. That's because what's happened in the American was this whole "political correctness and wokeness stuff"—that's the idea, that's what's *au courant*. In my view, it makes *JAPA* less scientific, less scholarly, and a less valuable journal.

* * *

A very, very significant thing we did, in all the books and journals I've published or helped to publish, has been to be more inclusive. That been a *leitmotif* of my professional life. And it's made a big difference, because it brought the larger analytic community into what we were doing. Of course, one of the most significant things for scientific scholarship is to have a website, a place where you can access papers from all the journals. That's been my shtick, to be more inclusive. Include everybody, and not to just give in to the American Psychoanalytic chauvinism and arrogance—that goes back to the lawsuits. My work to open up contemporary psychoanalysis illustrates my efforts to promote inclusion, professionally and scientifically, in psychoanalysis. That's what I do. That's who I am.

Exclusion is limiting for psychoanalysts and for the profession of American psychoanalysis. The story I tell is from when I was five years old. The lady who sold lemons—they wouldn't let her into the Thirteenth Avenue retail market that Fiorello La Guardia inaugurated. I think that incident had a profound effect on me. I believe that people shouldn't be left out. I have an image of that lemon seller, right outside the market at this little stand, selling lemons, and it really bothered me. A five-year old. Of course, my grandmother, who died, either just before I saw that lemon seller or just after, was also an old lady.

The papers I published in *JAPA* were not part of the mainstream. Therefore, they were controversial. Whom did I publish whom other journals might not have published? Well, the first paper that I accepted was a paper about the irrelevance of child observation to child analysis. Of course, child observation—Hartmann, Kris, Lowenstein, the cycle and study of the child—was very much part of the zeitgeist. The author I published, Peter Wolf, wrote this paper challenging the accepted wisdom. The issues he raised were similar to challenging the belief that neuropsychology has a lot to do with psychoanalysis; some people feel that it doesn't. Again, you see, we get back to controversial positions. I wasn't the heretic. I'd written a paper about extenders, modifiers and heretics; essentially, I was someone who was not any of those. I wasn't Melanie Klein or Heinz Kohut. Certainly, I wrote a lot of papers critical of those who were critical of all the Freudian stuff. That's true on the one hand. But on the other hand, I was open to new ideas. Being open to new ideas is very, very important. For example, compare Harold Blum's issue on female psychology, from when he was *JAPA*'s editor, and mine. I included Arlene in the issue, which set out different views about penis envy, and female sexuality, and so forth. People perceived me as a dissenter, a heretic.

Look, the problems began with Freud and Freudian orthodoxy. And that's why Bleuler left Freud. He said, "I'm not going to be part of a religion. I'm not going to be part of a dogma." The problem is, the early group felt under siege and therefore they had to defend themselves. That's why Freud got rid of Adler and Jung and Stekel. You know, *Az di rebbe tanst, tansen alle chassidim.* It's a wonderful Yiddish song: "When the Rabbi dances, all the Chassidim dance." In other words, whatever the rabbi does, the followers do. I think Freud is culpable for that approach. But it was made worse by the Americans who became more orthodox, more establishment, and more dogmatic.

No, I was not a heretic, not a dissenter. But I was willing to oppose. And, of course, all of my long and arduous efforts questioning certification—that was certainly questioning the establishment.

* * *

As Tamar and Larry published *JAPA,* they acquired the skills to publish books. That led to IPBooks (International Psychoanalytic Books, now incorporated as IPBooks Inc).

"When my dad was switching to self-publishing *JAPA*," says Tamar, "he wanted someone to do the typesetting. My parents encouraged both Larry and me to learn to do typesetting, but somehow we agreed that only Larry would do it. I did the other stuff. For example, we had a copy editor who didn't want to use a computer, so I entered the copyedits from many pages of hand-marked paper faxes to the computer.

"The *JAPA* period was a very good period for both of us, I think, and for my father, as well. We had a routine. We had work that was steady. We could handle it. My dad loved being the editor. He read lots of articles, and we worked on the peer review process. We'd send out the letters with a form the reviewers would fill out, and then we'd send the completed forms to the author. My dad also worked with a secretary at the American Psychoanalytic Association named Andrea. She did some of it, too, but we took over more and more of it. I became his full-time secretary or Administrator when she left the project.

"We transitioned to IPBooks a year after Steve Levy became editor of *JAPA*, and Sage Publications had taken over its publication, and made it more of an online entity."

"There was this psychoanalyst named Sylvia Brody," says Tamar, "and she wanted to publish a book. So because Larry knew typesetting, we figured that we could publish it—or Arnie figured that we could publish it—and that was our first book.

"After Sylvia Brody's book came out, my dad said, 'Why don't we publish other books?'

"We started for a number of years, working with a printing company that printed self-published books, and we stored *all* our salable copies here in-house. We don't use them much anymore. We now work with IngramSpark which also prints books for self-publishers, but it's better for us as they also print and distribute to the wholesale market worldwide, and they print on demand so we don't have to warehouse all of our inventory in advance, even for what we retail ourselves on IPBooks.net and Amazon.com."

"We acquire our book manuscripts in a few ways. Some authors contact us at conferences; sometimes, friends of Larry's want to publish. But most of them are through Arnie—his colleagues want to publish books. The collected-papers books are very labor-intensive, because we have to format all the articles and correct them. Sometimes they're from pdf's, sometimes scanned from print, which means there will be lot of errors in the format conversion. We also publish novels, which are much easier, because usually they're in good shape when we receive them. We also hire outside colleagues and friends to be manuscript editors.

"After our work on *JAPA* was finished, and IPBooks had already started, my dad also created a website in 2007 called: InternationalPsychoanalysis.net, which we call 'The Blog.' He started this site after being passed over for the editorship of the *International Journal of Psychoanalysis* in favor of Robert Michels who got the job.

"It was an opportunity to share his own take on psychoanalysis, on the broader field of psychology, and even current events. It became a sort of online 'Psychology *Readers Digest*,' featuring articles from all over the internet relating not only to psychoanalysis but topics further afield but of interest to the professional community. Included are regular monthly features like "Photography Friday," and "Poetry Monday," among links to other articles, and book reviews, and new announcements, and links to a wide range of subjects on other websites including science, history, and literature. There is an emphasis on psychoanalysis and Jewish-related topics, Arnie calls the blog is "a labor of love," and it does have devoted followers and fans, and is supported by advertising and paid announcements from several sponsors. Many articles are chosen by him personally come from other websites, and we re-post them via links. The site continues to this day, though at a slower rate of new posts since the start of the new online *International Journal of Controversial Discussions*."

184

"IPBooks is my main job. I do some work for other people. I worked with an analyst named Chuck Rothstein, typing his papers for a while. I work for Vivian Eskin, who's a social worker. And we also have our conferences, which my dad originated—they started in 1998 at Mount Sinai. He used to be very involved, but now the role has gone on to someone else, although we still work as the registrars for the conferences. Larry works for the American Association for Psychoanalysis in Clinical Social Work (AAPCSW) Conference. I do that, too, although he's much more involved with it, working closely with the Chair of their organization a the Administrative Conference Coordinator involved in all their conferences. Nevertheless, I'd say that the vast majority of our work is for IPBooks.

"My dad calls me several times a day. It's fine. I think I'm more comfortable working with him than with some of my other clients. He's a good boss. Sometimes he doesn't know what's involved with the work, but if you tell him, he learns it. Especially in the beginning, he used to think some things were hard that were easy, and some things were easy that were hard. But if you explain it to him—'This is going to take time'—he usually says, 'Okay.' Sometimes he gets a little over-enthusiastic, but he's generally very supportive. A lot of things are great in IPBooks, so he's pleased. And that's good.

"On the other hand, sometimes he calls me early in the morning and says, 'This author complained to me.' Larry has been taking over working with some of the authors I find difficult. Some people are very detail-oriented ,or I find that I can't understand what they want. Larry usually can. He's more patient than I am."

IPBooks has published over 250 titles (see IPBooks.net). We've won three *Gradiva Awards,* a publishing award given by the National Association for the Advancement of Psychoanalysis, and many, many laudatory reviews, including a review of one of our books in the *Times Literary Supplement* (*TLS*), which is, for a book, as good as it gets.

Then I started the *International Journal of Controversial Discussions*, which is free by subscription. We're up to thirteen hundred subscribers. We recently published the second issue of our second year—the whole issue centered on the theme "Jew-Hating, the Black Milk of Civilization," which has since been published as a book with that title. Arlene is editor of the next issue, titled *Is the Dream the Royal Road to the Unconscious?*. So that publication has been another major contribution to the field.

Of course, I owe a lot to Arlene, and also an awful lot to Tamar and Larry. I couldn't have done any of this without them. Tamar and Larry, essentially, run my publishing and professional life. They keep track of everything. They published the journals, starting with *JAPA,* and they publish the books.

People have said that I've done more to change psychoanalysis professionally than anyone else. It's the truth, if I may say so myself. Who else has accomplished what I have accomplished?

CHAPTER 13

MEMORABLE, INDEED
Seeing the World

We've always traveled—Arlene and I together, and with all the kids when they were younger. Our first long trip took place in the summer of 1962, between finishing my residency in Topeka and starting at the prison in Petersburg, Virginia. We took an indirect route—we went via Seattle, where we visited the World's Fair.

"This was our first big family trip," recalls Stephen. "We drove in a station wagon from Topeka to the World's Fair. Tamar was—I don't know, two, three? We kids were all in the back of the station wagon. We all had crayons, and we made a big mess."

We had a trailer, and camped in a field in Bothell, Washington, which is now a very developed urban area.

"It was all of us together," says Stephen. "There was camping out. We saw all these sights. I remember bits and pieces of the Seattle World's Fair. I remember there was an exhibit of art, and I rushed ahead. (My parents were always distressed with me because I would see how fast I could go through museums and the like.) This art exhibit consisted of sculpture based on crashed cars. I ran back to my parents and said, 'In this next room there's a whole bunch of junk. You have to see this!' That was pretty, pretty, pretty exciting to a seven-year-old boy."

From Seattle, we made our way east via a series of national parks. "If there were hotels along the way," Stephen says, "there weren't that many of them.

187

It was mostly camping. We went to Grand Teton National Park, Yellowstone, Dinosaur National Monument, and Rocky Mountain National Park in Colorado."

When we lived in Petersburg we camped in many of the state parks in Virginia and visited many Civil War battlefields. One of the most famous, after Gettysburg, was in Petersburg itself—site of the Battle of the Crater. After we moved to New York, the ritual was to take August off and travel during that month. We camped and rode bicycles. To begin with, we mostly went to Italy, camping again much of the time. We visited Rome—we camped on one of the seven hills. Of course, we saw Florence, Orvieto, Mantua, Padua, Lago de Como. I remember vividly the fireworks in Venice for the *Redentore* (in July, not August). The *Museo Poldi Pezzoli* in Milan. Art, art, and more art—we returned to Italy again and again.

"My dad loved going to churches," recalls Tamar. "We visited a lot of archaeological sites everywhere we went, cultural things. Greece and Italy one year, Spain and Portugal another. One time we all went to Mexico and Guatemala and climbed the pyramids."

We visited many other places in the world. One of the most exciting trips was to Russia in the 1990s. We went to Lake *Baikal,* in Siberia, the deepest freshwater lake in the world, on a Sierra Club work trip—we helped build campsites for eco-tourism. We had a wonderful group that worked together, with very little help from the Russians who were there. The Russian women did pitch in, but all the men were drunk by noon. We went to *Khabarovsk,* in *Irkutsk.* What do I remember most about those cities? I didn't come away from the Soviet Union with a sense that this was a country that would succeed because the population would work hard. It was just the opposite.

There were many other travels. Stephen remembers a ski trip he and I took: "My father and I once went to Killington, Vermont," he says. "Neither of us knew what to do. At one point, I decided, and he was persuaded, that we shouldn't use the ski lift, we should just try to walk up the mountain. We actually did it—once. That was the last time. We then decided it was better to buy lift tickets. There was another skiing trip, to Quebec. We went with the two boys who were foster children to us, James and Leslie Gara. It was very, very cold."

We made many trips to Israel, where we visited almost all of that country's archaeological sites. Out first trip was in 1968, the year after the Six Day War. We took a bus from the *Egged* bus station in Tel Aviv, and rode to the Mt. Sinai Monastery of St. Catherine at *Abu Rudeis.* We got up early in the morning and climbed Mt. Sinai, traditionally supposed to be the mountain where Moses received the Ten Commandments, although archaeological investigation shows that this is not the case. The monastery was inhabited by monks who guarded the icons that had not been not destroyed by the iconoclasts. Arlene slept in the section with the women and I in the section with the men. We stayed in *Sharm El Sheikh,* which, at this time, just after Israel captured Sinai in the war, was a new resort area. It had just one hotel, The Caravan, basically a Quonset hut. The waiters were on strike because they wanted to eat with the guests. We went snorkeling in the Red Sea. This was as spectacular a place as we ever visited in Israel. On a later visit we went to Petra in Jordan; the structures there are breathtaking.

We've visited Brazil and Rio de Janeiro twice to see my family, one time joined by our grandson, Joshua. And then there was the Far East—teaching in China for the last fourteen years, we combined every trip with a visit to some important place in that country. We saw the five gorges, Shanghai, and Beijing. We saw Xian, with the terra-cotta warriors in the part of China that's close to Tibet. Once we went to Japan, visiting Kyoto, which was a particularly memorable excursion. We've never been to Hawaii, but we did take a cruise to Alaska with the Division 39 psychologist group. We took one cruise to Bermuda with Alma Bond, another cruise there with Chuck Fisher. Most recently we went on the Turner Classic Movies cruise in the Caribbean to watch movies and listen to prominent filmmakers.

Machu Picchu in Peru was another spectacular place—we went there twice. We visited many Aztec and Mayan sites in Mexico and Central America.

Finally, there were bicycling trips. Once, Arlene and I cycled from Dublin to Galway. She wrote up the trip; her account was published in the *New York Times.*

* * *

Many of the trips Arlene and I made abroad were in connection with IPA congresses, which were held every other year. I think the first Congress we went to was in 1965, the year I graduated, in Copenhagen. I don't remember the trip as being memorable, but the next trip, to Rome in 1969, was memorable indeed. Leo Rangell was the president of the IPA and there was a counter-convention held by radical candidates in protest. But the memory that stands out most was the reception at the *Villa Giulia,* with a wonderful culinary spread which was devoured by the attendees in a few minutes—like locusts! This was the meeting where Heinz Kohut had hoped to preside but Anna Freud selected Leo Rangell instead.

The 1971 congress was held in Vienna; its claim to fame was that it was the setting for Erica Jong's novel *Fear Of Flying.* Another memorable aspect of that trip was that we went to the opera in Salzburg, seeing *Orfeo* by Monteverdi. We also went to congresses in Mexico City, Barcelona, Chicago, and Prague. The architecture in Barcelona was outstanding, as it was in Mexico City, where we visited Leon Trotsky's house and connected with the art of Diego Rivera and Frida Kahlo.

We didn't go to Chile in 2001. In 2005, we went to the Rio meeting, which was not memorable, but that was when we got to visit my family in Rio, Recife, and Sao Paulo. My uncle's grandson Ricardo, in Rio de Janeiro, has two sons. Bryni, my first cousin, is in *Recife.* My father and her father were brothers; my father went to New York, hers went to Brazil. Her granddaughter is in Sao

190

Paulo and works for Chabad. My uncle also has two granddaughters in Israel; they have lots of children and grandchildren.

In 2007 both Arlene and I went to Berlin, and this trip was a powerful reminder of the quote "What we are we are. But we are Jews." We visited the Holocaust Museum designed by Daniel Liebeskind and the Memorial to the Murdered Jews of Europe, designed by Peter Eisenman. Also the German Resistance Memorial Center, which had an exhibit recognizing the "Red Orchestra," which was a spy network run by a Polish Jew, Leopold Trepper, from an raincoat company in Brussels. The information he sent to London contributed to the destruction of two German divisions. He was held in the USSR for ten years after the war, then returned to Poland. After the Six Day War, the Polish government stepped up its anti-Semitism and was pleased to see thousands of Jews leave. Trepper wanted to join them and emigrate to Israel, but for some reason the Poles wouldn't let him go. In protest, his sons chained themselves to the fence at the UN. The Poles ultimately allowed him to leave after a resolution was passed by every Western European parliament.

We also went to congresses in Paris, London, Montreal, and San Francisco.

* * *

Years before we began our teaching association with Wuhan, we went to China and other parts of Asia. The trip, in 1978, was sponsored by APsaA and arranged by its travel agent. The trip was initially open only to members of APsaA; when not enough members signed up, a few others travelers were invited to join. We knew some of the APsaA travelers and also several who were not members, including close friends in both categories: Henry Rosner, a member of the American, and his wife; and Elaine Steiner, a non-member, and her husband. Margaret Brennan Gill was one of the travelers, a well-known and illustrious psychoanalyst, who had been married to Merton Gill, who was a close friend of ours. In addition to being a psychoanalyst, Margaret was an activist and humanitarian. I will never forget, when we were in India, she seemed to want to feed everyone who approached us asking for food. Another couple on the trip was Herb and Stephanie Newman, friends from our synagogue, SAJ. She was a professor of political science at the New School specializing in transfer of arms to underdeveloped countries.

The first leg of the journey turned out to be quite an adventure. Our first stop on the trip was supposed to be Teheran, where, we had been told, there was a revolution happening. So, it made sense when, at Kennedy Airport, we heard that Air Iran was on strike. We'd lost our airline and we were concerned about the political situation where we were headed. Stephanie called the State Department, and was told that all she had to worry about was packing enough evening dresses for parties in Tehran.

The travel agent arranged for us to fly Air France to Paris. When we got there our guide arranged for a flight to Rome; there, we found a flight to Teheran. When we arrived in Tehran, the city was in turmoil; the revolution had begun. We were told that we could not go to our other planned destinations in Iran, and that we would have to go directly to our next stop, China. We went jogging at *Shah Pahlevi* Park, partly because we had been sitting for so long, and partly for a chance to see something of the city. I remember seeing jogging women wearing hijabs over blue jeans and sneakers. While our travel agent scrambled for a flight East, our group visited the shop of a rug merchant—the store was located just opposite the American Embassy where the hostages would be taken a few weeks later. Arlene saw a beautiful silk rug that the storekeeper was willing to sell for six hundred dollars, about a tenth of what it would go for in New York. He said we could take it now and send the money to his bank in Israel when we got home. But we decided carrying the rug all through China would be too much of a liability, so we passed.

Back to the hotel for a lavish lunch. We got no news of a flight out; it would take at least another day. In the meantime, Arlene and Henry, and Lillian Rosner were determined to see the crown jewels and they arranged for a taxicab to take them there. I had decided I'd rather be safe than sorry, and did not join them. They drove through a demonstration; concerned for his passengers' safety, the driver told them to get down in the well behind the car's front seat so they would not be visible. They did get to see the crown jewels and returned to the hotel, where the group was lining up for a flight to New Delhi. We stayed there one night until we got a flight via Air Ethiopia to Beijing. When we saw the interior partitions of cardboard on the airplane we became concerned about its mechanical state, but we arrived in Beijing at the appointed time.

We were met by our interpreter, who had translated for Nixon and Mao in 1972. He said, "First, we will take you to change your money and then we will take you to the cleaners." He was not talking about getting our clothes cleaned. They proceeded to sell us everything they could—jade and paintings, especially. That was the beginning of the accumulation of dollars by the Chinese government, a sum that eventually added up to trillions. We were given accommodations in the Russian Hotel which was one of the best hotels in Beijing.

In Beijing we visited the most distinguished mental hospital in the city. We participated in a conference in which a Chinese psychiatrist presented a patient who had been treated with drugs and what they called "heart-to-heart" talk, which we call psychotherapy. The treatments seemed fairly standard to us except that there was much more involvement in the patients' community, their family, and their workplace. I was surprised by how sophisticated the psychiatrist was. He wanted to know about the state of psychoanalysis in the United States. He was familiar with the *Journal of the American Psychoanalytic Association*, and he asked about Margaret Mahler and separation/individuation. We visited Hang Chow and West Lake, which I think is one of the most beautiful places in China. There's a Chinese saying that the lucky person was born in Suchow, eats in Sichuan, and lives in Hang Chow. Shanghai, of course, was of great interest. We spent time on the boat, stayed at the Plaza Hotel, and visited the Jewish quarter.

We've been to Shanghai several times since, and the difference between what we saw then and what we saw later was quite dramatic. In 1978 there were very few cars; most people rode bicycles. Clothing was drab and uniform except for that of the children. It was also a politically interesting time. Mao had died only few years earlier. The "Gang of Four" had been executed. It was a time of opening up, the beginning of a transformation of China economically which began with importing technology from the West and selling goods to countries abroad. But in 1978, the transition hadn't happened yet. The China we saw then was not very far from what we had read about as schoolchildren or in the novels of Pearl Buck.

CHAPTER 14

TREATED LIKE GURUS
Our Work in China

Arlene and I began our work in China in 2013. She was invited by a director of the Hospital for Psychotherapy in Wuhan to come lecture and provide supervision for the staff. She said she would come if they invited me as well. They asked her to send my CV; apparently, I passed muster, and my invitation followed. Arlene gave five lectures on the psychology of women, and I gave five lectures based on my published papers. Arlene interviewed a patient for the staff and conducted four supervision sessions. I ran five group sessions on the ward for the patients and in the presence of the staff.

Although group therapy was not my area of expertise, I had experience running groups for the inmates and staff of the reformatory in Petersburg, Virginia. In Wuhan, dealing in group with more and less seriously disturbed patients was challenging. Before the last session, I asked them to talk about traumatic experiences in their lives. Several talked about childhood memories of parents or grandparents who had committed suicide. I talked about memory loss and the ending of our group experience. They offered to sing for me. The first song they sang was a Chinese pop tune. Another patient, who had cried for my attention, sang a Chinese classical song. I was then asked to sing a song myself. I was taken aback by the request. The only song I could remember the words to was a West Virginia anarchist song, "In an Anarchist Garrett." After I finished, the group stood up and sang "The Internationale" in Chinese. I was told that they hoped very much that we would return the following year.

"The last evening," Arlene recalls, "we met for a going-away banquet. I had a conversation with an official who was the Chair of the Wuhan Communist Party. He confided that he deeply regretted not having been close to his daughter, his only child, while she was growing up and he was busy working for his party and his country. Now he wanted to retire to help bring up his granddaughter. I said that I had been brought up by my grandfather, while my mother was busy working to support the family, and that it had been wonderful for me. I also told him what was difficult about it—for one thing, other children had teased me about not having a mother around. This official talked about the sacrifices people have to make, ordering priorities and seeing how decisions have unintended consequences. By the end of the conversation, he asked: 'Is this what you do?' I said: 'Yes.'

"As a result of the conversation, we were invited to nominate faculty members for a psychotherapy program, which would meet twice a year for three years. Some 225 psychiatrists from all over China took part. There were a thousand applications for this program. As a result of its success, we helped organize a second program. We recruited the faculty: senior American analysts plus one analyst from Australia. There is also an additional Chinese faculty. After the second program, there were two additional programs, each meeting twice a year."

There has been some turnover in the American faculty of nine. The program is quite intense. Each of the American and Chinese faculty members gives one lecture—those lectures take place in the morning. In the afternoon we meet for three hours of supervision of a case presented by the participants. My group is a group of supervisors who present their own supervisions. Our feedback ranges from the positive to the enthusiastic. The skill of the Chinese translator helps a lot. We feel we are being treated like gurus, rock stars. The participants are hungry for knowledge and say they love psychoanalysis and Freud. On the wall in the auditorium are pictures of famed psychoanalysts: Anna Freud, Melanie Klein, Heinz Hartmann, et al., as well as several famous Chinese psychiatrists.

The participants are also offered individual psychotherapy sessions with the faculty at a very low fee.

The program is funded by the Chinese government and driven, I am told, by the high rate of suicide in the country, including suicides by adolescent children of the nation's leaders. Five years ago our building was demolished and a new ten-story structure was erected in record time.

Our involvement is not limited to our in-person visits to Wuhan. Most of us continue with weekly online supervised and didactic sessions with our group and additional sessions with other groups arranged by the participants themselves or by several Chinese companies who do this as a business. Arlene holds five groups that meet every week. I lead one group, attending supervision and didactic sessions. My group is reading and discussing my theory papers in Volume 1 of my selected papers, *Critical Conversations* (2015), which has been translated into Chinese, as has Volume 2.

Arlene has completed three online courses of ten sessions each, the first on films used as examples of how to analyze dream material, the second on the psychology of women, and the third on the psychology of men. All of these have been recorded on video and are available online. She will be starting a new course on film in the fall.

What is striking and gratifying is the level of interest and enthusiasm, and the high degree of understanding of both clinical and theoretical issues. This group of people is as smart as any candidate group either of us has ever taught.

During the ten years of our involvement with China, we have tried to learn as much as possible about Chinese history, Chinese culture, and the Chinese family. There have been instances in which we seem to be more knowledgeable about Chinese history than some of our students. Some topics, however, are off-limits. You can talk about the Cultural Revolution—which often is relevant to the history of the parents of the patients—but not about the Great Leap Forward. You can talk about the psychological effects of growing up in a one-child family—an arrangement mandated by the regime for many years—but there is much shame and guilt about the infanticides and forced sterilizations of that era.

Currently, there is much concern among our students about events in the US. They perceive saber-rattling moves by America in the South China Sea. Those with relatives and friends in America worry about US policy that threatens the WeChat app. For some, money transmitted via WeChat is necessary for survival. For those who send their children to be educated here, the threat of loss of communication is frightening.

"Telling the China psychotherapy story without the impact on participants, supervisors, and teachers," says Arlene, "would be missing the most important impact of the program. Some of the participants went on to get 'personal experience,' which is their name for individual psychotherapy for therapists. Doing sessions for three or four people a day, I was, at first, shocked by what I heard. Stories of families forced to decide which child would be fed and which left to starve, of grandmothers found hanging in the kitchen by schoolchildren, of beatings, rapes, earthquakes, drownings, and unbearable loneliness when children were left at home alone all day while their parents worked in the fields—these tales had such an impact that I felt flattened by the end of each day.

"The tellers of these stories reported relief and gratitude, and that kept me at it even when they and I parted. I continued to listen to them via Skype, Zoom, and WeChat. Years of talking about the impact of their traumas had an effect. Some left prestigious but unfulfilling hospital jobs for the private practice of psychotherapy. They wanted and got analytic training through the International Psychohistorical Association while others were empowered to have families or to leave empty marriages and seek love. All of this gave me great satisfaction, albeit little money. In the process of doing four analyses, I gained as much self-esteem as the analysands did. I became profoundly grateful for the trust they gave me.

"Supervisees were reluctant to tell me of their failures; needing to save face, they often showed their understanding of theory rather than report on a session (referred to as an 'hour'). Gradually, by accepting their reluctance, I managed to convince them that they were the authorities on what happened in the hour, and that they could teach that to me. Over time, they began to present both hours and questions, mirroring the questions I asked them. Eventually, they were criticizing me and each other without fear of losing face or insulting the person whose work was being discussed. This process was been profoundly satisfying to me.

"Finally, I was forced and inspired to write papers for lectures to give in the program. The questions participants asked at the lectures were so satisfying because they showed how carefully the participants had attended to the shortcomings and the strengths of my thinking. I decided to give up retirement plans. As long as I can think clearly and maintain an empathic yet clear-minded stance, I hope to go on with this project."

One note, on China and recent events: We had been going to Wuhan for almost ten years, during which time hardly anyone we knew had ever heard of Wuhan. That all changed with the advent of Covid 19. Early on, Wuhan locked down completely, and all our patients and supervisees in Wuhan, and in other parts of China, saw their patients only virtually, just as we did in the United States. That change did not seem to have a major adverse effect on the treatments, as far as we could determine. For a time, the lockdown in China ended, and Wuhan returned to normal, but after a time the restrictions were reimposed. We were concerned about the situation of our supervisees and patients in Wuhan and the rest of China, but they were more concerned about us. Because there was a shortage of masks in America, they sent us a large supply of them. They were pleased to have this opportunity to help us.

CHAPTER 15

WHAT'S IMPORTANT
Looking Back, Looking Forward

How did I get to be so old? I certainly don't feel old, and one doesn't feel old when doing new things, as I am, including writing this memoir, starting a new journal, publishing new books, offering new courses.

I remember watching a short film called *Chicken Soup*. Set in southern New Jersey, it's about an elderly Jewish couple who are chicken farmers. The man kills the chicken and the wife makes chicken soup, and then they sing a Yiddish song which asks, "Where have my young years gone? They have been played out like cards." In that song, aging has to do with chronology not with mental age, which in my view is what really counts. Doing new things requires physical and mental ability but it's the mental ability that's most important. We recently met a man on a cruise who was able to tell us that he had to sell his house in Palm Beach and move to an assisted living facility because his memory was fading. I was impressed that he was able to share his story with us. He was a widower, and very fortunate to have a partner, a woman he'd been with for twelve years, who was clearly willing and able to take care of him.

I love to reassure myself about what I *can* remember: names of movies, historical figures. And I reassure myself by remembering things from my own distant past. Thus, it's reassuring to write a memoir because a memoir is a permanent record that does not get erased. A memoir is also an opportunity for self-analysis and self-evaluation. It's an opportunity to consider things that have happened to you and to find explanations for things you did that had not occurred to you before.

Acquiring new skills also counters the feeling of aging. My most recently acquired skill is photography; I've included some of my more recent shots in this book.

Looking back at my professional life, I can say that I faced up to the politics of exclusion and the iron law of oligarchy. It's been my effort to reform institutional psychoanalysis, and I think I've made a major contribution in that regard. The American Psychoanalytic Association will never be the same after me as it was before me. So I think that's a very important part of what I've accomplished, in addition to the day-to-day, month-to-month of helping patients.

Becoming a publisher has been central. Giving Tamar a livelihood has been central. My connection with Yiddish has been central. And these days I'm very much involved with terrible stuff about Israel and Zionism. I feel like I'm compelled to defend Jews and Zionists and Israel in the face of endless attacks. I now tell people I'm a Zionist. Of course, that drives people up the wall because that's obviously a bad thing to be. Did you know that? There's this professor who says that Zionism is a mental illness. It's getting worse and worse, especially in academia, here in the United States, and around the world.

My Jewish identity is very important. My Yiddish identity is very important. My psychoanalytic identity is very important. My family relationships are very important.

For many decades, I would see patients for as many as forty hours a week; that was a major, major involvement. It's all about connection with people. Take that amount of time, plus the time for organization. During this period I wrote papers that fill five volumes. Plus, I did all that writing and communicating with peers about psychoanalysis and psychoanalytic issues. And of course, we lived in New York. We went to the theater, the opera, concerts. It was, I would say, a very full and rich life. And we had our children to raise; eventually they all left and were off on their own, and it was just the two of us. It's been a long time since we had any children at home.

Overall, I'm very proud of what I've been able to accomplish with my patients. The first thing that comes to mind is that in my fifty years of practice, I have not had a single suicide. The only suicidal patient I had was when I was covering for my friend, Harvey Bezahler, who was away for the summer. This patient called me just before Labor Day. He wanted to see me, and I said fine. I came in on a Sunday to see him, but he didn't show up. And then I learned the next day that he'd killed himself.

I've certainly treated many patients in analysis. I've also treated some celebrities, whose names I cannot divulge. I'm very pleased about that. All I can say is, I think I've helped a lot of people, and have had an impact on them, their spouses, and their children. Very few of my patients have terminated with me because they were dissatisfied. I've had patients I've treated a long time, even thirty or forty years, and other patients I've helped in a much shorter time. I'm there for people as long as they need me to be there. I don't allow my own interests and wishes to intrude on the treatment. And that, of course, is very much welcomed and appreciated.

It's been said that the main criterion of a successful treatment is that the person's income increases. That's a joke, of course, but there's some truth in it. Obviously, however, that's not the whole thing. A successful treatment is about the person's personal satisfaction, and their improvement in interpersonal relationships. For example, I started to see one patient when she was in college. I treated her, and then she went to medical school, she went to residency, and then she became a psychiatrist. She got married, she has three children, and *they* have children. She calls me from time to time—I see her for a single session or talk to her on the phone. I've made her life and changed her life. There's another patient I see now—well, I talk to him on the phone, because I don't see anybody in person anymore—whom, again, I started seeing when he was in college. He went from college to law school, became a lawyer, got married, and has two children. I help people have a life and have pleasure. More pleasure, less pain. And avoidance of the *Sturm und Drang* that people get caught up in. I do this not by giving them advice about how to live their life, but by helping them to understand the nature of their conflicts. Part of their treatment is to have them consider alternatives.

It's interesting. We were in a restaurant in West Palm Beach not long ago, and someone came up to me and said, "Dr. Richards." I said, "Yes." He said, "Don't you remember me? I was your patient." I didn't remember him, and I didn't remember his name, and he wouldn't tell me his name. He felt he needed to maintain his anonymity. But he certainly looked like he was doing well. He must have been somebody I treated forty years ago, because I didn't recognize him. I'm sure he didn't look the same as he looked before.

I've written four papers on specific patients, with extended analyses. I published a paper on self-mutilation and father-daughter incest. I published a paper on hypochondriasis, and a patient with that. And a paper on the patient's experience on the couch. I never treated children, but I did treat adolescents. And that was always a challenge because you had to deal with the parents as well as with the adolescent. After a while, I stopped treating adolescents.

Some of the patients I had—at least my first two—were very disturbed. The reason is that I was sent patients from Topeka, and there were only three of us in New York from Topeka. The patient suffering from father-daughter incest was one who was from Topeka. So I developed a reputation in my institute for seeing more seriously troubled patients. That didn't go over so well with colleagues, because you're supposed to see neurotic patients. The belief was that you couldn't do analysis with more severely disturbed individuals, which I tried to do. Psychoanalysis, it was said, was for "the worried well." If you want to do analysis, lying on the couch five days a week, a patient has to be very healthy. Freud didn't feel that way, but that's what happened with the profession.

There's a stereotypic impression of psychoanalysis. In fact, I had one patient who said, "Analysis is lay, say, and pay."

But there's a misconception about that. No, I don't intrude, but sometimes I say a great deal. Nevertheless, I emphasize the need to say less rather than more. And not to intrude on the patient's individuality. I recognize that I have to restrain myself, because I know that I like to talk. I was just telling someone about having a writer's block. I said, "I *do* have a writer's block, but I don't have a *talking* block." I write by talking, I dictate. It's easier for me to talk than to write. I was well-known in college for brevity when writing: I would write one-page papers and get an A.

I had some patients who were really quite difficult and would call me all the time. Every weekend, in the middle of the night. I would struggle with them, but I would hang in. Eventually, they gave up and got better. Look, my view of treatment is: Attendance counts. You have to be there for people, you have to be available to them. That theory limited the number of trips we took. Since Arlene and I were both in practice, we tried to limit our vacations. We went away only for one month in August, although later on we would go to Palm Beach in the winter. We would go to the US meetings and the international meetings. But we kept limits on our travels. The important thing is to be there for your patients, and for your patients to depend on you. That's crucial.

I've often said that I've been devoted to lost causes: to Yiddish and to psychoanalysis. But Yiddish survives among the Chassidim or Haredim, here in America and in Israel. I think I've made a lasting contribution to preserving Yiddish culture, both with my work in YIVO and with the Yiddish Film Festival, which was a huge success.

Is psychoanalysis in decline? The American Psychoanalytical Association is in decline. But other organizations are very much not in decline. Look what's happening in China. We have this training program in two sections, and a total of five hundred students. Psychoanalysis is very much in the ascendancy in China, and in other parts of the world. Argentina, for example. Arlene and I have made a major contribution to promoting psychoanalysis in China, more so than any other two people in the world. I'm referred to as an ancient fossil by the Chinese. And Arlene is Guanyin, the Goddess of Kindness.

The experience in the United States is a separate matter. APsaA may be in decline, but some of the institutes outside the American, that are more independent, are getting more students. The problem with the decline in the United States has much to do with insurance. Folks can't afford psychoanalysis, and it's not covered. All that kind of thing. That's a whole other set of issues. Still, I think that there is a future for psychoanalysis in the United States, as well as abroad. Because there's more interest among younger people, in Freud in particular, and in psychoanalysis in general. The title of Arlene's book is *Psychoanalysis: Listening to Understand.* Instead of calling psychoanalysis a talking cure, I would call it a listening cure.

* * *

In 2002, I was having symptoms: I had ataxia; I couldn't walk. I had dysgraphia; I couldn't write. I had computer apraxia; I couldn't use a computer. I went from doctor to doctor to doctor, and nobody could diagnose it. But I told my situation to our friend Mara Schwartz, who relayed it to her son, Teddy Schwartz, the head of neurosurgery at Cornell Hospital. "Something is going on in his head," Teddy said. "Take him to Cornell." They did a CT scan and found that half my brain was covered with blood.

A subdural hematoma is when you have a leak of fluid, and blood forms under the dura, the membrane that encases the brain. So they drilled what's called a burr hole and drained the blood. It was very dramatic; I was lucky to be alive. I was in the hospital and rehab for a total of a month. It was very interesting, because I was editor of *JAPA* at the time. I'll never forget. They give you occupational therapy—cognitive therapy, where they ask you questions: "How do you get from Times Square to Central Park?" Things like that. I found it very, very annoying. I said, "Wait a minute." I had just gotten a paper to review. So I got the paper out and I began to read it to them.

While I was in rehab at Mount Sinai, I overheard the head of the department telling the nurse, "He'll probably never work again." I didn't believe him. I felt much more unimpaired cognitively than they thought I was.

And then I went back to work. I told my patients what was going on, and then I returned to seeing them. I didn't miss a beat.

Psychoanalysis isn't dead, Yiddish isn't dead, and neither am I. We all have plenty of life left.

POEMS

Poem in Progress

My poems
are personal
forged
in the oven
of my discontent
tempered by the fire
of my passion
which burns words
on white paper
like an electric tool
marks wood
and smoke
into the nostrils
perfumes
the page

on which I
the artisan
sets down
my lusts
and rage.
But art abhors
the confessional.
I will use artifice
to engage

my audience,
disguise to veil
the obvious,
guile to create
illusion
as I ply my trade.
The Troubadour to His Lady
My poems are narrow lined
Short staccato sentences
Assault the senses
Consonants cracks like machine gun fire
Your poems are filigree lace lined
entwined like tendrils
soothing senses
sibilant sounds like zephyr wind

My poems are solid grounded without allusion
or artifice
heavy-handed
perhaps too precise
footfalls on earth
Your poems are porous, evocative
dip below the surface then soar
above like whales
dancing in Baja waters

Fire, Earth, Air and Water

Aristotelian elements
Separate, yet all that is matter and us.

Father's Day

My father had a stubble beard
a crippled gait, a sad face, a quiet voice
My father had a troubled life.
Mother died before her time.
Brother struck by Cossack blade.
Father carried the body home.
Sister shot in dark ravine.
A world destroyed, A god that failed..
My father grew old. His hair turned white.
A wrinkled suit wrapped his frame,
He walked home.
Stooped, returned to wife
Bandit waited in darkened hall
Blood unstopped stained the wall.
My father had a troubled life,
a crippled gait, a stubble beard
a sad face, a quiet voice
A troubled life|
And then he died.
Rhyme or Reason
I write a
poem search
for rhyme
and rule
but line

falls flat
I juggle
words
In desperation
Should I stick
to science?
Galileo said
the laws of
shadow making
are the same
on the moon
as on the earth
and apples fall
like planets
said Newton
But I like
Surprises

Mother's Day

My mother was
a Hallmark junkie.
Collected cards
Dates received
recorded in her book
pages wide-ruled
black-and-white
speckled cover
the gift noted
where applicable
House plant:
"It lasts but it needs
watering"
Flowers by telegraph:
"A visit would
have been better"
A thimble to add
to her collection.
She hung the cards
on a line strung
across the rough stone
basement wall
white powdered surface
sheets out to dry
printed wishes

flower-bordered
rhymed couplets
written by
the poet laureates
of Kansas City.

Petersburg, Va. 1965

I was the jailor
You were the jailed
We plotted your escape.
Dark night at Southern Depot.
First stop on the underground railway
Route to freedom.
No more chain gang dogs Greyhound
route to freedom.
Missed by a minute or less
Sinking heart, sweaty palms
Who decided you or I Impala
Route to freedom
No more nigger work wife I 95
Route to freedom.

Firefly

Fireflies communicate
with phosphorescence
Fill the humid air
with flickering
greetings
You and I meet at night
Brief hellos or sterile
semaphores in the
morning
politeness
In the evening lovers
talk in whispers
Words caress
I write but
cannot break
the silence.

For My Much Younger Sister on the Occasion of Her Birthday

Shall I mark your birthday when you did not mark mine?
We both started in same space but at the wrong time.
I too soon. You too late.
You Sara's gift.. I a mistake
Down the same canal. Greeted by the same face
Brought to the same place.
Crowded and cluttered rooms with little view.
Windows covered with damask opaque to leaves and sky
Furniture covered with plastic.
Transparent in pattern shielding texture from the feel of sticky fingers
yours and mine.
We both ate In the same kitchen. Sanitas on the walls,
linoleum on the floor
Fox Ubet Chocolate MyT Fine
We shared space and place but not time.
I came to love the man who also made us both.
You were taught otherwise.
Who cut our ties of birth?
I am our father's son.
You are our mother's child.

A Wreath of Verses

(On the Fresh Grave of Toni Greenberg)

Color it black

If you don' t mind
Her eyes shut tight
"Shakhor b'eynatim"
Black decorates our hall
Our no longer happy
Birthday Party and hers
Danzig/Vilna 1925
God would not delay
Her departure for our
Benefit
Color it black
Color of mourning
Darkens our vision
"Tunkl in di oygn"
She carried history
On her person
Khasidik Queen
Superordinate to Kaiser
And Emperor
God would not delay
Her departure for our

Purpose
Color it black
If you don't mind
Her eyes shut tight
"Khoyshekh b'eynayim"
Curtain falls
On Central Park window
Dusk drops early in December
But it was a warm autumn
Did God delay winter
This year to ease her exit?
Color it black
Funereal
Yankele, Toni's emissary
And God's messenger
Followed her instructions
To the letter

stamped with date/time

Color it dark
Like death
Eros and Thanatos
Frozen in a final
Embrace

Like a computer
She summoned the players
for the final performance
She was a star
She had the right
To schedule closing night
For her benefit
"Finster in di oygn"
Color it darkness

Elegy for Muriel

You celebrated your self
and rightly so.
You reveled in your senses,
pampered them with aliment
sonatas and sauces
flavorful.
You tuned your body
Sharpened its sensuality
prepared for its adornment,
clothes your advertisement.
You wrote your own
jacket copy
prideful
before your
fall.

Muriel Weistein, PhD died two summers ago. She fell off a mountain in Switzerland where she loved to climb

Boro Park

Color it red
If you don't mind
I will call
a spade a spade
was it a buck knife
or switch blade impaled the painter' s chest wall
red blood spurting
on tiled floor
of dark hallway
headline in The Forward
CRIPPLE STABBED IN BORO PARK
red blood like spray paint
my father's last job
price complete
includes labor and materials.

He always lived dangerously
soldier-librarian
in Trotskyis army
he escaped bandits
and commissars
British shells
crashing on Odessa
Romanian border guards
Arabs In Gallilee

He came to America
land of promise
He died the day after
the Fourth of July
red white and blue
celebration of
our revolution
ironic, ex-Bolshevik
killed by worker
dead like brother
bayoneted by Pitlura
He should have stuck to books
or stayed
a worker, Mottle
the boss not the
operator. Or kept
the payroll In the bank,
skipped the evening news
and advertised in the
Yellow Pages:
Workmen's compensation
fully covered
estimates cheerfully given
windows for eight dollars
fire escapes for twenty-five
Benjamin Moore paint the best
but don't forget
Dutch Boy red lead
undercoat first
if you don't mind.

Brighton Private
Color it gray
If you don't mind
I will settle for
less passion
and more peaceful
time no more roller
coaster ride
Coney Island cyclone
steeplechase and
Luna Park the
funny place before
It went up in fire
did he jump or was
he pushed from
Half Moon window
Honeymoon hotel
for flappers
Gamblers pay the
price for adrenaline
surge I'd rather
not live dangerously
sell Good Humor
on the beach no time
for broads or under
boardwalk look at
private parts
fudgsicle for a nickel
toasted almond for a dime

Like Zola egg cream you bet
I'll skip the black and white soda
if you don't mind.

A Picture at The Prado

Fiery Night, Regulus light pierces Leo's sky
On earth leaves rustle. A lion roars,
Teeth gape from open jaws.

David's son minds his father's flock.
White headed rams and ewes. We watch in horror.
Do we dare to tame the beast?
Do we rather run and hide?
A story is a tale, one as good as any other.
If it works, no matter

Where is truth? God knows.
But is God dead?
That puts de cart before the hearse the darkie said
God a she, God a 'mere' God is philosophy
Is that the point?
Who cares about the answer?

Philosophy is edified or dead,
Both or neither? Deconstructed

There is truth but who knows it?
Philosophers perhaps not dead.

Embedded.

Hayden Planetarium

Color it dark matter
Dispersed exactly
In the universe
The cosmos poised
Precariously at conception
On a teeter totter

Density is destiny
Miscount six atoms
Per square meter
And the Big Bang ends
In burp or blast
Or whimper

Mass is critical
Cold dark matter
Even if invisible
Gathers up the galaxies
Like love the great
Attractor

Theology is Cosmology or Before the Weighed the Neutrino

Density is critical
Our fate hangs on one letter
Not alpha but omega.
Weigh the universe
Find a number.
Weight over space is what it takes
To stop expansion from going on
Forever.

More than one back come mass.
to a bang not a whimper.
Less than one stars are dim
Cosmic soup keeps getting colder

Omega at one
The world goes on
Balanced on its own teeter totter

Earth and moon
Stars and sun
God is one
No matter.

Study Group

Freud asked what do women want

Not so wise a man

I thought maybe he didn't know everything

My students are women groupies hang on my every word and

I tell good jokes besides they think I know everything.

I dazzle with my erudition

I know them better than they know themselves .

I bask in their adoration.

They think I know what women want and I should tell Freud

But do I know myself or anything?

Summertime

Last night Leontyne Price
sang "Summertime"
in fire red dress
iridescent
arms outstretched
in benediction

I remember
summer times
Sunset Park
boyhood backyard
watching fire flies
phosphorescent
semaphores
in the dark
I played at war
Caught fire flies
with cupped hands
imprisoned in
empty Ovaltine
cans
and strawberry
jam jars
luminescent
beacons

Fireflies

my
imaginary
Armada
Zeros and
Messerschmitts
Dive bombers
Hornets and
Spitfires
Flaming
Incandescent

Summertime

Last night
Leontyne Price
Sang summertime
arms outstretched
fingers pointing
to the sky
While missile
Streaked over Tel Aviv
flashed
and died

Scissors and Paste

Poetry
Cuts up life
Into pieces
And pastes them
On a page

Introspection

my happiness
is the happiness of others
not martyr
not victim
not self sacrificing
giving
is satisfying
life meaningful
the order of my world
in my remaining
time

Yom Kippur

my father went to the movies
on the day of atonement
he was an atheist
he did not believe
in ritual
or superstition
he ditched his Bolshevism
but his belief in mankind
replaced his belief
in a deity
which he conveyed to
me. he loved language
Russian
Hebrew
him
Yiddish

me
central to my identity
thinking
speaking
doing
mind
is first
good deeds
primary
foundational
religion
replaced
by righteousness
his Yom Kippur
my Kol Nidre

Universe

has no rhyme or reason to exist
born from a quantum fluctuation
escaped annihilation
it's own reason for being
transcendent
a big bang at the beginning
but what came before
mystery
mathematics
perhaps
mankind
an anomaly
in an anomaly
a deity is comforting
but not dispositive
we lay down our arms
ignorance
and humility
sustains
perhaps

something's are certain
but more are uncertain
what is certain

is uncertainty
the size of the universe
how it began
how it will end
is Fermi right
do we have alot of company
or are we alone
are we a singularity
or part of a multiplicity
we are burdened by ignorance
knowledge beyond our grasp

humility
doesn't come easily
to any of us
sadly

the universe began in a big bang
monstrous stars
each ending in a bang
from bang to bang
from explosion
to explosion
incomprehensible
our world
unknowable
what connects
you and me ?

Bodies

Everybody has a body
does shape matter?
does size matter?
what matters is mind
mind matters more than body
mind also has a size
mind also has a shape
mind can be exercised
like the body
the body ages
the mind grows
the body loses its beauty
the mind retains its wonder
awesome mystery
remains in memory
but sometimes the mind goes before the body
tragedy
and in this poem
on this page
and in our mind
and the mind of others
body gone
body no longer matters
mind remains in history
memory is legacy
eternal

PICTURES

PICTURES

My Uncle David & My Grandfather in Russia

My uncle David in Russia

My Father and his Sister in Russia

My Maternal Grandparents and Their Children

**My Father (standing) and a Friend,
in Ukraine before WW I**

My Father (Center) 1920 in Haifa, Palestine...

My Father (far right) in Quarry Nahala, Palestine (1923)

My Father in New York City

4-My Father in USA with 2 Friends (1930s)

My Parents in Brooklyn (1940s)

Lillian & Sam: My Parents and friends

Aunt Milia with Libby and Me

My Parents, Libby, and Me on Boat

My Sister Libby and Me

Mother, Sister-in-law, and Other Richards Family—New Year's Eve (c. 1940)

MY BAR MITZVAH, 1947

Cousin Yita

My Cousin, David Gorodovits

My Father Samuel, on a Plaque

My Uncle Simon's Painting (naieve art)

My Mother's Needlepoint, 1929

Steve & Rebecca

Rebecca with Cast on one leg (1960)

Rebecca & Tamar (early 1960s)

Tamar, Arlene, and Rebecca (1960s)

Rebecca Plays the Harp

Tamar at Airport (1970s)

Rebecca, Around 10 Years Old (Late 1960s)

Tamar, Rebecca and Steve (1970s)

Like Mother, Like Daugher:
Arlene (1960s);
Tamar's HS Graduation (1978)

Rebecca (Late 1970s)

Carol and Josh (late 1980s)

Carol and Steve (1990s)

Justin (early 1990s)

Justin in Boat (later 1990s)

Josh's Hebrew School Graduation

Larr Tamar, Arlene, Steve,
Libby, David, Gail & Brooke (1991)

Arlene, Me, Tamar, and
Mother-in-Law Edith (1994)

Justin's Graduation

Family at Justin's Graduation

Rebecca and Me

Tamar & Larry (2016)

Tamar & Larry (2021)

Tamar (2022)

A Signed Sketch of Karl Menninger

Yivo Benefit with Joe Papp, Stella Ader, et al. (1985)

Charles & Irma Brenner at Arlow Book Party

Leo Stone at Arlow Book Party (1988)

Jacob Arlow at his Book Party

Bringing Cake to Arlow Book Party

HARVEY BEZHALER
(1930–2023)

Arlene and Me in China (1978)

On the Great Wall of China (1978)

**Arlene, & Lilian Rosner in Tehran,
en route to China (1978)**

In the Forbidden City with Turtle Statue (1978)

Arlene & Me in Ningbo, China (c. 2018–2020)

Arlene & Me in Wuhan, China (c. 2018–2020)

Dr. Tong, China Faculty

Class in Wuhan with their Diplomas

At Dinner With Students in Wuham, China

Dr. Tong Lectures, Wuhan, China

Top Row: D.W. Winnicott, Melanie Klein, Jacques Lacan, Wilfred B:
~rgaret Mahler, Heinz Kohut, Sigmund Freud, Anna Freud, Arnold Richards
Bottom Row: Ronald Fairbairn Karen Horney, Peter Fonagy, Otto Kernberg, Hans Loewald

Wuhan Hospital Analysts Plaque, Including Me

Two Tall Pagodas

With Daniel and Adriana Benveniste

Wuhan, China Group

Full Wuhan China Class

With Arlene at Farewell Party in China

West Lake, China (1978)

Single Small Boat on West Lake, China (1978)

Shanghai (1978)

Forbidden City, Beijing, China (1978)

Beijing, China (1978)

Petra Treasury, Jordan

Arlene walking at Lake Baikal, Siberia, Russia

Irkutsk, Siberia, Russia

Nova Utshitza Holocaust Memorial, Ukraine

Disney Dream Cruise Ship (2022)

Cruise Ship Crow's Nest (2023)

Cruise Ship Upper Deck (2023)

Cruise Ship Deck Chairs (2023)

Palm Beach, FL

Urban Sprawl Wuhan, China

Brooklyn Bridge

Draw Bridge in Palm Beac h, FL

Passing Cuba

Dali Bai.jpg

Palm Beach, FL Sunset

Sunset over New York City

Man on Beach, Maceio Brazil Cruise April 2023.

WINSTON CHURCHILL POODLE
Our Beloved Dog, Winnie
18 Years, May He Rest in Peace

9 781956 864502